PEOPLE AT PLAY:
Sport, Culture and Nationalism

PEOPLE AT PLAY:
Sport, Culture and Nationalism

Edited by

Amitava Chatterjee

Setu Prakashani

Kolkata Delhi

People at Play: Sport, Culture and Nationalism
edited by Amitava Chatterjee

First Edition: January, 2013

Cover Design: Dilip Ghosh

ISBN: 978-93-80677-46-0

Published by:
Archana Das & Subrata Das
on behalf of **Setu Prakashani**
12/A Sankar Ghosh Lane, Kolkata-700006
Phone : +91 33 2219 0704, +91 94330 74548

Outlet :
2, Shyama Charan Dey Street,
Kolkata - 700 073

Delhi Branch Office :
A-43, Mahendra Enclave, Galli No. 3,
G.T. Karnal Road, P.O. : Azadpur, Delhi - 110 033
e-mail: setuprakashani@gmail.com
Website: www.setuprakashani.com

Price: Three hundred fifty

Setting by: Cynosure, 3/37A, Bejoygarh, Kolkata - 700 032
Printed by: Sarada Printing Works, 7/1, Gurudas Dutta Garden Lane, Kolkata - 700 067

To

My Sir Prof. Bhaskar Chakrabarti

this book is for him ...

because of him

Acknowledgement

I would like to acknowledge all the individuals who played a direct or indirect role in publishing this book. I am indebted to my doctoral supervisor Professor Bhaskar Chakrabarti for his positive influence in the development of my intellect. He has been supportive in all my endeavors; his critical comments have always squeezed the best out of me. My heartfelt gratitude goes to Prof. Kausik Bandopadhyay, whose advice means a lot to me, whose encouragement resolved my dilemma whether to delve into such a serious project. He also kindly wrote the foreword of this book amidst such a busy schedule. Special thanks go to Prof. Peter Robb who actually opened up some new dimensions regarding sporting identities of a nation during our discussions in SOAS. I sincerely thank Richard Alford, Secretary, Charles Wallace India Trust for offering me the Charles Wallace Fellowship, 2012. It was this fellowship which helped me to open up new vistas as far as sporting culture of Bengal is concerned. Special thanks to Prof. Ranjan Chakrabarti, Hon'ble Vice Chancellor, Vidyasagar University, my teacher in Jadavpur University who taught me to write alternative histories. I am indebted to Prof. Nirban Basu and Prof. Sajal Nag for their continuous guidance and encouragement that substantially improved my research abilities. My heartfelt regards for Prof. Chittabrata Palit who was always by my side in my formative years. I profoundly thank Professor Boria Majumdar who has always been an outstanding role model as a sports historian, scholar and person.

I greatly appreciate and recognize the effort and dedication of all the contributors, without whose active support I could not have completed this task. I am grateful to my institution, Ramsaday College, Howrah, my institutional head Prof. Pralay Talapatra and my colleagues for their reassuring presence. I appreciate the support of the entire teaching fraternity of the department of History of Rabindra Bharati University, Kolkata, where I serve as a guest lecturer. Special thanks go to Mr. Subrata Das of Setu Prakashani for his willingness to publish this book.

Special consideration and thanks to Souvik Naha and Avipsu Halder, brilliant research scholars at JNU, for their support and unbridled enthusiasm. They helped me to gather, manage, and organize endless streams of data over regular, long discussions in pursuit of completing this book. They actually corrected many flaws of mine as well as checked almost all the articles between the lines. This volume would have never materialized but for their active involvement. My friend Binayak Datta is also to be thanked for his active support. Special thanks go to Sean Brown for his active support and encouragement in all of my academic endeavours. I am thankful to Sabyasachida who has always stood by me like an elder brother.

I could not produce a list of acknowledgments without addressing my Dada- I am truly blessed to have such a supportive pillar right beside me in every step of my life even after his sad demise. Mamoni, who left me alone couple of years back, would have been the happiest person to witness this volume. Finally the task of editing this book could not have been accomplished without the support of my wife, Aparna, and my little daughter Anushka. I attribute all my successes in life to their continuous inspirations. My family's sacrifices and belief in me made this venture possible and life a joy.

Amitava Chatterjee

Contents

Preface

There can be little dispute regarding the crucial role of modern sport in recent and present global history, in terms of sport's political, cultural, social, educational, gender and economic significance. Eric Hobsbawm, it is well known, believed modern sport to be one of the most significant social practices of the late nineteenth century. In the twentieth century, increasing professionalization of sport and the growth of club culture across the world, growing commercialism associated with mega events like the Olympics and nationalism, which is at the root of contemporary sporting discourse, took the importance of sport to new heights. In the twenty-first century, as the world becomes a global village thanks to the internet and social networking sites, for many the English language, music and sport will be the central subjects of debate across the world.

I have elsewhere in several of my books raised the question of the inexcusable neglect of sport in Indian social science writing. The reason, however, is not hard to find. Sport, till recently, was branded as leisure and entertainment and not deemed a serious subject of academic debate by scholars of modern India. In doing so they neglected an importance lens to study Indian society better, an attempt made well by Amitava Chatterjee in this book. Take the case of the Olympics for instance.

In most accounts of Olympic history across the world, India's Olympic journey is a mere footnote. A detailed probe, however, demonstrates that India was an important strategic outpost in the Olympic family, which started as a global phenomenon at the turn of the twentieth century. The nascent movement's strategic alliance with the YMCA in Latin America and China, and subsequently in India, proves this point.

The Indian Olympic story conclusively validates the contention that the essence of Olympism does not reside only in medals won, records broken, or television rights sold. Particularly for India, the Olympic movement is important because it provides a unique prism to understand the complex evolution of regional and national identities.

Amitava rightly suggests that Indian sport has been a battle-ground where an emerging nation's internal dissensions were given full play: issues of national representation, colonial and post-colonial resistance, women's empowerment were all hotly debated and discussed and eventually and played out.

Each chapter in the book has been written with the intention of exploring the complex relationship between sport, identity and nationalism. At the same time, there is a conscious effort to come to terms with the philosophical debates that emerged in course of India's engagement with sporting ideals.

This book does not seek to ascertain the pre-eminence of one nation's tryst with sport over that of others. Rather, it emphasizes that claims to understand the true nature of sporting histories in certain countries or regions area studies, as it were -- are simplistic and short-sighted. Finally, it alludes to the fact that the story of India's engagement with sport is acutely political and provides a unique prism to understand the complex evolution of modern Indian societies through the lens of sport. Carefully edited, this book is a good addition to the growing corpus of scholarly research on sport in India.

Boria Majumdar
Kolkata, December 2012.

Foreword

In the modern world, sport has become an interesting and complex aspect of social life. Eric Hobsbawm once described sport as 'one of the most important new social practices' of the Europe of the late nineteenth and early twentieth centuries. [1] In the twentieth century, sport has emerged a major social phenomenon with political, cultural, economic, spiritual and aesthetic dimensions. Harold Perkin wrote two decades back: "As such the history of sport gives a unique insight into the way a society changes and impacts on other societies it comes into contact with and, conversely, the way those societies react back upon it." [2] As J.A. Mangan remarked on the eve of the new century, "... across the globe, sport is now too important to be left in the hands of sportsmen and women. More and more, it is the property of the 'People' in their various manifestations as politicians, entrepreneurs, educationists, commercialists, publicists, and, not least, academics." [3] When James Walvin wrote his influential essay "Sport, Social History and the Historian" [4] for the first volume of the *British Journal of Sports History* in 1984, he was fully convinced that "the history of a particular game had an importance which far transcended the game itself" and that "ultimately, sport could (and perhaps ought to) provide a reflection of wider issues and relationships in society at large." [5] Yet what seemed difficult for him to reconcile at that time was "the manifest discrepancy between the undeniable significance of sport in the contemporary world and the refusal of many to accept the importance of sport in its historical setting." [6]

While sport in the modern world is a proper subject of study for historians, it has taken an inordinately long time for them to appreciate its relevance for the lives of both the influential and the insignificant of past communities. [7] Failure to get sport into sharp academic focus may be 'a form of intellectual myopia born of long-established prejudice'. [8] Sport now has a significant place in Indian life. The study of sport as a serious intellectual discipline, however, remains not-too-developed in India. [9] While the Western academic world in the past two decades has appreciated the relevance of sport in the history of past and present communities, [10] India remains far backward in its appreciation of the role of sport in Indian society. In fact, the history of Sport is only in its adolescence in Indian academia. To establish its credibility as a viable academic discipline has proved something of a struggle for those Indian historians engaged in its research for the past one decade or so. The struggle is overcome elsewhere in the world. To overcome it in India, the teaching of sports history within the broader discipline of history from school to post graduate level must go hand in hand with serious research. While it is surprising to note that the modern Indian historian has more or less neglected sport as worthy of serious historical scholarship, cricket came to attract serious scholarly attention from the late 1980s. Hence, the production of scholarly studies on the social and cultural history of sports *sans* cricket in India has been few and far between. *And* as one crosses the still-somewhat-sacrosanct 'lakshmanrekha' of 1947, one is struck by an utter lack of academic appreciation of the significance of sport in modern Indian life in historical perspectives. The problems and prospects of sports history in India emanate mostly from this lack of appreciation on the part of Indian historians. [11] Yet, amidst this long-term neglect of sport as a proper subject of historical study, quite a few studies have tried to redress this imbalance in the past one decade. The result is the generation of steady interest in the subject, leading to quality researches on various aspects of the history of Indian sport. It is in this context that the present work edited by Amitava Chatterjee assumes enormous significance.

Like many other forms of social behaviour, as Walvin rightly noted, sporting activity is largely socially and historically determined. [12] He further pointed out that "the sports historian and sociologist need to reach beneath the surface, behind the obvious facts of sporting history, if their studies are to be any more than yet another quasi-antiquarianism masquerading as serious social history." [13] Following Walvin, Boria Majumdar argues that "a study of sport history is crucial not only for an understanding of the evolution of the sporting heritage of the Indian nation, but for a deeper appreciation of the seemingly unrelated political processes such as nationalism, [and] colonial culture ...." [14] According to Ramachandra Guha, there have been two approaches to the Indian history of sport. [15] The first has focussed narrowly on its practice, the background of its patrons and players, the evolution of its associations and tournaments, and on how it pays or does not pay for itself. The second approach, which Guha himself prefers, uses sport to illuminate themes of wider interest and relevance. "It views sport as a *relational idiom,* a sphere of activity which expresses, in concentrated form, the values, prejudices, divisions and unifying symbols of a society." [16] The present work seems to have taken the second approach.

There has also been an irrational yet popular belief that only the 'committed', the insiders or the practitioners are qualified to pursue sports history. This is certainly a flawed assumption. Personal experience or membership of course can be useful at times in understanding 'certain distinct sensibilities which outsiders could never experience'. [17] But that should never be considered a deciding factor in pursuing academic research on sport. Walvin is again pertinent in his comment:

> (S)uch claims to exclusivity are intellectually crippling and depend ultimately for their *rationale* on the belief that there

> is, or ought to be, only one particular approach or interpretation of historical experience. It is to be hoped that sports history will avoid such factional fights, although this is not to claim that sporting practitioners have *nothing* to tell us. Far from it. What is quite clear however is that one does not need to be player, spectator or *aficionado* of any sport to appreciate its broader social, or historical significance.[18]

It is not necessary therefore for social historians to describe events or matches that they never saw or to engage in discussions of the tactics employed in a match. Nevertheless, it can be useful to have knowledge of the evolution of a game's technicalities, which sometimes exerts important sway on its social history and vice versa.

The problems faced by a sports historian in India are both frustrating and challenging; frustrating because the essentially 'non-academic' character of sports authorities, personalities and spectators in India makes the task of collecting primary materials hopelessly difficult; challenging not only because researchers have to establish the credibility of this new domain of research by overcoming all the odds that commonly accompany an under researched field, but because they have to confront a conscious, sophisticated exploitation of this under developed state of research by some not-too-learned academic or non-academic writers. It is therefore high time for Indian historians to include sports studies as an integral part of social historical research *and* teaching. Quality publications on the history and culture of sport are a prime requisite to promote the teaching and research in the field. Such efforts will help dispel the erroneous views about the relative unimportance of sport in the shaping of modern Indian society and culture and make students aware of the extent to which entertainment and leisure have a compelling influence on their lives. As important, these will certainly encourage them to pursue research on sports history in future.

Chatterjee's effort is a significant contribution to fulfill the above objectives. The work reinforces the premise that the history of South Asian sport and its relation with nationalism can be meaningfully understood only by looking beyond the sports field. Again, any study of the history of sport is intertwined with important issues of political and cultural history. The issues addressed in the volume albeit a random sample of themes include some of the most pertinent ones that concern any social historian of modern South Asia & physical exercise and mass culture; colonial masculinity and game hunting; gender and sport; crowd violence and India-Pakistan relations; literary representations of sport; national identity and fandom; diverse sports and nationalist consciousness, with examples ranging from Bengal and Northeast India to the United States of America.

The attempt here is therefore to bring to light the importance of sport in colonial and postcolonial societies as an essentially cultural experience, political tool, social instrument and nationalist force. In this sense, it contributes to the growing body of literature on the history of sport in South Asia. The work has attempted to identify questions that still need to be asked, raise issues that urge serious debates and offer insights that can stimulate future research. One may recall J.A. Mangan's much celebrated emphasis on 'a triadic approach' in this context: '...the analytic approach will be multicultural; balance, breadth and depth will be the ambition; completeness of perspective will be the aim.'[19] Amitava's effort has made a significant contribution in this direction in the Indian context. More studies, I hope, will follow to supplement this smart effort.

Kausik Bandyopadhyay
Associate Professor in History
West Bengal State University
Academic Editor
Soccer and Society (Routledge)

References

Eric Hobsbawm, "Mass-Producing Traditions: Europe, 1870-1914", in Eric Hobsbawm and Terence Ranger, eds. *The Invention of Tradition* (Cambridge: Cambridge University Press, 1983), p. 298.

Harold Perkin, "Teaching the Nations How to Play: Sport and Society in the British Empire and Commonwealth", in J.A. Mangan, ed. *The Cultural Bond: Sport, Empire, Society* (London: Frank Cass, 1992), p. 212.

J.A. Mangan, "Series Editor's Foreword", in Mike Cronin and David Myall, eds. *Sporting Nationalisms: Identity, Ethnicity, Immigration and Assimilation* (London: Frank Cass, 1998), pp. Xi-xii.

James Walvin, "Sport, Social History and the Historian", *British Journal of Sports History*, Vol. 1, No. 1 (1984), pp. 5-13.

Ibid., p. 6.

Ibid., p. 13.

J.A. Mangan, "Introduction", in J.A. Mangan, ed. *Pleasure, Profit, Proselytism: British Culture and Sport at Home and Abroad: 1700-1914* (London: Frank Cass, 1988), p. 1.

Ibid.

Boria Majumdar, "The Vernacular in Sports History", *Economic and Political Weekly*, Vol. XXXVII, No. 29 (2002), p. 3069.

Academic pursuit of sports history in the West began in the 1970s and got concretized in the next decade with the publication of a series of works by a galaxy of social scientists that included such names as J.A. Mangan, Wray Vamplew, Tony Mason, Allen Guttman, Richard Holt and Peter McIntosh. Institutional organization to support their efforts began in 1982 when the British Society of Sports History was founded. Distinguished publishers such as Frank Cass offered instant active support and launched *the British Journal of Sports History* that was later transformed into *The International Journal of the History of Sport*. These institutional efforts met with welcome parallels in other Western countries like Scotland, Finland, Sweden, Denmark, Brazil and the USA. Scholars from Asian countries like China, Japan and South Korea as well as Australia too were quick to recognize the importance of sports history and joined the venture in right earnest since the early 1990s. Finally, the Cass launched three more journals, viz. *Culture, Sport, Society; Soccer and Society* and *European Sports History Review* and most importantly *the Sport in the Global Society* Series in the late 1990s under the auspices of the International Research Centre for Sport, Socialization and Society instituted at the Strathclyde University, Scotland with J.A. Mangan as the executive academic editor. The huge success of all these ventures further points to the current healthy state of sports history in the West.

11. For an in-depth discussion on this, see Kausik Bandyopadhyay, "Sports History in India: Prospects and Problems", *The International Journal of the History of Sport*, Vol. 22. No. 3-4 (2005), pp. 708-721.
12. Walvin, "Sport, Social History and the Historian", p. 8.
13. Ibid.
14. Majumdar, "The Vernacular", p. 3069.
15. Ramachandra Guha, "Cricket and Politics in Colonial India", *Past and Present*, No. 161 (November1998), p. 157.
16. Ibid.
17. Walvin, "Sport, Social History and the Historian", p. 7.
18. Ibid.
19. Paul Dimeo and James Mills, eds. *Soccer in South Asia: Empire, Nation, Diaspora* (London: Frank Cass, 2002), p.xiii.

INTRODUCTION

The traditional consignment of sport to the margins of academic interests and respectability is by no means confined to any one discipline. Nevertheless, anthropologists who have been persuaded to take games and sport as legitimate subjects of study have learned much about how best to link this field to their discipline's core analytical concerns. In John MacAloon's view, sport sociologists were late to take sport as seriously as did the world around them. Sport scholars, he opined, should 'stop perceiving ourselves as Quixotes if we are ever to cease acting and writing as Sancho Panzas'. Sports, loosely defined, are found elsewhere in the world in which anthropologists work: in 1945 George Peter Murdock listed 'athletic sports' as a human universal. Anthropologists and particularly folklorists have paid attention to sports and games throughout the history of discipline. However, these treatments of sports were typically peripheral to the central problematic of the discipline, such as kinship, ritual, evolution of state and so on.

The study of sport has endowed a fruitful empirical challenge for sociologists, social historians and cultural analysts, informing major debates on structure and agency, globalization and identity, and its sources and determinants. It has proved to be a critical lens through which we understand the impact of major social processes and changes both upon the fabric of everyday life in the modern period and upon the genesis and character of related cultural forms such as the media. Sport and leisure can also illuminate the nature of ideologies in a society. Sport should be understood not as some quasi-autonomous institution, as some kind of self-sufficient social institution or sub-system related in various ways to parallel institutions within the society, but rather as a constructive element in everyday life and popular culture, within particular social and historical settings.

The construction of sport through individual personalities- the creation of individuals with whom we, the audience, can identify- is also one of the means by which the value of "immediacy" is realized. We are taken closer to the action and the participants than we could ever be as mere spectators at the event. Sports coverage is also literally immediate, in the sense that much of it is broadcast live from sports stadia and race courses. Much of the appeal lies in this rapidity- though 'recorded highlights' are not exactly poor substitutes for live coverage. Nevertheless, they require condensing and dramatizing to restore their attractiveness. Yet this sense of immediacy- the transparency of media presentation- is illusory to some extent. The immediacy is, in fact, mediated between us and the event stands the cameras, camera angles, producers' choices of shots, the commentators' interpretations the whole invisible apparatus of media presentation. We can hardly view the whole event; we see the parts filtered through this process of presentation. It locates us as watchers in a very different position from the spectators at the event itself we cannot see what goes on out of sight of the cameras. Even live spectatorship is not wholesome; as no one occupies the same space they are bound to produce multiple perspectives.

Therefore, sport and leisure cultures must be researched first-hand and in close-up for the meanings and values that they express, represent, confirm or challenge and for their varying relationships with other (to paraphrase P. Bourdieu) social fields. Such analysis can demonstrate the importance of cultures in times of seismic cultural change oras is more widely and commonly the case in times of cultural stability and continuity and, most importantly, in relation to more broadly impacting social forces and trends. Two such trends underline how sport resonates with the sounds the signs of the times: firstly, the making and remaking of modern nations with the concomitant expression or formulation of national identity; and secondly, the rise of consumer culture lived locally but manifestly global, in both public and more privatised and individualized forms.

Nationalism is essentially political but is often fostered through nonpolitical channels such as sports in various contexts. Colonial India was no exception. Political leaders were acutely conscious of the integral linkage between the two different manifestations of nationalism. They appreciated the mission of the silent nationalists to elevate their country to the highest pedestal of triumph. They were the visible emblems of India's honour at a time when it was customary for the British to humiliate the Indian in every walk of life. Macaulay's famous diatribe, describing Bengalis as a race of cowards, inflicted a permanent festering wound in the latter, which was reflected in two distinct spheres. On the one hand, it spurred them to specialize in physical culture. On the other hand, this goaded them to excel over the British in the field of play. While the former was integrally linked with the mainstream nationalist movement, the latter was connected tangentially though not without political ramifications. Herein lays the paradox of the Indian nationalist movement where physical culture, a part of sports, became the abettor of militant nationalism. Most of the revolutionaries happened to be sportsmen of high caliber, endowed with strong physique. Thus, despite its insularity from the arena of politics, sports proved the paradoxical catalyst of nationalism in India. It symbolized a new martial spirit, inculcating masculine attributes and youthful effervescence which matched the integral philosophy of the revolutionary movement. The literature on national identity and nationalism is enormous, some of which has been reviewed in the context of sport. National identity can be powerfully felt, as sport provides a vehicle for the articulation and often public demonstration of national identity and nationalist sentiments. It can also be garnered for political purposes, sport providing a means for the expression of national pride on an integral stage.

Another vital influence, sadly neglected by many aspirationally ethnographic sociologists, has been the everyday version of the French model of total history. The everyday-ness of material life has become a major focus for the Annales School. Oral historical accounts of sports and leisure cultures and qualitative data on leisure lifestyles and practices are vital sources to arrive at a comprehensive argument on behalf of the sometimes marginalised cultures of consumption and leisure.

Sport draws on and gives a symbolic value to particular local identities, constructing "communities" of interest and support. This is probably most visible in professional football, which was historically provided to a mass working class audience by local businessmen and traders as one of the means through which cross-class loyalties could be established beyond the local and regional identities. It exemplifies the most socially visible identification constructed and maintained through sport as a cultural symbol. This is the connection between sport and nationalism whose best example in the Indian context perhaps is Mohun Bagan's Shield Victory of 1911 & barefooted indigenous youth challenging the mighty colonizers in the football field and against all odds snatching the shield from the East Yorks. Sport is a forum that allows the construction of the nation as "us"- rising above and displacing whatever minor divisions there may be.

Essential to the revolutionary movement of India and Bengal was the urge to discover spiritual fulfillment in the display of masculine traits in the battle of life. One of the earliest advocates of physical culture as a means of national emancipation was Swami Vivekananda. It was he who directed Jatin Mukherjee, the firebrand revolutionary, to join the wrestling centre of Kshetracharan and Ambikacharan Guha near the Hedua lake of

Kolkata. Srish Chandra Guha, grandson of Ambikacharan was the President of the Indian Association of Singapore and provided financial assistance to the Azad Hind Fouz of Netaji Subhas Chandra Bose. Another grandson of his, Jatindranath Guha commonly known as Gobar Guha who won the award of Champion of the Empire in wrestling in 1938, was also very close to Subhas Bose. Vivekananda himself practiced wrestling at the centre of Nabagopal Mitra and also the Simla Byayam Samiti of Jogen Pal.

Sport was not simply a matter of imperial domination or indigenous subversion; participation in sport did not imply acceptance of colonial class order. Influences moved in both directionsthe top-down approaches went alongside bottom-up activities. Sport also came to be supported by colonial subjects for reasons that were indigenous, which neither supported nor challenged the British. Organised games functioned crucially within imperial contexts as a means for disseminating British ideals of masculinity as well as constructing alternate and constructing masculinities around which colonial subjects could mobilize. By and large, false consciousness and social control are inherently specious explanations for popular enthusiasms and actions. Working class and colonial spectators were not duped into carrying about sports as a way to distract them from revolutionary activity; rather it is clear that a passion for sports was genuine and deeply held across the Empire and the class spectrum. Although elites might have promoted sports for one set of reasons and the subordinate parts of society might have embraced them for another, there was a certain commonality which is evident in newspaper accounts, letters to the editor, sporting memoirs and the like.

Sports play a key role in legitimising particular ideologies around masculinity and femininity that support the subjugation of women. While male domination is challenged in nearly every other sector of society, there is a whole field of activity where male dominance just seems to be taken for granted. The implications of this range from the exclusion of women from workplace discussions of sporting events, through the ubiquity of sporting metaphors in the language of business and politics; to the legitimisation of male violence. The link between sport and violence or sexual abuse by men against women has become one of the key issues within sports sociology. Women's increased success in sport could play a major role in challenging exclusive representations of masculinity as the gender of physical prowess. The shared masculinity upon which subordinate men seized to stake their claims to nationalised conceptions of manliness was based on banishment of women from public sphere. While sports represented an avenue for counter hegemonic form to be publicly produced and trumpeted, they rarely, at the authentically elite level at least, were beneficial to women regardless of their national, class or racial background. Pressures outside the actual games also influenced the manner in which they were played and organised. Colonial subjects acted as class surrogates for British. Colonial resistance to British supremacy was seen to have domestic ramifications.

Marxism and cultural studies represent contested and heterogeneous bodies of thought and their application to the study of sport has not been conducted in any uniform or systematic way. Furthermore, as theoretical traditions, Marxism and cultural studies are not necessarily synonymous, though there are clear overlaps between the two. Within sports studies, for example, the main thrust of cultural studies emerges out of a critique of orthodox Marxist approaches which raises the question as to what extent and in what ways do scholars working within an explicitly cultural studies framework remain within the Marxist problematic of interpretation and transformation. However the first phase in more formal Marxist influenced approaches to the study of sport and society emerged in the wake of cultural and political radicalism of the mid to the late 1960s.

This decade was the 'high point' for forms of anti-colonial resistance and Thirldworldist nationalism that had emerged during the 1950s. Variously labelled as neo-Marxism, Frankfurt-Marxism and structural Marxism, writers from the nascent Marxist sociology of sport eschewed the false neutrality of extant positivist paradigms.

After analysing almost all possible theoretical perspectives on the history of sport and its relation with other disciplines it is important to mention what the present volume seeks to achieve. It provides some of the substantive concerns, theoretical perspectives and interdisciplinary approaches that can usually be brought to the study of games, sports and cultures. In the first chapter, Boria Majumdar and Sean Brown picks up the question as to why, on the one hand, did cricket flourish in Pakistan and India? And why, on the other hand, is cricket not much played in the United States, with its heritage and 'special relationship' with Britain? For decades, historians have debated this question. This is yet another attempt to explicate how and why cricket and baseball, both with century-old histories, became national passions in two of the world's biggest erstwhile colonies, and was appropriated by indigenous peoples for purposes of confronting the Empirethe common reference point in both contexts.

Unfurling the thread of anti-imperial nationalism, Souvik Naha analyses the historiography of cricket and nationalism in colonial India. It is beyond doubt that sporting activities carried nationalist connotations, but the story of cricket was exceptional due to the variety of actors and processes involved. Unlike football or hockey, cricket was unable to elude the imperial label. As a result, it justified and undermined colonialism at the same time, depending on the meanings ascribed to it by various agents such as European officials and civilians, different indigenous religious communities, and secular cricket enthusiasts, in specific contexts. Naha evaluates the major debates around these acts of meaning-making notably the works of Ashis Nandy,

Ramachandra Guha and Boria Majumdar along with his personal observations. His article envisages colonial cricket as two distinct phases of collaboration and subversion. In the third section, he analyses the academic perspectives on the textual significance of *Lagaan*, discussing relative merits of the nationalist paradigm of resistance, modern nationalist consumerism, subaltern consciousness, and caste hierarchy and gender dynamics of the film. He concludes by suggesting a number of areas in which research on colonial cricket and nationalism can be furthered.

Jishnu Dasgupta analyses moments of crowd violence during India-Pakistan matches in the 1990s and early 2000s as part of a broader spectrum of post-independence nation-building. Although cricketers remained above hate-mongering, these cricket matches provided a space for religious and political antagonisms. The press bore much responsibility in drawing 'battlelines', highlighting the history of military conflict and strained diplomatic relations between the countries. Such reports have often been seen to have informed group sensibilities among spectatorsdivisions which are not restricted to class identities. According to Dasgupta, tensions escalated during the Kargil War, when certain political factions criticised acts of supporting Pakistan among certain sections of Indian Muslims, and suggested that they make open exhibitions of their patriotism. The martial imageries used in match reports helped little but polarise the communities further, provoking clashes at times. The hyper-nationalism was manifest in the World Cup 2003 contest between the countries as news snippets unfolded stories of Muslim supportwhose voluntariness was debatable, and communitarian victory celebrations. The 'revival series' of 2004 resonated with diplomatic initiatives rather than public interest. Notwithstanding the military rhetoric deployed to advertise the series, the warmth of Pakistani fans and the temperance by supporters of both sides sugar-coated the rivalry. However, the press made oblique references to specific fan behaviours, nationalities and the distinctive pride of winning against one particular country. Political parties tried to make the most of India's victory. The BJP initially emerged the clear winner, but their ensuing fall from power proved that electoral politics do not revolve around sportsthe two share contiguous but separate spaces. On the other side of the border, parties and factions of the press blamed the loss to a secret pact between the two countries. Hence, the proclaimed unity remained a pipe dream; the cloak of harmony often slipped to reveal the underbelly of political motives and national sentiments.

Avipsu Halder explores the potent force of civic and ethnic sporting nationalism in integrating the nation. Despite the theoretical distinction between the civic and the ethnic dimension of nationalism, sporting nationalism successfully merges the two. Sporting nationalism acts as a protective shield in preventing any symptoms of sub-nationalist tendencies. Finally, he shows how it weathers the storm of the globalizing tendencies in sports. The national identity in sport plays a critical role in the development of fandom, manifest in the support for football clubs in the transnational football leagues. For instance, the jerseys of several national teams attain brand value due to its association with the multinational corporations. Simply put, the national jerseys become renowned merchandize product. Halder's article ponders these multimodal attachments of the nation and contemporary commercial culture.

Suparna Ghosh contextualizes the participation of women in sporting activities during the colonial era, and the nationalist consciousness it underlined. Women's participation and triumph in sports was perceived as a victory of the colonial Indian masses against their colonizers. Besides, the article draws a parallel between the participation of women in the Indian national movement and in sports events to drive home two important claims. Firstly, sport is a representative of national identity. Secondly, as a corollary, sport becomes the theater of nationalist struggle for independence. The study uses numerous historical instances to consolidate this claim. Moreover, it highlights the process of conceptualizing the nation from the perspective of gender. In this context, it provides ample scope for its readers to explore the dynamics of Indian masculinities as viewed by the British. It concludes by claiming that the acts of participation and competition of Indian women with their European counterparts do reveal the ambivalence of neither emulating the imperial culture nor succumbing to it. Additionally, the triumph of Indian women in these sporting events added a dimension to the indigenous the nationalist ideology of the resilient Indian.

My article argues that the cult of manliness in the physical culture movement represented was the answer to racism of the white ruling class. The colonial stereotype of the 'effeminate' Bengali babu, for example, was challenged by the protagonists of physical culture. Sports were encouraged to make Bengali men healthy and instill the necessary moral virtues. In the second half of the nineteenth century bodybuilding and wrestling became a common feature in the districts of Bengal. Middle class Bengalis made several efforts to revive the culture of akharas or gymnasiums in order to cultivate and instil a sense of pride in the physical prowess of the Bengalis. These akharas were the cradles of many wrestlers who earned name and fame internationally. They succeeded in defeating almost all the foreign opponents whenever they faced each other in wrestling rings irrespective of places in India and abroad and truly fought for the sake of their nation's pride. In my article I have tried to explore into such issues in the context of late colonial Bengal with particular reference to emergence of physical exercise as an aspect of mass culture.

Binayak Dutta investigates attempts of constructing colonial masculinity in North East India through European practice of gaming. While it is admitted that colonialism represented both an ideology and practice, construction of colonialism through sports is a recent effort. In this process, it is imperative to examine such practices in colonial North-east India, in order to give such studies an inclusive character. This study is interesting as it makes this reconstruction of colonial masculinity through the diary noting of three European Military officers, who were in this peripheral region at some point of their life and which have seen the light of print today. The importance of these diaries lay in the fact that they hold the evidence for narration of 'native' gaming practices, a counter to colonial claims justifying hegemony.

Debashis Majumder makes a comparative analysis of the role of three sports-cricket, football and hockey-in arousing nationalist consciousness among the people of India. He envisages the manner through which football scored over cricket and hockey to become the representative of national identity in colonial India. The paper traces out the history of the national movement and the role that football played in this context. The paper discusses important theoretical underpinnings of nationalism. It replicates the manner in which nation and nationalism has been conceptualized in the realm of sport. The paper tries to communicate the idea that there are two ways of conceptualizing a nation: firstly, through an elitist perspective; secondly, from the point of view of the masses. It offers an interesting explanation of the elite-mass dichotomy in the context of sporting nationalism. The paper refers to the fact that it was mainly the maharajas and the elites who patronised cricket. In contrast, football manifested the 'Indianness' in sports, evident by team composition, the style of play. The paper communicates the idea that the colonized people conceived the football field as a battleground between them and the colonizer. Hence, the famous IFA Shield victory by Mohan Bagan is viewed as a triumph of the Indian masses against the imperial might of the British. To put it differently, any sport that possesses a mass appeal becomes successful in representing the nation/national sentiment.

The article co-authored by me and my colleague Amitabha Bandopadhyay builds on the secondary literature on sports spectatorship by revealing critical issues related to the cultural, social and economic dimensions of a sport victory in colonial society. The article grapples with the process through which these elements influence football fandom in Bengal. It pivots around the argument that football fandom emphasized the political and cultural factors in conceptualizing notions of identity. It illustrates Mohan Bagan's triumph in the 1911 IFA Shield and the bitter rivalry between two premier football clubs, East Bengal and Mohan Bagan to reveal important facets of identity formation and fandom in the realm of sport. The victory of Mohan Bagan in 1911 portrayed the role of sporting fandom in representing a nation. The support for the home team was perceived as a reaction against the British imperialism in India. In other words, it was an alternative way of addressing the political grievances by the Indians. In contrast, the rivalry between Mohan Bagan and East Bengal focuses on the role of sport in extrapolating the phenomenon of sub-nationalism. In this case, sport resembles the differential cultural and ethnic traits of the people of these two communities. The paper concludes by proposing the view that football in Bengal has played a critical role in defining both nationalism and sub-nationalism.

Shubhankar Roy explores the representation of sport as a central idiom of American society in two novels by F. Scott Fitzgerald. Sport was one of the vehicles of American exceptionalism which formed the ideological foundation of its cultural and commercial expansion in the early twentieth century. Fitzgerald's allusions to sports spectators and practices posit a critical account of this social history. In *This Side of Paradise,* Fitzgerald used football in Princeton as a device to demonstrate the prevalence of class strata and meritocracy, establish social homogeneity as a myth, and indicate excellence at cultural activities as a tool for social mobility. In *The Great Gatsby,* references to cricket and football signify personality traits and class locations of two of its protagonists. The novel used baseball as a symbol of American identity and nationalism. With reference to the novel, Roy shows how baseball embodied middle-class rectitude as against the supposed elitism of cricket and was used as the mortar in the edifice of the American nation. In contrast, instances of cheating at a golf tournament or fixing the World Series exhibit the infirmity of value construction and conspiracy within particular classes. A nation remains elusive to the proponents of a sport-loving society, yet the credentials of sport in constructing traditions and milieus are self-evident.

Though from the nineteenth century the domain of sports remained confined to elitist colours of the society but gradually it penetrated among the masses. Sport became a part and parcel of Indian society. The ambiguities between the two theoretical stances the colonial and elitist nature of sport as it was enthusiastically espoused from the middle decades of nineteenth century in India and the recent theoretical identification of sports as an essential component of popular culture have accounted for relative shyness among historians in grappling with the subject. Sports history till date is not so much a widely accepted form of history which is often kept aside of mainstream historical discourse by historians of repute in India. But interestingly many academics especially from Kolkata, Delhi and Assam have started showing their passion for sports in its historical form. As far as Kolkata academia is concerned different universities like Calcutta University, Rabindra Bharati University, West Bengal State University and Jadavpur University have included the history of sports in their post-graduate curriculum. The curriculum of C.B.S.E has of late included the cricketing history of colonial India. Interestingly, the dimension of sports and nationalism (with special reference to the historic I.F.A shield victory of Mohun Bagan against the colonizers) has been included in the newly structured syllabus of West Bengal Council of Higher Secondary Education. This will obviously be helpful for the students who will develop an understanding of "total history" from a very tender age.

This volume is an earnest effort on the part of a young researcher to gather different aspects of sporting culture of India in the form of historical discourse. My students of post graduation level has been a source of immense inspiration who questioned me about various aspects of sports history thus insisting me to edit this volume which will quench the thirst of 'n' number of students who seriously express their concern for the most neglected aspect of social history- 'sports history'.

Amitava Chatterjee
Kolkata
December, 2012

References

Alan Tomlinson, *Sport and Leisure Cultures*, University of Minnesota Press, 2005.

Jeremy MacClany (ed) *Sport, Identity and Ethnicity*, Oxford, 1996.

John Mac Aloon, *This Great Symbol: Pierre de Coubertin and the Origin of the Modern Olympic Games*, Chicago; Chicago University Press, 1981.

Pierre Bourdieu, 'Programme for a Sociology of Sport', in P. Bourdieu, *In Other Words: Essays Towards a Reflexive Sociology*, Stanford: Stanford University Press, 1990.

R.D. Mandell, Sport: *A Cultural History*, New York, Columbia University Press, 1984.

Roger Caillois, *Man , Play and Games*, New York, Free Press of Glencoe, 1961.

Why Baseball, Why Cricket? Differing Nationalisms, Differing Challenges

Boria Majumdar and Sean Brown

> Cricket, the quintessential English game, is nonetheless one of the most international of sports. It is a dominant game in more countries than any other sport except soccer, in lands as varied as Australia, India, Pakistan, South Africa and the Commonwealth Caribbean. But a glance at the global map of cricket poses a remarkable cultural puzzle.
>
> Why, on the one hand, does the game flourish in lands like Pakistan and India. ... And why, on the other hand, is cricket not much played in the United States, with its heritage and 'special relationship' with Britain?
>
> The puzzle only deepens when one considers that cricket was once popular in the... United States. It rivaled baseball for most of the 19th century, with as many stories in the sports pages of The New York Times until 1880.
>
> So the puzzle is not so much why it was never adopted in North America, but why in the early 20th century it was subsequently rejected in favor of baseball. [1]

For decades, historians have debated this question. In fact, its significance is such that publishers have also been drawn into its fold, albeit unknowingly. The best exemplar of such inadvertent participation is the most recent New York Oxford University Press edition of the Thomas Hughes classic *Tom Brown's Schooldays*. On the cover jacket of this title, Tom holds a bat; that it is a baseball bat and not a cricket bat is almost certain. It can be conjectured that this is because Tom is more drawn to baseball in the United States. [2] Contrastingly, editions of *Tom Brown's Schooldays* popular in the Indian subcontinent clearly depict cricketer Tom standing to take guard. [3] In other words, the cover jacket of *Tom Brown's Schooldays* unknowingly serves as an entry point to explicate how and why cricket and baseball, both with century-old histories, became national passions in two of the world's biggest erstwhile colonies, and were appropriated and subverted by indigenous peoples for purposes of confrontation against the British Empire. In both cases, the common reference-point remains the empire. While in the Americas the desire was to dissociate American sport from British sport, in countries such as India, where the empire lasted far longer, the intention was to appropriate and subsequently indigenize British sports for purposes of resistance. In fact, the American reaction to empire sport was simply the opposite of the Indian retort to imperial games. One need only compare the American and Indian responses to cricket to see this great chasm in views towards the game. In doing so, the historian ends up with the same theme - nationalism - asserting itself in completely inverse ways across the globe.

In India, the nationalist movement from the close of the nineteenth century made it imperative that cricket be taken up as a non-violent means to compete with the ruling British. In the United States, where independence was achieved a century and a half earlier than India, this need was totally irrelevant. Rather, what was important in the US was to sever all sporting connections with the empire to emphasize an independent American identity. It is this inverse invocation of nationalism, we have argued, that best provides the key to unwinding the old dichotomy 'Why baseball, why cricket?' in differing global contexts.

Sport is a most pervasive and enduring theme in the history of British imperialism. The central feature of its power is the subconscious influence it has exerted in both colonial and post-colonial conditions'. [4] Despite the obvious influence of British games, few issues are clear when thoughts turn to the origins of baseball in the United States. That the governing body of organized baseball knowingly perpetuated a myth regarding the game's creation further complicates the issue. For the casual fan, the debunking of the Abner Doubleday myth left is less than satisfying, as nothing is likely to have taken its place. [5] Once the invention of baseball is taken from Cooperstown, where is it to go? For the purpose of this essay and in order to gain a sense of the historical context, it is necessary to construct a rudimentary history of early baseball in the United States. This is more an attempt to synthesize multiple sources into a coherent if incomplete idea of the early structure of what eventually became modern baseball. [6]

First, it is generally accepted that modem baseball owes a debt to the British game of rounders. [7] At the very least, historians place baseball on the same evolutionary chain of stick and ball games that produced rounders in England, as well as townball and variations of 'old cat' in the United States, seen as American versions of rounders. [8] In all these games some common elements existed: a pitcher tossed a ball to a batter, who attempted to hit it and traverse a set of'bases' before being put out, which usually happened when the batter was struck with a thrown ball while not safely at a base. In fact, the term 'base ball' is itself not peculiar to the United States, being a game known and played in England in the eighteenth century. [9] These games were generally played by children before 1840, and were mostly looked upon with disdain by American peoples who had yet to be exposed to any muscular Christian doctrine.

Most of these games progressed with children playing by more or less similar rules, variations of which were constructed to suit the needs of particular contexts. As industrialization changed the leisure habits of the American people, [10] ball games such as townball experienced a growth among adults: 'As industrial technology and the expansion of commerce forced city people to adjust their work and play habits, mass production and new inventions in transportation and communications facilitated modern forms of sport'. [11] As early as 1831, young adults were regularly meeting for games of townball between Philadelphia and New Jersey. The group eventually merged to form the Olympic Ball Club in 1833. The dub in little time drew up a constitution and rules of play for what was soon to become a standardized game. Meanwhile, dubs possessing similar structures but significantly different rules were coming up in Boston and New York. They generally distinguished themselves by their geography, such as the 'Massachusetts game' or the 'New York game'. These regional differences coexisted for some time.

Eventually, it was the New York version of the game that was accepted as modern American baseball, an acceptance engineered by the most prominent club in New York, the Knickerbockers. [12] The Knickerbockers' chief organizer was Alexander Cartwright, a fireman and bookstore proprietor. In 1845, it was Cartwright who was responsible for the codification of the Knickerbocker rules, and if credit is due to any one person for the version of baseball that nearly everyone today would recognize, it is Cartwright. New York's peerless standing among American cities helped ensure that the Knickerbocker style of baseball would spread much more quickly and efficiently than the versions played in Philadelphia or Boston. As Melvin Adelman notes, 'sporting practices in New York City were more likely to shape sporting practices throughout the country'. [13] When the National Association of Base Ball Players (NABBP) was formed, it adopted almost verbatim the Knickerbocker rules. [14] With the wide acceptance of the New York game, modern baseball was born.

Though claims of baseball as the 'national' game of the United States originated as far back as 1856 with the New York Mercury's coining of the phrase 'national pastime',[15] it was not until after the Civil War that baseball's supremacy was assured. Before 1860 (and to a limited extent afterwards), cricket enjoyed its own popularity in the US, and the question as to whether cricket or baseball would ultimately capture the American sporting heart was still unanswered. The earliest record of cricket in the Americas was found in the 'secret diary' of William Byrd II of Virginia and the date, believe it or not, is 25 April 1709.[16] Subsequent references to cricket date back to Georgia in 1737 and an advertisement in a New York paper for players in 1739. The first recorded American cricket match was in New York in 1751 on the site of what is today the Fulton Fish Market in Manhattan.

Cricket, records indicate, remained popular in the Americas until the 1860s and the first recognized international match between Canada and USA was attended by over 10,000 spectators at Bloomingdale Park in New York in 1844.[17] Tours to and from the US were common until the 1880s, and the best moment for US cricket came when a United States side defeated the West Indies in an international match in British Guyana in 1880. Though matches between Americans and British residents were played on the American West Coast right through the 1880s and 1890s,[18] cricket, by the turn of the century, had given way to baseball. By the end of the Civil War, baseball's ascendance to the top of the American sporting pantheon was inevitable, if not already complete. Though cricket would experience a revival in the 1870s,[19] it would never again compete with baseball as either a participatory or a spectator sport in the United States. The most compelling question to emerge from this development is simply 'Why?' What were the factors that allowed baseball to prevail over cricket, despite the latter's longer history both inside and outside the United States? It is to this question that we now turn.

In the existing historiography that attempts to reconcile the cricket vs. baseball conundrum, two interrelated themes emerge: the structure of the games themselves and the pervading cultural values of the United States and other countries. Structurally, issues have tended to revolve around the time differential between baseball and cricket, the pace of play and the spectator- and player-friendliness of the two sports. Temporally, it has been explained that baseball offered a distinct advantage over cricket because it could be completed in a matter of hours instead of days. [20] The difference in the pace of action between the two sports has also been emphasized.

However, these barriers are not necessarily insurmountable or even valid. Melvin Adelman has in fact challenged both of these arguments in pure empirical terms. Temporally, he cites the fact that baseball teams met during two afternoons a week for practice as well as the fact that in England and the United States, artisans had found the time to play the game. In effect, it seems that at least from a participation standpoint time was not a crucial element. Rather, it is baseball's ability to allow for a more intimate involvement of fans that is seen to stimulate its appeal. While this argument may possess a certain amount of merit in that it is factually correct, it does not help explain the popularity of cricket in other parts of the world, especially the Indian subcontinent. [21] Is the American sporting fan so unique as to require a more intimate view of the action? Additionally, these arguments fail to explain the enormous popularity of American football, which, when viewed live at the stadium, is notoriously 'fan-unfriendly'. The large field and the distant stands that characterize professional American football stadiums in the United States have in no way hurt the sport's popularity, and attendance for the National Football League is healthy. [22]

Culturally, the supposed advantages of baseball over cricket become more diffuse. Cited reasons that baseball is culturally suited for the United States rest on (among other things) its association with the season cycle, its trend towards extreme quantification, rural nostalgia, its ability to produce folk heroes and as 'a compensatory mechanism for the travails of industrial life',[23] all of which are seen as something intrinsic to the American character. In trying to contend with these arguments, Jules Tygiel begins to scratch the surface of what seems to be the most compelling advantage of baseball over cricket. In labelling the preceding arguments as ahistorical, he states: 'They describe values and attributes that Americans have grafted onto baseball after it became embedded in our culture'.[24] In essence, because baseball was not established the way cricket was, it was shaped by the people that began to standardize it. It was natural that baseball would reflect the values of nineteenth-century America, because it was forged during that era by people who held those values. Its destiny as a 'national' game rested on its relative formlessness during that era compared to cricket, with its long (and foreign) history. Baseball's malleability during this time period inevitably led to it taking on 'national' characteristics, a flexibility seen at the time as notable. In 1868, the American Chronicle of Sports and Pastimes claimed that baseball had changed more in ten years than cricket had in the last 400. It also noted that this change had allowed baseball to reflect American values.[25]

It is this question about the foreign nature of cricket that leads to the most compelling of arguments surrounding cricket and baseball. There exists a body of evidence that points to emergent American nationalism as a critical component of the battle for American sporting loyalty. American nationalism in the mid-nineteenth century was still somewhat a novel concept. Carl Degler has argued that the American nation emerged in part due to the Civil War, before which American nationalism was lacking. The threat of southern secession and the potential for the United States to break up less than a century after independence provided an arena where the nation was truly formed. It is therefore no surprise that an American sporting nationalism would assert itself at this time as well. Thus, the 1850s became the critical moment in this battle for sporting supremacy. As American nationalism emerged and strengthened, baseball, continually forged and moulded to suit the needs of Americans, began to assert a stronger hold on the American public, eventually pushing cricket forever into the margins of American sporting life. It was during this decade that calls for a national game were heard, and it was this decade that saw the term 'national pastime' first written. The need to create a national game grew out of the American desire to 'emancipate their games from foreign patterns'. [26] Additionally, Porter's *Spirit of the Times*, a prominent sporting periodical of the time, demanded a game peculiar to the citizens of the United States, one distinctive from the games of the British or the Germans. The *New York Times* also pined for the independence of American sports. [27] Once baseball had become the unequivocal American sport, great pains were undertaken to protect its American heritage. It was this desperate need to divest baseball of its British origins that led to the creation and perpetuation of the Abner Doubleday myth surrounding baseball's creation. It began with a speech by Abraham G. Mills in 1889, [28] given in New York upon the conclusion of a baseball tour led by sporting goods magnate Albert Spalding. [29] During the speech Mills, who was president of the National League at the time, claimed to have found definitive proof of the American origins of baseball, stating that 'patriotism and research alike vindicate the claim that [baseball] is America in its origin'. [30] This claim was met quite enthusiastically by the crowd with shouts of 'No rounders!' [31]

This speech and the subsequent media support led sportswriter Henry Chadwick to defend the rounders theory, which had enjoyed popular support up until that point. Chadwick's 1903 article reasserting the English origin of the American game riled Spalding, a vehement defender of the American origins of baseball. Upon reading the article, Spalding set out to settle the issue once and for all. At his request, a special committee was formed to ascertain the true origins of the game. It included men of 'high repute and undoubted knowledge of Base

Ball' as well as two United States senators and A.G. Mills. According to Seymour, 'While the committee supplied the window dressing, A.G. Mills did what actual work was done'.[32] After gathering evidence from a variety of sources, the committee issued its final report, the Mills Report, three years later. The report, dated 30 December 1907, affirmed the American origin of the game, and officially ordained the myth of Abner Doubleday. The committee based its final report largely on the letter written by Abner Graves, who had claimed to have played baseball with Doubleday in Cooperstown. Graves claimed that Doubleday had spontaneously invented baseball in 1839. However, three central problems cropped up immediately: the Graves letter was written based on memories well over half a century old; Doubleday had never mentioned any exploits on the ball field and certainly hadn't made any claim to have invented a new game; and the fact that in 1839 Abner Doubleday was enrolled at the West Point Military Academy and did not take leave that year. It is possible that Doubleday had never even been to Cooperstown. However, the commission had spoken, and the myth was set into motion.

In 1939, organized baseball used the Mills Report to justify the celebration of its 'centenary'. As part of these celebrations, the formation of the Hall of Fame in Cooperstown was announced. The United States government even issued a postage stamp to commemorate the event. It is almost certain then that the adoption of baseball over cricket, even if structural arguments are given credence, had much to do with nationalism. The establishment of an 'American' game was an extremely popular topic of the sporting media of the time.[33] It was also very prominent in the minds of the keepers of the game from the 1850s onwards. The creation and perpetuation of the Doubleday myth only reinforces the idea that baseball was to be protected from its own origins, that it was to be an American game, and that it was to always have been an American game. Baseball had truly invented its own tradition, having 'actually invented, constructed, and formally instituted' its own creation story.[34]

What is most interesting about this desire to separate American sport from British games is that it was aberrant. As emphasized at the start, the American reaction to the sport of the empire was simply the opposite of the colonial reaction to imperial sport. Despite American independence, English influence was still prevalent in the United States and cricket had a much longer history in the United States than baseball did. This made it imperative for Americans to appropriate/indigenize baseball to the extent that its British roots would be totally forgotten. On the other hand, in India, as the next section will demonstrate, conditions of colonialism made it imperative for the nationalists to take up cricket as a way to compete with the British.

Cricket in India owed much to the patronage of the educated, well-to-do classes, the Parsees in the west, the Bengali bhadralok in the east and the affluent upper caste/class Brahmins in the south.[35] Desire to attain recognition in British eyes, together with the longing to defeat the British at their own game, were, among other reasons, at the root of this initiative and, to that extent, Indian cricket was a nationalist enterprise. The Indian middle classes, products of the public-school system the English had imported into India, though openly advocating the 'games ethic',[36] often employed sport as a tool of subversion. It was a well-thought-out strategy. On the surface, it demonstrated to the colonial masters the success of the 'games ethic' as an imperial tool. Accordingly, British administrators hardly ever thought of suspending empire sports promotion in the colonies. Rather, the ruling British, on many occasions, took the lead in providing equipment, necessary infrastructure and funding so that sporting activities could flourish.[37] That the 'games ethic' was actually subverted makes the story of Indian cricket all the more intriguing.

In South India, Indian patrons of cricket such as Buchi Babu Naidu, designated the father of Madras cricket, looked on the annual Presidency match with the British as an opportunity to meet and defeat European cricket sides. As V. Ramnarayan asserts, 'angered by the apartheid practised by the Madras Cricket Club, which required Indian players to sit under the tree and eat their lunch in the shade, while the Europeans enjoyed the comfort of the club's pavilion', [38] Buchi Babu conceived the idea of the Presidency match. Commenting on his father's move, C. Ramaswamy has declared:

> My father's main idea in launching this series stemmed from his desire to uplift the Indians who suffered step-motherly treatment at the hands of the British. In the pre-independence days, the British players enjoyed the privilege of using the Chepauk pavilion, while the Indians had to sit outside, beneath the trees. Hurt by the treatment meted out, my father felt that the Indians deserved better treatment and mooted the idea of the Presidency matches so that at least on the cricket field they were recognized better. [39]

Cricket in Bombay, on the other hand, propped up by the Parsee business classes, was initially rooted in an urge for social mobility within the colonial framework. [40] However, even within this context of upward mobility, 'nationalism' was not altogether absent. As both Mihir Bose and Ramachandra Guha have shown, [41] the cricket field in Bombay did become a site for indigenous assertion against the colonizers in the late 1870s and early 1880s. To quote Guha:

> The agents of disruption were the European polo players ... The coming of the polo players [to that area of the maidan where the natives played cricket] led to a bitter protest by the native cricketers. Their struggle to evict polo from the maidan provides a fascinating window on the cultural life of Empire, and demonstrates how quickly and how energetically Indians had made cricket their game. [42]

This contest is described in detail in Shapoorjee Sorabjee's *A Chronicle of Cricket among Parsees and the Struggle: European Polo versus Native Cricket* published in 1897. [43] The struggle began in 1879 when a native cricketer first described how the polo players enclosed their playing area with black flags, prohibiting native cricketers from playing within its boundaries. He suggested that 'nearly two thirds of the parade ground is occupied by Europeans to the great inconvenience of the school boys wishing to play cricket'.[44] Two years after this report, Shapoorjee Sorabjee wrote a letter of protest to the Bombay gymkhana[45] on behalf of the Persian Cricket Club. However, the polo secretary of the gymkhana dismissed his complaint, asserting their determination to play polo as before. The contest continued until the mid-1880s and though the natives won a temporary victory in 1882 (an order was passed in April 1882 allowing the Parsees exclusive use of the Esplanade Parade ground), this decree was revoked in 1883 permitting the European polo players' use of the native cricket ground.[46] In this fight, which ended in a defeat for the natives, the Asian game of polo became the emblem of patrician power, and the English sport indulged in by the natives the mark of plebeian resistance.[47]

Interestingly, the struggle between polo and cricket is not the only occasion when the cricket-playing natives of Bombay clashed with their European masters.[48] The final episode of the struggle was fought out in 1929-30, when native cricket administrators made common cause with the Gandhian call for civil disobedience and the British were on the receiving end. This final chapter of the struggle started when the Marylebone Cricket Club (MCC) was invited to tour India in November-December 1931.[49] This tour received full support from the Viceroy, as also from most cricket associations of the country. The MCC too was very keen to undertake the tour and passed a series of motions supporting the visit. Even the County Cricket Advisory Committee expressed keenness about the tour with a view to encouraging cricket in India.[50] However, when everything seemed to be going right, the Bombay Hindu Gymkhana announced its decision not to support the tour. Commenting on the move by the Hindu Gymkhana, the *Times of India* declared:

> The Hindu Gymkhana has, however, refused to cooperate with the Bombay Cricket Association. At a recent meeting of the Association when the proposed tour was discussed, a letter from the Hindu Gymkhana was read in which they stated that they were unable to participate in any of the matches with the MCC.[51]

In another report entitled 'What is the truth about the proposed boycott of the MCC cricketers by the Hindus and Parsees of Bombay?' the newspaper suggested:

> It will be remembered that last year the intended visit of the English team was cancelled on account of the political troubles of the country. It was hoped, however, that this year when another invitation was sent to London, all would be plain sailing but alas, all is not plain sailing and rumours have been current in Bombay for some time now that all was not well.[52]

The reason assigned by the Hindu Gymkhana for its refusal to cooperate was that the country was facing an uncertain political situation and that Gandhi had given a clarion call for civil disobedience against the British. Also, because the participation of the Congress in the Second Round Table Conference was still uncertain, it was unwilling to play cricket against a touring British side. The continuing opposition from the Hindu Gymkhana eventually forced the MCC to cancel its visit to India.

Soon after the news of postponement was made public, the Hindu Gymkhana withdrew the ban on the tour, lending strength to the conjecture that the earlier policy of the gymkhana was a clear-cut 'strategy', adopted to thwart the visit. In contrast to Bombay, nationalist intentions were much more pronounced in the Bengali patronage of cricket. Bengali middle-class promotion of cricket, it may be argued, was rooted in the urge to negate the British charge of effeminacy leveled against the Bengali male.

In existing works of Indian sport, cricket patronage in Bengal has been confined to the initiatives of the royal families of Natore and Cooch Behar. While acknowledging that the royal families of

Natore and Cooch Behar played key roles in promoting cricket, it needs to be asserted that such initiatives were part of a broader interest in the game among the educated Bengali middle class. [53] Princely patronage was a later development, which made an appreciable difference from the early twentieth century:

> Sports in Bengal in the early years of the nineteenth century present a peculiar incongruity. While games like cricket and football were looked upon as exclusive European preserves, indigenous sports like wrestling were confined to the lower classes. The educated middle class remained aloof from all kinds of sporting activity. In the years 180060, the bhadralok patronized indigenous sports like wrestling, though they did not themselves participate in such activity. They organized competitions in which their servants fought against each other amidst great excitement and enthusiasm. [54]

This picture underwent a transformation from the second half of the nineteenth century, a transition that may be dated from the 1870s and 1880s. From this period onwards, the educated Bengali middle classes attempted to integrate sporting activity, rooted in physical culture, into their everyday lives. This transition may be located in the changed political conditions of Bengal in the aftermath of the Sepoy Mutiny of 1857. In the post-mutiny period, the educated Bengali middle class found it imperative to devise an effective strategy to counter the colonial charge of inferiority.

As argued by Mrinalini Sinha, in the second half of the century, middle class Bengalis made several efforts to combat the problem of the emasculation of the Bengali male. Prominent nineteenth century Bengali intellectuals were indeed concerned about the consequences of effeminacy. In the 1860s the famous Tagores of Jorasanko and the organisation with which they mostly associated, the Adi Brahmo Samaj, launched a concerted drive for the physical regeneration of Bengalis. Bankimchandra Chatterjee, one of the most famous Bengali writers, oscillated between mocking the modern babu and attempting to answer the charge of Bengali effeminacy which he called Bharat Kalanka or Indian Stigma. [55]

Barred from staging violent demonstrations or other acts, which would be symbolic of 'physically challenging' British superiority, educated Indians thus looked upon 'leisure' pursuits with new eyes. Colonialism and the realities of being a subject population were the conditions that informed Bengali middle-class investment in sport. Drawing on real-life encounters between colonizer and colonized, leisure settings provided an exciting imaginary, minus the attendant risks that would otherwise characterize such situations. That a new breed of Bengali intellectuals extolled the virtues of physical prowess is evident from the following account of an interaction at a gathering in the Sovabazar Palace involving Nagendraprasad Sarbadhikary, leading Bengali sports patron of the time:

A young family member ridiculed Nagendraprasad's powerful stature and stamina saying that a man needed only that much strength that would enable him to drink a glass of water by himself! Surrounded by armed retainers the babus present broke into laughter at the comment. Not amused in the least, Nagendraprasad stunned everyone present by lifting the young man off the ground and asking 'now that I shall fling you down, what do you imagine you will require to escape that fate?' It was only after the man apologised that Nagendraprasad set him down. He declared in disgust, 'those who speak like this they are the ones who are afraid to step out on the streets with their wives and daughters; and when they do [they] are unable to safeguard their honour. Bengalis are effete, let them gain in physical strength with the return of masculine splendour, will come respect from others.[56]

This investment in physical culture reached a climax with the organization of the World Wrestling Championship under the patronage of the Maharaja of Cooch Behar in 1892. It was as part of the new vision outlined above that the bhadralok began their tryst with European sports such as cricket; one which intensified in the 1880s. Noting that the charge of effeminacy continued to be levelled against them, evident during the Ilbert Bill controversy, the bhadralok realized that an investment in physical culture was not enough. The Ilbert Bill controversy, as Sinha argues, 'rearticulated the broader shifts in colonial economic, political and administrative imperatives in the politics of colonial masculinity: it substituted for a straightforward defence of racial exclusivity a supposedly more natural gender hierarchy between "manly" and "unmanly" men'.[57] From this time onwards, the bhadralok realized that prowess in European sport was essential to infuse in the Bengali a sense of pride and purpose.

Even Swami Vivekananda, the famous Bengali religious and social reformer, imbibed this view. He argued that 'you will be nearer to god through football than through the Bhagwad Gita'.[58] Children also imbibed the feeling of satisfaction that came from victories in competitions against the British. A passage from the contemporary journal *Sakha* is redolent with these sentiments. The editor recalls a conversation he had one evening with a 'young friend' who reported with glee that he had successfully beaten the sahib in a game of 'bat-ball'. 'I wondered', he writes:

> What is so great about defeating the sahibs? Boys of all nations indulge in play. So what is it that has marked out English boys as superior to their young counterparts especially the Bengalis? The answer lies in the fact that while the sahibs play these manly games almost regularly Bengalis are averse to any form of physical exhaustion. Since the sahibs practice athletics, cricket etc. their bodies are strong and they acquire skills, which cannot be matched by the natives. Manly sports are therefore an exclusive English preserve. It was the act of defeating the coloniser on his own turf that filled his young friend with such glee.[59]

This interaction indicates that the 'significance' of defeating the sahibs at their own game had already filtered down to young Bengali/Indian boys by the middle of the 1880s.[60] Interestingly, even princely patronage of cricket was at times rooted in ideas of nationalism. Existing studies of princely patronage have assumed that all princes saw cricket as a means of associating with the ruling British. This view ignores evidence of native princes' determination to set up cricket teams comprising of Indians only, an initiative deriving from the belief that this was the only means of challenging the British. The Maharaja of Natore was an ardent nationalist, having been an active member of the Indian National Congress for some years. Soon after turning 18, he became president of the Natore Political Association at the request of Surendranath Banerjee. In 1894, he joined Banerjee and Anandamohan Bose as member of the Rajshahi municipality. After the partition of Bengal in 1905, he was a key figure in the anti-partition movement, delivering a famous speech against the partition at the Calcutta Town Hall. That his nationalist credentials were well-known is evident from the following testimony by Charuchandra Mitra:

> Prior to him, no other member of the royal family, either in Natore or in other families of the state, had actively supported the nationalist agenda. This was because they wished to be close to the ruling classes. It was to break this tradition that the Maharaja of Natore had joined the National Congress and had actively advocated the demands raised by the nationalists. This was best evident during his speech at the Town Hall in protest against the partition of Bengal.[61]

However, he differed from the nationalists in his modes of resistance. Until 1914, he used the cricket field to challenge the English; after this time he invested in the evolution of the vernacular press. That he was to a large extent successful in rousing nationalist sensibilities among his subjects is evident from contemporary accounts:

> Whenever the Natore XI defeated the European teams of Calcutta, our chests swelled with pride. Before the formation of the Natore XI, we, Indians, were losers on most occasions. But with the formation of the Natore XI, Maharaj Jagadindranarayan turned the tables on the

> English. Whether it is a fault of ours or not, we do not regard games as something simple, rather we are affected by the results of these encounters. This is because this is the only arena where we are allowed to compete on even terms with the English. The English have always ridiculed us as 'effete'. It is on the sporting field that we may counter such false allegations. This is why we justifiably perceive a victory on the sporting field as a 'national victory' against the British. Though the English mock us for our perceptions, it is evident that whenever they lose to us, they are filled with rage and humiliation. Thus, whatever is said on this count, that the Natore XI stimulated nationalist instincts among the youth is doubtless. This is a great achievement and has given the Maharaja immortality.[62]

Indian cricket thus was not simply an act of mimicry,[63] but was conceived of as a tool for remedying deeper, more serious allegations that underplayed native abilities. The roots of cricket in India went deep to help ideas of self-respect, manliness and self worth to permeate among the natives. Educated men from middle-class backgrounds promoted cricket, trying to legitimize physical activity in society and win respect for the players. The sport had emerged as the mirror wherein an Indian identity started to reassess itself, and in that sense was certainly part of a nationalist enterprise. What do the above sporting myths, played out in contexts grossly dissimilar, say about the dívergent expressions of nationalism? Why did American and Indian nationalisms necessitate the promotion of separate sports? Why baseball and not cricket in the United States? Why cricket and not wrestling/hockey in India? Answers lie in the George Orwell axiom 'Serious sport... is war minus the shooting'.[64]

If sport is in fact a metaphor (and in some cases a metonym) for war, then cricket simply was not necessary in the United States, as it was in India. The United States, having prevailed militarily already against the British (twice) had no need for 'war minus the shooting'. The early date of American independence, coupled with the arrival of American nationalism in the 1850s and beyond, meant that cricket was inevitably the game that had to lose in the battle with baseball. [65] In India considerations were exactly the reverse. Prowess in sport wasn't enough. Accomplishments had to be demonstrated in empire sport, which would mark a symbolic victory against the ruling colonial state. To substantiate the point: even when India won gold medals in field hockey in the Olympic Games in the years 1928-56, hockey could never rival cricket in colonial India. This is because Britain refused to participate in Olympic hockey contests in the years 1928-36 knowing that the Indians were favourites to win the gold. This is especially interesting because Britain had won the Olympic gold in field hockey in 1904 and 1920, the only years when hockey was played before 1928 and years when India did not participate. [66] Absence of competitions against the colonizer, it can be argued, relegated hockey in the Indian sporting hierarchy. In contrast, in America there was a need to move away from British sport in order to produce an American identity. The newer stick and ball game, even before concerted efforts had commenced to make it 'American', had already efficiently separated itself from any of its British forebears. In 1860, Henry Chadwick eloquently made this point noting that baseball, though 'of English origin, has been so modified and improved of late ... in this country, as almost to deprive it of any of its original features beyond the mere groundwork of the game'. [67]

This American sporting nationalism has manifested itself almost continually since that time. American sports fans still prefer sports that they can identify as 'American'; the internationalization of professional basketball and baseball in recent years may actually be hurting their domestic popularity. Meanwhile, the least integrated of the major sports in the United States the National Football League and NASCAR have not seen concomitant declines in viewership. [68] The need to assert Americanness in the sporting field still remains a vigorous part of the culture of spectatorship in the United States. This need to separate predates the rise of the United States to its own imperial status. It first began in the rejection of a decidedly British sport for one that was more 'American'. The actual origin of the game was simply not as important to the popularity of the sport as the perception of the essence of the game. Almost from the beginning, the essence of baseball was American. It was only later that its origin became American as well.

Notes

1. Orlando Patterson and Jason Kauffman, *New York Times*, 1 May 2005 (emphasis added).
2. Though the cover illustration is stated to have been taken from 'The Cricketer, 1850', anyone who has played and watched cricket would know that the illustration does not depict an accepted cricketing posture.
3. Some editions, though, depict the playing of rugby, equally popular in Britain towards the close of the nineteenth century.
4. Stoddart, 'Sport, Cultural Imperialism and Colonial Response', 673.
5. Doubleday, according to sanctioned myth, was said to have invented baseball during a sudden brainstorm in Cooperstown, NY, in 1839. Though the story came into almost immediate question and has since been conclusively delegitimized, the story still holds a place in the popular imaginings of casual baseball fans.
6. For several competing secondary histories of the game, see: Adelman, *A Sporting Time*; Alexander, *Our Game*; Block, *Baseball Before We Knew It*; Goldstein, *Playing for Keeps*; Kirsch, *The Creation of American Team Sports*; Rossi, *The National Game*; Seymour, *Baseball: The Early Years*; and Tygiel, *Past Time*. For a look at the history of early baseball through primary sources, see Sullivan, *Early Innings*.
7. For a recent attempt to liberate baseball from rounders, see Block, *Baseball Before We Knew It*. However, even Block places baseball in a stick-and-ball matrix, but from a variety of sources, not all of them English.
8. Seymour, *Baseball*, 7.
9. Goldstein, *Playing for Keeps*, 10.
10. For a succinct description of the impacts of industrialization on American leisure, see Kirsch, *The Creation of American Team Sports*, 58. In this description, Kirsch derides the simple 'industrialization equals more free time' trope as oversimplified. Instead, he argues that industrialization obliterated traditional forms of play, which tended towards sporadic periods of play during the work day and season. Industrialization, with its emphasis on routine and homogeneity of experience, eliminated sporadic play. It had to be replaced by specifically scheduled times that workers could set aside for play activities.
11. Ibid., 8.

12. The Knickerbocker Base Ball Club of New York began as a group of men who met regularly to play baseball, beginning in 1842. Upon the suggestion of Alexander Cartwright, the men formed a club, and secured the rights to play at the Elysian Fields in Hoboken, NJ. Originally more a social club than a baseball team, the Knickerbocker Club incorporated baseball into a fraternal structure, which emphasized gentlemanly conduct on and off the playing field. The original codification of their rules in 1845 is the basis on which modern baseball now rests. For more on the Knickerbockers, see Seymour, *Baseball*, 1523.
13. Adelman, *A Sporting Time*, 112.
14. The term 'National' is largely hyperbolic here, as the association initially consisted of clubs from New York and Brooklyn only.
15. *New York Mercury*, 5 Dec. 1856; During this time, other publications, including Porter's *Spirit of the Times* and *The New York Clipper*, had begun calling baseball the national game.
16. Singh, *A History of Cricket in America*, 1.
17. Deb Das, 'A History of Cricket in the USA', available online at http://content.cricinfo.com/usa/content/story/ 141158.html, accessed 26 May 2006.
18. For details see; http://www.cricinfo.com/db/ARCHIVE, accessed 26 May 2006.
19. According to Adelman (*A Sporting Time*, 116), the number of cricket clubs in the United States increased during the last quarter of the nineteenth century. Adelman credits the wealthy segments of American society as well as several elite educational institutions for this growth. Additionally, Kirsch (*The Creation of American Team Sports*, 214) credits the continued 'migration of British officials, businessmen, and skilled craftsmen' as well as continued media support for the brief and modest cricket revival after the Civil War.
20. It would be interesting to know how modern limited-overs cricket and more recent innovations such as Twenty20 cricket, which finishes in a little over two hours would have influenced this argument.
21. For a detailed analysis of Indian cricket and its social, cultural and political moorings, see Majumdar, *Twenty-Two Yards to Freedom*.
22. Since 1990, National Football League stadiums have been quite full. Overall, the league has averaged almost 91 per cent of its possible attendance, based on stadium capacities and actual attendance from 1990 to 2003. Statistics compiled by authors.
23. Tygiel, *Past Time*, 4.
24. Ibid., 4.
25. Rossi, *The National Game*, 5.
26. Adelman, *A Sporting Time*, 136.
27. Tygiel, *Past Time*, 6.
28. Abraham G. Mills was the fourth president of the National League, and a pivotal figure in baseball's history. He brokered the National Agreement, which brought the American Association and the National League together and extended the reserve clause to all three leagues, which kept players from 'jumping' from one league to another.
29. Spalding, also president of the Chicago Club, had just led a professional team of players on a worldwide tour. The dinner was given in honour of this team. Spalding was also a fierce defender of the American origins of baseball.

30. Block, *Baseball Before We Knew It*, 89.
31. Ibid. This cry was in obvious response to the popular notion that baseball was an extension and Americanization of the British game rounders.
32. Seymour, *Baseball*, 9.
33. See, for example, Porter's *Spirit of the Times*, *The New York Clipper* or *The New York Mercury* for baseball writing of the time.
34. Hobsbawm and Ranger, *The Invention of Tradition*.
35. Bhadralok is a generic term used in Bengal since the second half of the nineteenth century to denote the upper and middle classes of Bengali society, who are distinguished by their access to a liberal education and the English language.
36. For an in-depth discussion on the impact of the 'games ethic' in the colonies, see Mangan, *The Games Ethic and Imperialism*. Also see Stoddart, 'Sport, Cultural Imperialism and Colonial Response'.
37. In Presidency College, Calcutta, one of the foremost educational institution of the country, efforts to promote European sports reached their apogee under Henry Rosher James, principal of the college during the years 1906-16. James tried to make Presidency a self-sufficient civilized academic community, a world dedicated to excellence in the English language with friendly relations between European members of staff cemented through involvement/participation on the sports field. For details on Presidency College sport see Majumdar, 'Nationalist Tool for Imperial Resistance'.
38. Ramnarayan, *Mosquitoes and other Jolly Rovers*, 24.
39. Commenting on Buchi Babu's efforts, Rayan Amal Raj states: 'He wanted a club for the locals, a club that would rival a white man's club, like the MCC ... where even ordinary Indians could enter, play and mix freely with others'. Quoted in Muthiah, *The Spirit of Chepauk*, 118.
40. Most published works on Indian cricket have portrayed the game in these terms: Docker, *History of Indian Cricket*; Cashman, *Patrons, Players and the Crowd*; Bamzai, *Guts and Glory*.
41. For details, see Bose, *History of Indian Cricket*, 22; Guha, 'Searching for Space', in *A Corner of a Foreign Field*.
42. Guha, *A Corner of a Foreign Field*, 20.
43. Sorabjee, *A Chronicle of Cricket*. While focusing on important events that shaped the nation's early cricket history, Sorabjee has also left his readers a chronological narrative on the development of cricket in colonial India. A must-read for cricket scholars, A Chronicle of Cricket does a great job in detailing the landmarks in the course of the game's early development. One thing that Sorabjee makes clear which may well be his fundamental contribution is that in India cricket is often politics and politics is often cricket.
44. For details see Sorabjee, *A Chronicle of Cricket*, 20.
45. An Indian term for a sporting club.
46. On 9 February 1883, Shapoorjee Sorabjee and others addressed another petition to Sir James Fergusson, Governor of Bombay. This petition asserted: 'We, therefore, on behalf of the cricketers, humbly pray to your Excellency to direct that proper effect be given to the resolution of 17 April 1882, so that polo may not be played on the ground in question, and the plot of cricket ground kept enclosed by the Gymkhana may be open for cricketers'. Responding to their petition, W.A. Baker, under-secretary to the government wrote: 'It was never intended to

deprive the cricketers of the Gymkhana of the reserved ground they at present occupy without occasion and due notice and that their request in this respect cannot be acceded to'. Subsequently, Mr Cecil Gray, polo secretary of the Gymkhana submitted a petition to the government on 30 May 1883, 'praying that, as the only open space of sufficient size and in other respects suitable for polo is the Parade ground, His Excellency in Council will be pleased to cancel the Government Resolution No. 139E 620, dated 13 April 1882'. In response, the government passed the following resolution: 'In modification of the orders contained in Government Resolution No. 139E 620 dated 13 April 1882, Government are now pleased to rule that the Esplanade Parade ground may be used for Polo on one evening of the week and also in the morning of the Brigade Holiday'.

47. Guha, *A Corner of a Foreign Field*, 28.
48. The struggle over polo was in fact the second phase of this struggle. The first was fought out in the years 1868-69 over whether native cricket playing was dangerous for European inhabitants of the city. For details of this struggle, see Majumdar, *Once Upon a Furore*, 19.
49. *Times of India*, 15 April 1931.
50. *Times of India*, 18 April 1931.
51. *Times of India*, 16 May 1931.
52. *Ibid.*
53. This fact hardly finds mention in existing works on Indian cricket, which equate the early phase of Indian cricket with a phase of princely patronage. It is erroneously asserted that 'cricket, as an elite sport, required the sort of time and money not available to the bourgeois elites of colonial India' (Appadurai, 'Playing with Modernity, 29; Mannathukaren, 'Subalterns, Cricket and the "Nation"'.
54. Ghosh, *Byame Bangali*, 100.
55. Sinha, *Colonial Masculinity*, 21; For a discussion on the Bengali efforts at emasculation, also see Roselli, 'The Self Image of Effeteness'.
56. Ghosh, *Krida Samrat Nagendra Prasad Sarbadhikary*, 1801.
57. Sinha, *Colonial Masculinity*, 5.
58. Football and cricket, both European manly sports, were given equal importance in late nineteenth-century India. Accordingly players who played football also excelled in cricket and vice-versa.
59. *Sakha* 12 (Dec. 1883). Also see *Sakha*, Feb. 1891.
60. Bengalis took similar pride in the achievements of their Parsee counterparts. Commenting on the Parsee victory against the touring English side led by G.F. Vernon, the Bengali journal *Sakha* urged the Bengalis to take pride from the Parsee victory and motivate themselves to achieve similar feats on the sporting field. The notion that defeating the English at their game was no mean achievement was not unique to Bengal. For similar parallels in Australia see Mandle, 'Cricket and Australian Nationalism'.
61. *Manasi o Marmabani*, 1925-26, 5524 (Bengali literary magazine, published in Calcutta).
62. *Ibid.*
63. For an entirely different understanding of mimicry, see Bhabha, *The Location of Culture*.

64. Orwell wrote this in an essay entitled 'The Sporting Spirit' in 1945, in the wake of a visit to Britain by the Russian football club Moscow Dynamo. The essay concludes: 'There are quite enough real causes of trouble already, and we need not to add to them by encouraging young men to kick each other on the shins amid the roars of infuriated spectators'.
65. Jules Tygiel has asserted that baseball and cricket were not actually in competition with each other, as cricket never gained a foothold with native-born Americans. It seems from consulting other sources that Americans would likely have ultimately taken up the game had an alternative not existed. For more on his position, see Tygiel, *Past Time*, 78.
66. See India files at the International Olympic Museum, Lausanne: IDD CHEMISE 9404 CIO CNO INDE CORR, 192463.
67. Chadwick, *Beadle's Dime Baseball Player*, 5.
68. Brown, 'Exceptionalist America'.

References

Adelman, Melvin. *A Sporting Time: New York City and the Rise of Modern Athletics, 182070*. Urbana, IL: University of Illinois Press, 1986.

Alexander, Charles C. *Our Game: An American Baseball History*. New York: Henry Holt, 1991.

Appadurai, Arjun. 'Playing with Modernity: Decolonization of Indian Cricket'. In *Consuming Modernity: Public Culture in a South Asian World*, edited by Carol Breckenridge. Minneapolis, MN: University of Minnesota Press, 1996.

Bamzai, Sandeep. *Guts and Glory: The Bombay Cricket Story*. New Delhi: Rupa and Co., 2002.

Bhabha, Homi. *The Location of Culture*. London: Routledge, 1994.

Block, David. *Baseball Before We Knew It*. Lincoln, NE, 2005.

Bose, Mihir. *History of Indian Cricket*. Bombay: Rupa and Co., 1990.

Brown, Sean F. 'Exceptionalist America: American Sports Fans' Reaction to Internationalization'. *International Journal of the History of Sport* 22, no. 6 (2005): 113672.

Cashman, Richard. *Patrons, Players and the Crowd*. Calcutta: Orient Longman, 1979.

Chadwick, Henry, ed. *Beadle's Dime Baseball Player*. New York: American News Co., 1864.

Docker, Edward. *History of Indian Cricket*. Delhi: Macmillan Co. of India, 1976.

Ghosh, Anil Chandra. *Byame Bangali*. Calcutta, 1928.

Ghosh, Saurindra Kumar. *Krida Samrat Nagendra Prasad Sarbadhikary 18691940*. Calcutta, 1964.

Goldstein, Warren. *Playing for Keeps: A History of Early Baseball*. Ithaca, NY: Cornell University Press, 1989.

Guha, Ramachandra. *A Corner of a Foreign Field.* London: Picador, 2002.
Hobsbawm, Eric and Ranger, Terence, ed. *The Invention of Tradition.* Cambridge: Cambridge University Press, 1983.
Kirsch, George B. *The Creation of American Team Sports: Baseball and Cricket, 183872.* Urbana, IL: University of Illinois Press, 1989.
Majumdar, Boria. *Once Upon a Furore.* New Delhi: Yoda Press, 2004.
–, *Twenty-Two Yards to Freedom: A Social History of Indian Cricket.* New Delhi: Viking Press, 2004.
–, 'Nationalist Tool for Imperial Resistance: The Games Ethic in Indian History'. In *Sport in South Asian Society Past and Present,* edited by Boria Majumdar and J.A. Mangan. London: Routledge, 2005: 4865.
Mandle, William H. 'Cricket and Australian Nationalism in the Nineteenth Century'. *Journal of the Royal Australian Historical Society* 59, no. 4 (1973).
Mangan, J.A. *The Games Ethic and Imperialism: Aspects of the Diffusion of an Ideal.* London: Frank Cass, 1998.
Mannathukaren, Nissim. 'Subalterns, Cricket and The "Nation": The Silences of Lagaan'. *Economic and Political Weekly* (2001): 45804.
Muthiah, S. *The Spirit of Chepauk.* Chennai: Eastwest Books, 1998.
Ramnarayan, V. *Mosquitoes and Other Jolly Rovers: The Story of Tamil Nadu Cricket.* Chennai: Ind-Com Press, 2002.
Roselli, John. 'The Self Image of Effeteness: Physical Education and Nationalism in Nineteenth Century Bengal'. *Past and Present* 86 (Feb. 1980): 12148.
Rossi, John P. *The National Game: Baseball and American Culture.* Chicago: I.R. Dee, 2000.
Seymour, Harold. *Baseball: The Early Years.* New York: Oxford University Press, 1960.
Singh, Amar. *A History of Cricket in America.* Philadelphia, PA: University of Pennsylvania Press, 1996.
Sinha, Mrinalini. *Colonial Masculinity: The Manly Englishman and the Effeminate Bengali in the Late Nineteenth Century.* Manchester: Manchester University Press, 1995.
Sorabjee, Shapoorjee. *A Chronicle of Cricket among the Parsees and the Struggle: Polo Versus Native Cricket.* Bombay, 1897.
Stoddart, Brian. 'Sport, Cultural Imperialism and Colonial Response in the British Empire: A Framework for Analysis'. *Comparative Studies in Society and History* 14, no. 3 (1987).
Sullivan, Dean A., ed. *Early Innings: A Documentary History of Baseball.* Lincoln, NE: University of Nebraska Press, 1995.
Tygiel, Jules. *Past Time: Baseball as History.* New York: Oxford University Press, 2000.

Brown Man's Burden?: The Historiography of Cricket and Nationalism in Colonial India

Souvik Naha

Introduction

> And across the globe, sport is now too important to be left in the hands of sportsmen and women. More and more, it is the property of the 'People' in their various manifestations as politicians, entrepreneurs, educationists, commercialists, publicists, and, no least, academics. [1]

The academic attention devoted to sport in Europe and America has broadened considerably in the last few decades. Sociology was the first discipline to examine sport as a meaningful human activity, and the literature on sport and leisure has grown substantially since the early 1990s.Historians too have engaged with the cultural, economic and political manifestations of sport and identified the latter's hitherto unrecognised historical contingencies in social formations. Stephen Jones, for instance, wrote of sport in industrial societies as an important economic, social and political activity yielding vital insights about labour market, capital investment, class, gender and even international relations. [2] A history of sports, in addition to evaluating sporting traditions, myths and identities, illustrates past themes of culture and society and produces an epistemology of understanding their journey into the present.

Appraisal of the history of cricket in India is important especially since the sport had been associated with a number of institutionsfrom macro entities (empire, dominion) to walks of everyday life (sports press, advertising)the interplay among which reveals a complex history of Indian society. Although cricket's origin can be traced to Early Modern folk games in France, its modern form was developed in Britain. In the nineteenth century, cricket was an important element of the colonial 'civilising mission' albeit without overt official encouragement. [3] The sport was invested with ideals of sporting spirit and fair play, and promoted as an ideological templatea design to strengthen the player's moral and physical character, thereby producing exemplary citizens and subjects. Education and religion were the primary media of propagating cricket, eliciting asymmetric responses in different contexts. [4] Americans reportedly distorted cricket into baseball to articulate their dislike for everything British. [5] South Asians, on the other hand, enthusiastically took to cricket, transforming it into an instrument of at once imitating and interrogating imperial institutions. Cricket in India has therefore emerged as a site of contestation among forces of colonialism, nationalism, communalism, race, caste, religion etc. Linkages with transnational sporting philosophy, 'native' princely patronage, corporate sponsorship and public opinion have increasingly widened the reach and complexities of cricket; so much so that South Asia has emerged as the economic and performative nerve centre of global cricket, displacing the sport from its British 'home'.

The beginning of academic studies of cricket in India coincided with the country's first victory in the Cricket World Cup in 1983 and its entry into the global network of sport capitalism. Aided by the relative profusion of sources, historians of Indian cricket have reframed many age old ideas and stereotypes about the game. Their works not only evaluate sporting traditions, myths and identities but also illuminate cultural and social pasts, producing in the process a way of understanding their transformation into the present.

In this article, I review the most debated question among historians of Indian sport show fundamental cricket was to colonial-nationalist encounters in British India? Sport is considered an important cultural aspect of imperialist expansion. The colonial response to it was characterised by, argues Allen Guttmann, the drive to emulation the success of which accorded the literal or metaphorical colonials 'a splendid opportunity to enhance their self-esteem, for nothing can be more delightful than "beating them at their own game".[6] The act of emulation has often been endowed a nationalist/anti-colonial agency in which subversion of the colonial regime came though apparent imitation. C.L.R. James' *Beyond a Boundary,* which discusses the centrality of cricket in Caribbean social formations, foregrounds the discursive functions of sport as a cultural form which alternately upholds and/or sabotages colonial hegemony.[7] Kausik Bandyopadhyay's excellent research on the nationalist significance of Mohun Bagan's famous Shield win of 1911 in the context of the Swadeshi movement is a case in point.[8] Joseph Maguire is not wrong when he argues that:

> Historically, international spots contests, as they developed in the late nineteenth century, became a form of patriot games in which particular views of national identities and habitus codes were constructed and represented. Close links can be traced between the rituals of national identity practices and these sports occasions, and sport remains an arena where processes of habitus/identity testing and formation are conducted.[9]

This article traces the exploration of this sporting habitus in the historiography of cricket in colonial India. Since I confine the analysis to the colonial period (1757-1947), the various nationalisms associated with post-colonial cricket as manifest in diaspora support or fan behaviour during matches against Pakistan have not been addressed. Hence the works of scholars such as Christina Davis, Grant Upson, Thomas Fletcher, Jishnu Dasgupta and Kingshuk Chatterjee, in addition to a few writings by Guha and Majumdar, fall outside the scope of this review article. Having referred to the principal arguments, I identify some of the lacunae in which research can be furthered.

A Brief History of Cricket in Colonial India

The earliest reference to cricket being played in India comes from a war memoir by Clement Downing, naval officer and engineer with the East India Company. 'We lay here near a Fortnight ...', writes Downing in recollection of an afternoon spent near the Bay of Cambay in 1721, 'tho' all the Country round was inhabited by the *Culeys,* we everyday diverted ourselves with playing at Cricket and other Exercises, which they would come and be Spectators of.' [10] Bombay, Calcutta and Madras, the three major trading settlements of the Company, became and still remain the most important cricket centres in India. The Calcutta Cricket Club, arguably established in 1792, was considered the second oldest among existing cricket clubs in the world after the Marylebone Cricket Club (1787) before Majumdar discovered an entry in Hickey's *Bengal Gazette* dated 16 December 1780 which mentions the'Calcutta Cricket Club'. [11] Robert Vansittart hit the first recorded century on Indian soil. The first Indians to have started playing cricket were the sepoys garrisoned in various cantonments. [12] In 1848 the Parsees of Bombay established the Oriental Club as a formal cricket outfit. The history of first-class cricket in India starts with a match between madras and Calcutta in 1864. Two Parsee teams visited England in 1886 and 1888, prompting the MCC to send teams to tour India from 1889-90 onwards to strengthen the colonial cultural bond. The same tour saw the first instance of a 'native' team beating an English side, when the Parsee Gymkhana pulled off an astonishing win over them on 30 January 1890. In 1892-93, an all-India team was formed for the first time to face Lord Hawke's touring XI, though mainly Europeans were included.

Two Indians, Ranjitsinhji and his nephew Duleepsinhji, played for England with distinction. In 1911, the Maharaja of Patiala sponsored an all-India team's tour of England. On the merit of a few individual feats in this and in the 1926-27 series against an MCC side led by Arthur Gilligan, performed by the likes of Palwankar Baloo, C.K. Nayudu and D.B. Deodhar, a governing body to organise and regulate cricket in IndiatheBoard of Control for Cricket in India (BCCI) was formed in 1928. India played its first Test against the MCC in 1932, led by C.K. Nayudu. India did not win a single Test match official or unofficial until 1952 even though it had on its roster a number of brilliant players such as Vijay Merchant, Mushtaq Ali, L.P. Jai, Vijay Hazare, Mohammad Nissar and L. Amarsingh. In the 1940s, the progress of Indian cricket was disrupted by political disturbances. On the flipside, Indian spectators had the opportunity to watch foreign cricketers such as Dennis Compton and Keith Miller play for regional or regimental teams while on war duty in the country. Following India's partition in 1947, a few promising Muslim players migrated to Pakistan.

The most important fixture in the nineteenth century was the Bombay Presidency Match (starting from 1877) between the Europeans and the Parsees which evolved into the Bombay Pentangular with the subsequent inclusion of the Hindus (in 1907), the Muslims (in 1912) and the Rest comprising mainly Anglo-Indians and other religious groups (in 1937). Its popularity among the incipient urban consumer societies in the 1930s set in motion cricket's evolution to a market-oriented industry. It was, however, banned in 1946 on the pretext that the tournament's religion-centric spectatorship increased communal polarisation, though a stronger reason was that the BCCI needed to rejuvenate the inter-state Ranji Trophy tournament (run by the BCCI since 1934-35) which lagged in popularity and profit behind the highly successful Pentangular tournament.[13]

Cricket as 'Civilising Mission' The Phase of Collaboration

The British invested cricket with spirit of sportsmanship and fair play, and promoted it as a design to strengthen the player's moral and physical character. [14] Cricket was arguably a part of the colonial 'civilising mission', evident in the sport's propagation through the elite public and missionary schools as 'moral training'. [15] This is nowhere more apparent than in the words of Cecil Headlam who toured India in 1903-04 as part of the Oxford Authentics:

> ... cricket unites, as in India, the rulers and the ruled. It also provides a moral training, an education in pluck, and nerve, and self-restraint, far more valuable to the character of the ordinary native than the mere learning by heart of a play of Shakespeare. [16]

Cricket was believed to promote the English qualities of sportsmanship and fair play among the 'natives', and enable them to experience the altruism of imperialism as enlightened subjects. A number of scholars, notably among them Allen Guttmann, claim that the British governors such as Lord Harris and Lord Brabourne patronised cricket with the hope that the sport might 'bond together India's religiously, linguistically and ethnically diverse population'. [17] Lord Harris, governor of Bombay 1890-95, went on to say that, 'I really do not know a sight really more creditable to the British capacity for administration than that of a cricket match on the parade ground between the Presidency European Eleven and the Parsis.' [18] The pedagogic measures did not go beyond the premises of a minuscule number of institutions and the efforts of a few individuals. Not all Englishmen subscribed to this grand idea. They preferred to establish exclusive European clubs and defamed the appearances and playing styles of Indian cricketers in their chronicles. An army regiment, when pressed hard to play against a Parsee club, agreed on the condition that the match would be played as: 'officers with umbrellas versus natives with bats'. [19] Such contemptuous remarks spurred Indian groups to compete with more vigour, using paraphernalia as close to English customs as possible. [20]

Yet, the traditions, value systems and style of play associated with cricket received enthusiastic response initially from the Parsees, other regional elites and the educated middle-class and eventually from every socio-economic group. Ashis Nandy has rather uniquely interpreted this obligation of emulation. He demonstrates that Victorian discourses of cricket were coextensive with the conventional temperament and philosophy of Indians. [21] The idea of moral masculinity embedded in cricket dovetailed particularly well with the 'rather classical Brahminic concept' which stressed 'control over [one's] impulsive self', 'superiority of form over substance, mind over body, culture over nature' and 'serenity in the face of the vagaries of fate'. [22] Although based on sweeping generalisations which reinforced colonial myths regarding class, culture and society instead of interrogating them, Nandy's work should be credited as a pioneering effort in the cultural studies of sport.

Subsequent works point out that different Indian groups started playing cricket in different social contexts. The Parsees of Bombay were the first among these groups to be involved with the game. The cricket books authored by Parsees are the most substantial chronicles of early cricket in Bombay. They seemed to have taken the British rule as an opportunity to iron out a community identity which had previously lay unnoticed due to their social marginality and cultural insularity. The zeal with which the Parsee cricketers conducted the first-ever trip to England prompted an Englishman to remark that 'As pilgrims go to Jerusalem to worship at a shrine, so now the Parsees are going to England to do homage to the English cricketers.' [23] They were cordially welcomed on both the trips, perhaps to ensure their support for the British Empire whose integrity was being threatened by the alliance with revolutionary Ireland of a Parsee, Dadabhai Naoroji. [24] That imitation and loyalism were the major issues in Parsee cricket has been accepted uncritically by most historians. Even the works on cricket,argues Anthony Bateman, apes the Victorian celebration of cricket as the epitome of ethics and discipline. [25] Such understanding is too simplistic to cover the multi-layered reaction of a community to another.

Although a few texts such as Dosabhai Framji Karaka's *The Parsees* (1858) describe the community as loyal citizens of the Raj, closer scrutiny of the same works establishes that it was not so much a devotion to the coloniser but a desire to self-differentiate from Indians in general which drove the Parsees to play cricket seriously. [26] An examination of late nineteenth and early twentieth century Parsee texts reveals a number of self-attributes progressiveness, rationality and civilised masculinity which symbolically constructed the Parsees as the most Westernised community in India, wrote off their thousand year history of agricultural labour and reanimated the grandeur of the ancient Persian Empire. [27] Even J.M. Framji Patel, selective readings of whose text inspired the idea that early Parsee cricket was an explicit measure to gain British sympathy, argues in favour of a transcultural flow instead of mere imitation of the British: 'Who is the father of Indian cricket? It is the child of progress, of the friendly embrace of the East and the West.' [28] The course of Parsee cricket resembles the sport's development in Australia. Cricket became popular in Australia, according to Richard Cashman, since it allowed the Australians to negotiate their cultural identity amidst the transplanted British settler habitus. [29] Early Australian victories over visiting teams caused ambivalent nationalist sentiments, and were underlined by 'a very deferential nationalism which reinforced pro-imperial links'. [30] The celebration that ensued after the Parsees defeated G.F. Vernon's XI in 1891 mirrors the Australian experience. In the words of Framji Patel, 'the imaginative and emotional Parsee youth felt for a day or two that he was the victor of the victors of Waterloo'. [31]

This ambivalence is manifest in Shapoorjee Sorabjee's account of the negotiation between the Parsees and the European Bombay

Gymkhana over the acquisition of playing spaces in the Esplanade *maidan*. [32] The *maidan* turf had been spoilt by the Gymkhana's polo practice, so the Parsees petitioned to the Governor to save the field. Eager not to incur displeasure of the wealthiest Indian community, the government allocated to them a part of the newly reclaimed land in the Kennedy sea face. The struggle against the English for proper practice of their signature game serves a good example of how the colonial subject mimics the colonizer to ultimately undermine the latter's ideologies of superiority and apparently stable identity. [33]

Cricket in Decolonising India The Phase of Subversion

In an article on the imperial origin and indigenous elements of Indian cricket, Projit Bihari Mukharji draws attention to three distinctive functions of colonial cricket: as a powerful mechanism for questioning the dominant types of imperial organization, as an instrument for ensuring a broadening of social access to modern sport and as a creative means of re-negotiating gender politics. [34] While the second theme remains broadly untouched except in passages from Guha and Majumdar's works, the third theme has been partly discussed by Souvik Naha in an article on female spectatorship in Calcutta. He demonstrates that in the colonial period the idea of spectatorship in Indian grounds ran parallel to the conservative English paradigm which assigned women spectators the decorative role of lending a festive, civilising atmosphere in the closely guarded club houses and tents. [35] This practice was gradually destabilised in the postcolonial period as women acquired powerful agency as consumers of the game.

It is the theme of resisting imperialism through sport, however, which has been discussed in relatively greater detail. Cricket was not indigenised the same way as were similar British imports such as football and hockey. While the latter lost the English connection long ago, cricket always retained its British imprint. Keith Sandiford reckons this paradox the 'ultimate triumph of Victorian imperialism', but his approach has been criticised by scholars who view the sport as a site of cultural contestation instead of imperialist hegemony. [36]

According to Nandy, aside from enabling Indians to negotiate colonial modernity, the 'moral posture' of cricket empowered them to question the post-utilitarian colonial governance for not living up to their own standards of morality. [37] Guha's book demonstrates how imperatives of colonial politics often resulted in a sport's unique appropriation, with cricket emerging as an arena in which an indigenous brand of nationalism was articulated. Contradiction of the colonial ideology through symbolic resistance was the dominant feature of colonial sports, especially cricket and football, from the early twentieth century onwards.

When the Hindus defeated a European representative team in 1906 the news quickly spread all over the country and was celebrated as a feat comparable to the military victory of Japan over Russia in 1905. [38] A sporting victory subverted the discourses of British superiority. In 1916 an incident where a European cricketer disputed a Hindu umpire was labelled as 'unsportsmanike' by the Hindu Gymkhana and the European player was admonished. [39] During the MCC's tour of India in 1925-26, C.K. Nayudu became a 'national hero' after scoring 153 in 116 minutes with 11 sixes and 13 fours, an innings of prodigious attack even by today's standard of aggressive batting. Historians of Indian cricket later regarded this innings as a premier symbol of resistance against the British Empire. Nayudu's innings could not have come at a better time. With the path to political self-determination becoming uncertain after the non-violent Non-cooperation movement (1920-22) led by Gandhi petered out, people started looking for new heroes. According to Guha, this knock, coming against the representatives of the colonizers in the most British of games at an important ground, tapped into all sources of nationalist pride. [40] Majumdar too regards this epic innings as a 'moment of departure' which signified the juncture when 'an indigenous brand of Indian nationalism "took off" on the cricket field'. [41] Incidentally, not one contemporary account suggested any nationalist undertone of this innings.

The MCC returned in the winter of 1933-34. Nayudu lit up the gloomy political situation with a furious 116 at Lahore. Two young cricketers in the crowd later wrote of how his stroke-play signalled to them a broader political message. One of them, Prithvi Raj, expressed gratitude to Nayudu for driving away the 'fear of the foreigner' from his mind. [42] Prem Bhatia, the other student, wrote: 'Every sixer hit by 'C.K.' Nayudu against the visitors' slow bowlers was as good as a nail in the coffin of the British Empire... [each shot was] also an assertion of our resolve to throw the British out of India'. [43]

Beginning in the 1930s nationalist feelings pervaded the sentiments of cricket officials and scribes too. Hamidulla Khan, Nawab of Bhopal who served as the BCCI president too, asked the team to 'keep India's flag flying' at a farewell dinner given prior to departure for England in 1936. [44] In *Indian Cricket Uncovered*, Berry Sarbadhikary carefully highlighted the ingenuity of cricketing trends developing in spite of or in opposition to the colonial tradition. [45] A.S. De Mello, in the foreword to Sarbadhikary's *Presenting Indian Cricket* which was produced to mark the post-war resumption of cricketing relations between England and an all-India team in 1946, writes that,

> The goal is to play the game in the same spirit as it is played in England and also if possible to beat the Englishmen at their own game and on their own soil at the game of cricket, England's sunny gift to India! ... Whatever the results, this great sub-continent will be happy as long as her chosen representatives "play cricket" in every sense of the phrase. [46]

The aspirations clearly show the extent to which cricket had been accepted as a prime tool of subverting the dogmas of British superiority. De Mello's *Portrait of Indian Sport* continues to preach this moral high ground of cricket as achieved through its supposedly nationalist stance. [47]

Majumdar's *Twenty-Two Yards to Freedom* is by far the best account of cricketing nationalism since it establishes that 'Indian cricket' is far from a monolithic structure and highlights the local variations of nationalism. He explores how cricket differently served as a nationalist front against colonial dominance in Bombay and Calcutta, and how it subsequently embodied politics itself instead of remaining a metaphor for politics. In the Bengal Presidency cricket remained a British sport for a century until the educated Bengali middle class in Dhaka engaged with the game in the 1870s, followed by their counterparts in Calcutta in the 1880s. [48] Despite its political character, since cricket was accompanied by no discernible radical intonation associated with other proto-nationalist ventures, it was not suppressed. Contrary to the usual explanation of cricket's princely patronage as a quest for political mobility, Majumdar foregrounds a variety of underlying factors such as peer rivalries (as between the Maharaja of Cooch Behar and the Maharaja of Natore), self-aggrandizement (Ranji) or regional ascendancy (between Bengal and Mumbai). Contradicting the dominant argument that posits the princes and the educated middle classes as incompatible in enterprise, he comes to an unorthodox conclusion that the princes often joined hands with the nationalists, if only to ful?l personal ambitions. Cricket in colonial India was very much democratised and considerably more representative of the Indian society than its postcolonial counterpart.

Another symbolic function accomplished by cricket was challenging the consistent refrains running through European knowledge of the inferiority of Indian physicality. Indians were often portrayed as physically and hence intellectually incapable of keeping pace with the strides of modern civilization. A description of the Calcutta Cricket Club by George Johnson aptly summarises the contempt for 'native' physicality:

> The natives do not at all enter into the pleasures of this manly game, neither do the servants of the players, if

> desired to stop a stray ball, think it all meritorious to risk stinging their fingers by stopping it while in motion; they amble by its side until it has ceased rolling, and then pick it up![49]

From the mid-nineteenth century, groups of Indians strove to dispel this humiliating myth of the physical downfall of a once proud culture. Numerous *akharas* (gymnasiums) sprang up across India, mostly in modern-day Bengal and Uttar Pradesh. Quite a few political leaders and associations espoused the cause of cultivating strong physique in retaliation to European criticism of fragile Indian body and mentality.[50] A strong body started carrying nationalist connotation. The physical culture movement grew strong in the late nineteenth century, but its political overtone moderated in the twentieth century. As the once vibrant physical culture movement petered out, failing to motivate the masses and to counter the colonial stereotype of effeminacy, Indians stated using cricket and football as the non-violent means of challenging the Raj.[51] Texts played a critical role in this element of subversion. The cultural investments in Nayudu's body, for instance, made him appear an indefatigable colossus whose function was to batter the English on the field of play, whereas his real life nationalist activities were rather modest.[52] His ancestral connection with the Telengana region was appropriated by Andhra nationalists to carve a cultural niche. Moreover, commercial corporations selected him to endorse certain consumer items, making him the first Indian cricketer to do so. The advertisements consistently referred to his physical and sporting faculty.[53] The aspiration was similar to the Australian longing for sporting achievements in the nineteenth century which enabled them to dispel the suspicion that tropical climate might lead to genetic degeneration of the Anglo-Saxon race.[54] At another level, cricket cultivated in white Australians a strong sense of egalitarianism contrary to the amateur-professional divide in English cricket, though this outlook did not extend to Aborigines.[55]

Lagaan: Nationalist Romance in a Subaltern Past?

Bollywood shares a strange relationship with cricket. It has tried to capitalise on cricket's appeal as the biggest mass entertainer in contemporary India by making films on cricket or casting cricketers in lead or cameo roles. But it has spectacularly failed except on one occasion. *Lagaan* (2001), set in a nondescript village oppressed by high tax demands of the British Raj, became not only the greatest hit of the year, but a landmark in the history of Indian cinema. The villagers of famine-hit Champaner, led by the local prince, petition the local British administrator for a temporary remission of agrarian tax which has just been doubled. While the prince speaks to the officer, the villagers encounter the game of cricket for the first time. Having failed to negotiate the waiver, an impulsive young man named Bhuban (played by Aamir Khan) challenges the colonial officer to a cricket match, the wager being no tax for three years if the village wins. The entire village is furious since no one of them has even a remote idea of how to play cricket, and if they lose the tax would be tripled. But Bhuban reasons that cricket is merely a European improvisation of the *gilli-danda* played by children. By doing so, he not only de-colonises cricket but reduces it to a form of immature behaviour by the (British) colonizers. Coached by an English woman, the villagers master the art of cricket. A woman's appropriation of the (masculine) role of a cricket coach disrupts the phallogocentric preserve of the game. The peasants expectedly win the match after three dramatic days of cricket, aided by team play and Bhuban's heroics. The British are shown to have been humiliated so much that they desert the garrison near the village, granting Champaner symbolic independence.

Unlike previous films on cricket, *Lagaan* enjoyed both instant and lasting success since, contends Sharmistha Gooptu, it portrayed cricket as a sensational, 'spectacular' period drama instead of an everyday activity that the Indians frenziedly participate in.[56] Aside from the spectacle, the motif of conquering the British using their own weapon has prompted a variety of responses from historians. Majumdar contextualises the nationalist overtones in *Lagaan* in the retaliatory aspect of colonial cricket which, he says, accounted for the sport's expansion in Bengal and parts of north India in the 1880s-90s. Although the portrayal of cricket in *Lagaan* wanders into fantasy beyond the game's material reality in the period, it promotes an integrative nationalist imaginary in which people across class and caste make a stand, not exactly in harmony though, against the colonial masters. A major reason for the film's success was the time of its release the second half of 2001 when India recovered from the taints of match fixing allegations by winning memorable matches against Australia and Zimbabwe. The evocation of a marginalised past of white-bashing was well received, and cricket followers felt pride in being 'Indian'. [57] Srimati Basu argues that the unique selling proposition of Lagaan was its creative use of cricket, the sport which underlined the colonial civilizational mission, as an instrument which symbolically subverts the colonial regime by resisting tropes of European superiority. [58]

On the contrary, Dipesh Chakrabarty contends that the nationalism expressed in *Lagaan* echoes the aggressive 'mass mediatized nationalism' of the present. He says that the film 'deliberately mixes up historical chronology and uses the mediatized mass-spectacular nature of limited-over cricket now set back into the 1890s as a visual metaphor for Indian anti-colonial nationalism ...' [59] Brinda Bose identifies in the film a disconcerting conversion of sporting ideals into 'jingoistic nationalist ideology'. [60] She argues that the narrative transforms the cricket field into a 'veritable battlefield that pits native heroes against the suave and crafty colonizers in a do-or-die bid for hyper-patriotic glory'. [61] While Bose can be criticised as having read too little into stories such as the impartiality of an English umpire who is more loyal to the conventions of cricket than the exigencies of the colonial government, or the prince's refusal to help the villagers in order to preserve his personal convictions about vegetarianism, Majumdar and Basu's opinions have been challenged on the ground of privileging the master narrative of popular nationalism over the subtexted subaltern consciousness in the film.

Nissim Mannathukkaren criticises *Lagaan* as the manifestation of an essentially bourgeois nationalism which marginalises the subaltern, represented by the figure of Kachra which means 'garbage' in Hindi, in the national imaginary. [62] Peasant state of affairs in 1890s' Awadh, the time and place in which the narrative takes place, was characterised by large-scale exploitation not only by the colonial state and zamindars, but also by intermediary groups such as *taluqdars*, moneylenders and village heads a condition effaced by the binary conflict of Indians and Europeans in *Lagaan*. [63] Majumdar's reading of *Lagaan*, Mannathukkaren says, transposes meaning derived from different contexts into the film's narrative and invents historical parallels in a fictitious story in an unconscious attempt to 'nationalise the past'. [64]

Sirivayan Anand identifies in the film's success the proof that a rigid caste hierarchy still dominates social relations in the country. *Lagaan*, he observes, establishes the majoritarian vision of the nation. [65] Criticising both Majumdar and Mannathukkaren for having failed to recognise agencies of subalternity embedded in *Lagaan*, Chandrima Chakroborty argues that subversion of the colonial through mimicry (using a colonial inheritance to defeat the colonial) and indigenization (appropriating conventional methods to suit local requirements) manifests subaltern politics and mobilization. Chakroborty contests Mannathukkaren's critique of *Lagaan* for having failed to explain the peasants' inability to shift the focus of attack from European oppressors to the native collaborators of the Raj, arguing that the materiality of subordination in the screenplay had fixated subaltern identity in the film. [66] Moreover, while condemning the imposition of a nationalist paradigm over a subaltern discourse, she envisages

Lagaan as an extension of the subaltern studies project in the visual medium which has the power to decolonise popular mass imagination. [67] She argues that characterization of the peasants in the film contradicts the colonialist and nationalist historiographical stereotypes which assumed that ignorance and lack of resources had restricted the peasants' autonomy of selection and action, and only external stimulus could organise them as a unit. [68]

In a later article, Mannathukkaren demonstrates that contrary to what Chakroborty suggests, neither does *Lagaan* recover subaltern agency, nor can it be read as an extension of subaltern studies which itself had undergone an epistemological shift from the initial 'critical Gramscian thrust' to the later culturalist interpretive model inspired by the works of Foucault, Derrida and Said. [69] By identifying the English officer as the 'real enemy', the film omits the collaborative role of the native princes and feudal lords, and appropriates the peasant to the cause of an elite nationalism. [70] Hence, instead of questioning the social hierarchy of the colonial period, *Lagaan* perpetuates the existing social order. [71]

Afterword

Compared to other sports, the body of cricket writings in India is so large that it is not possible to imagine cricket without the literature it has produced. [72] Newspaper reports, tour books, biographies, autobiographies and literature on cricket are abundant to say the least. Dimeo holds that this tradition of cricket writings was hegemonic, having exclusively memorialised the development of cricket as representative of the nation while marginalising other sports. He explains how cricket writings as newspaper reports or books became fashionable owing to its patronage of educated elites and financial promises and continued to dominate indigenous sports writing because of the corporatization and centrist presence associated with cricket. Contemporary historians of cricket such as Guha, he argues, consider the sport a mirror of the nation since its past has been subconsciously mythologized as such. [73] Most of the recent histories, he continues, tend to 'nationalise' cricket as an element of India's anti-colonial past. The nationalist value has been so implanted in Indian cricket that, contends Satadru Sen, colonial cricket matches which did not convey overtly political messages left no impression on popular memory. This is why 'memorable' performances in regional tournaments have been forgotten, while brief episodes in East-West matches have been recorded with abandon. [74]

It will be worthwhile not to envisage nationalism in cricket as self-determination campaigns or ideological-physical confrontation with the core but instead as a discourse whose textual dimension, particularly the limits and excesses of its mediation, was primarily responsible for the spread of cricket in the colony. Instead of assuming cricket writings to be mirrors of ideologies or models of something, one should question the modes of representation itself since it is what mediates the liminal space in the sport-consumer dyad. By analysing representations of cricket in various media local and national newspapers, magazines and oral accounts it is possible to situate the sport not merely as a reflection of broader socio-economic history, but as a driver of modernizing some of the forces which had shaped lexical and visual consumerism in the late colonial and postcolonial India.

It is surprising that historians have seldom looked beyond reports in indigenous newspapers. A comparative analysis of Anglo-Australian and Indian media yields an excellent overview of the transnational dialectic of anti-colonial nationalism. Narrating a political disturbance in a cricket match during a Calcutta riot in which fifteen people were killed, the *Sydney Morning Herald* wrote that, 'A crocodile of children and men, followed by a screaming character wearing a Gandhi cap and waving a Congress party flag, wound its way to the wicket where Compton was batting, swarmed on to the cricket pitch'.[75] The 'rabble of dirty children and young students', it continued, shouted slogans of independence. The same incident was described in *The Statesman* with relative sympathy. Moreover, it is necessary that scholars start exploring expressions of nationalism other than the anti-colonial variety. Instances of civic and ethnic nationalism are abounding in the annals of Indian cricket. A deeper appreciation will not only enrich sport studies, but may lead to more nuanced understanding of nationalism as well.

Notes

1. Mangan, 'Series Editor's Foreward', pp. xi-xii.
2. Jones, *Sport, Politics and the Working Class*, p. 2.
3. Paul Dimeo, 'Sporting and the "Civilizing Mission" in India', in Harald Fischer-Tiné and Michael Mann eds., *Colonialism and Civilising Mission: Cultural Ideology in British India*, London: Anthem, 2004, pp. 165-78.
4. Brian Stoddart, 'Sport, Cultural Imperialism, and Colonial Response in the British Empire', *Comparative Studies in Society and History*, 30 (4), 1988, pp. 649-73.
5. Boria Majumdar and Sean Brown, 'Why Baseball, Why Cricket? Differing Nationalisms, Differing Challenges', *International Journal of the History of Sport* 24 (2), 2007, pp. 139-56.
6. Guttmann, *Games and Empires: Modern Sports and Cultural Imperialism*, p. 179.
7. C.L.R. James, *Beyond a Boundary*, London: Stanley Paul, 1963.
8. Bandyopadhyay, *Playing for Freedom.*
9. Maguire, *Global Sport*, p. 176.
10. Downing, *A Compendious History of the Indian Wars*, London: T. Cooper, 1737, p. 229. Neither of the quotes in Guha or Majumdar's book matches the original passage. Ramachandra Guha, *Corner of a Foreign Field*, p. 3; Boria Majumdar ed., *Indian Cricket through the Ages: A Reader*, p. 33. The passage published in these works is essentially reprinted from a note written by J.S. Cotton in the *Athenaum*on 27 May 1905, which had missed a few prepositions and punctuation marks.
11. Majumdar ed., *Indian Cricket through the Ages: A Reader*, p. 34.
12. Majumdar, 'When the Sepoys Batted: 1830-50 on the Playing Field'.
13. Majumdar, 'Communalism to Commercialism: The Bombay Pentangular 1892-1946', pp. 1050-51.
14. Williams, *Cricket and England*, p. 1.
15. Mangan, *The Games Ethic and Imperialism: Aspects of the Diffusion of an*

Ideal,p. 134.

16. Headlam, *Ten Thousand Miles*, pp. 169.
17. Guttmann, *Games and Empires*, p. 33.
18. Lord Harris, 'Bombay', p. 70, cited in Luhrmann, *The Good Parsi: The Fate of a Colonial Elite in a Postcolonial Society*, p. 119.
19. Guha, *Corner of a Foreign Field*, p. 17.
20. Ibid.
21. Ashis Nandy, *The Tao of Cricket: On Games of Destiny and the Destiny of Games*, 2[nd]edn., New Delhi: Oxford University Press, 2000, p. 1.
22. Ibid., pp. xx.
23. Luhrmann, *The Good Parsi*, p. 119.
24. Berry, *Cricket Wallah*, pp. 21-22.
25. Bateman, *Cricket, Literature and Culture: Symbolising the Nation, Destabilizing Empire*, p. 127.
26. Karaka, *The Parsees*, p. 226.
27. Luhrmann, *The Good Parsi*, pp. 96-99.
28. Framjee Patel, *Stray Thoughts on Indian Cricket*, p. 174.
29. Cashman, 'Australia', *The Imperial Game*, p. 40.
30. Ibid, p. 46.
31. Framjee Patel, *Stray Thoughts on Indian Cricket*, p. 55.
32. Sorabjee, *A Chronicle of Cricket Among Parseesand The Struggle: European Polo Versus Native Cricket.*
33. For theories of mimicry see Homi K. Bhaba, 'Of Mimicry and, Man: The Ambivalence of Colonial Discourse'.
34. Mukharji, 'The Early Cricketing Tours: Imperial Provenance and Radical Potential'.
35. Naha, 'Adams and Eves at the Eden Gardens: Women Cricket Spectators and the Conflict of Feminine Subjectivity in Calcutta, 1920-70'.
36. Sandiford, *Cricket and the Victorians*, p. 156.
37. Nandy, p. 7.
38. Guha, 'Cricket and Politics', p. 167.
39. Ibid., pp. 167-68.
40. Guha, *A Corner of a Foreign Field: The Indian History of a British Sport*, pp. 173-5.
41. Majumdar, *Lost Histories of Indian Cricket: Battles off the Pitch*, p. 118. It is arguable whether the term 'the moment of departure' appropriately describes the development, but the debate can be skipped without hampering our present argument. For theoretical explication see Partha Chatterjee's *Nationalist Thought and the Colonial World: A Derivative Discourse*.
42. Guha, *Corner of a Foreign Field*, p. 204.
43. Ibid., p. 205.
44. Mushtaq Ali, *Cricket Delightful*, p. 71.
45. Sarbadhikary, *Indian Cricket Uncovered*.
46. Preface to Sarbadhikary, *Presenting Indian Cricket*.
47. The book is remarkable in its laborious survey of a number of sports alongside cricket. He compares them on the grid of popularity, and tries to establish

cricket's claim as one of most popular sports despite being an elite preserve.

48. Ghosh, *Cricket Elc Banglae*.
49. Johnson, *The Stran;ger in India* or *Three Years in Calcutta*, p. 62.
50. Rosselli, 'The Self-Image of Effeteness: Physical Education and Nationalism in Nineteenth-Cent ıry Bengal'.
51. Majumdar, 'Cricket in Colonial Bengal (1880-1947): A Lost History of Nationalism'.
52. Naha, 'Producing the First Indian Cricketing Superhero: Nationalism, Body Culture, Consumption and the C.K. Nayudu Phenomenon'.
53. Ibid., pp. 575-76.
54. Mandle, 'Cricket and Australian Nationalism', p. 233.
55. Ibid., p. 241.
56. Gooptu, 'Cricket or Cricket Spectacle: Looking Beyond Cricket to Understand Lagaan'.
57. Majumdar, 'Politics of Leisure in Colonial India, Lagaan: Invocation of a Lost History', p. 3399.
58. Basu, 'Aamir's Fables: Lagaan as Phenomenon'.
59. Chakrabarty, 'The Fall and Rise of Indian Sports History', 341-42
60. Bose, 'Our Fate is in Our Stars: Gender, Culture and Sport in India', p. 249.
61. Ibid., pp. 249-50.
62. Mannathukkaren, "Subalterns, Cricket and the 'Nation': The Silences of 'Lagaan'".
63. Ibid., p. 4582.
64. Ibid., p. 4584.
65. Sirivayan Anand, 'Eating with our Fingers, Consuming Hindi Cinema and Watching Cricket'.
66. Chakroborty, Subaltern Studies, Bollywood and *Lagaan*', p. 1881.
67. Ibid., pp. 1879-84.
68. Ibid, p. 1881.
69. Mannathukkaren, 'Reading Cricket Fiction in the Times of Hindu Nationalism and Farmer Suicides: Fallacies of Textual Interpretation', p. 1203.
70. Ibid., 1204.
71. Ibid., 1209.
72. In the words of Benny Green, 'Not only does cricket, more than any other game, inspire the urge to literary expression; it is almost as though the game itself would not exist at all until written about.' *A History of Cricket,* London: Barrie and Jenkins, 1988, p. 14.
73. Dimeo, 'Cricket and the Misinterpretation of Indian Sports History'.
74. Sen, 'History without a Past: Memory and Forgetting in Indian Cricket', pp. 97-98.
75. *Sydney Morning Herald*, 14 Nov 1945, p. 1.

References

Anand, Sirivayan, 'Eating with our Fingers, Consuming Hindi Cinema and Watching Cricket', http://www.ambedkar.org/ research/ Eatingwith.htm, accessed on 12 June 2010.

Bandyopadhyay, Kausik, *Playing for Freedom*, New Delhi: Standard, 2008.

Basu, Srimati, 'Aamir's Fables: Lagaan as Phenomenon', in Boria Majumdar ed. *Indian Cricket through the Ages*, pp. 392-96.

Bateman, Anthony, *Cricket, Literature and Culture: Symbolising the Nation, Destabilizing Empire*, Farnham: Ashgate, 2009.

Berry, Scyld, *CricketWallah: With England in India, 1981-2*, London: Hodder& Stoughton, 1982.

Bhaba, Homi K., 'Of Mimicry and, Man: The Ambivalence of Colonial Discourse', *Location of Culture*, London & New York: Routledge, 1994, pp. 85-92.

Bose, Brinda, 'Our Fate is in Our Stars: Gender, Culture and Sport in India', in Martina Ghosh-Schellhorn and Roland Marti eds., *Playing by the Rules of the Game*, Berlin: LIT Verlag, 2008, pp. 241-52.

Cashman, Richard, *Patrons, Players and the Crowd: The Phenomenon of Indian Cricket*, New Delhi: Orient Longman, 1980.

—, 'Australia', in Brian Stoddart& Keith A.P. Sandiford eds., *The Imperial Game*, Manchester: Manchester University Press, 1998, pp. 34-54.

Chakrabarty, Dipesh, 'The Fall and Rise of Indian Sports History', in BoriaMajumdar and J.A. Mangan eds., *Sport in South Asian Society: Past and Present*, London: Routledge, 2005, pp. 1-7.

Chakroborty, Chandrima, 'Subaltern Studies, Bollywood and *Lagaan*', *Economic and Political Weekly* 38 (19), May 10, 2003, pp. 1879-84.

Chatterjee, Kingshuk, 'To Play Or Not To Play: Fabricating Consent over the Indo-Pak Cricket Series', in Boria Majumdar and J.A. Mangan eds., *Sport in South Asian Society: Past and Present*, London: Routledge, 2005, pp. 277-94.

Chatterjee, Partha, *Nationalist Thought and the Colonial World: A Derivative Discourse*, Tokyo: Zed Books, 1986.

Dasgupta, Jishnu, 'Manufacturing Unison: Muslims, Hindus and Indians During the IndiaPakistan Match', in Boria Majumdar and J.A. Mangan eds., *Sport in South Asian Society: Past and Present*, London: Routledge, 2005, pp. 239-48.

Davis, Christina P. and Grant P. Upson, 'Spectatorship, Fandom, and Nationalism in the South Asian Diaspora: The 2003 Cricket World Cup', in Boria Majumdar and J.A. Mangan eds., *Sport in South Asian Society: Past and Present*, London: Routledge, 2005, pp. 295-313.

Dimeo, Paul, 'Cricket and the Misinterpretation of Indian Sports

History', *Historical Studies* 24, 2005, pp. 98-111.

Downing, Clement, *A Compendious History of the Indian Wars*, London: T. Cooper, 1737.

Fletcher, Thomas, 'Who do "they" cheer for?': Cricket, Diaspora, Hybridity and Divided Loyalties amongst British Asians', *International Review for the Sociology of Sport*, published online on 29 July 2011 at http://irs.sagepub.com/content/early/2011/07/28/1012690211416556.full.pdf+html accessed on 30 July 2011.

Ghosh, Siddhartha, *Cricket EloBanglae*, Calcutta: Subarnarekha, 2002.

Gooptu, Sharmistha, 'Cricket or Cricket Spectacle: Looking Beyond Cricket to Understand Lagaan', in Boria Majumdar and J.A. Mangan eds., *Sport in South Asian Society: Past and Present*, London: Routledge, 2005, pp. 197-212.

Green, Benny, *A History of Cricket*, London: Barrie and Jenkins, 1988.

Guha, Ramachanda, *A Corner of a Foreign Field: The Indian History of a British Sport*, London: Picador, 2002.

—, 'Cricket and Politics in Colonial India', *Past and Present* 161, Nov 1998, pp. 155-90.

Guttmann, Allen, *Games and Empires: Modern Sports and Cultural Imperialism*, New York: Columbia University Press, 1994.

Headlam, Cecil, *Ten Thousand Miles Through India and Burma; An Account of the Oxford University Authentics Cricket Tour with Mr KJ Key in the year of the Coronation Durbar*, London: J.M. Dent, 1903.

James, C.L.R., *Beyond a Boundary*, London: Stanley Paul, 1963.

Johnson, George W., *The Stranger in India* or *Three Years in Calcutta* vol. II, London: Henry Colburn, 1843.

Jones, Stephen G., *Sport, Politics and the Working Class*, Manchester: Manchester University Press, 1992.

Karaka, Dosabhai Framjee, *The Parsees: Their History, Manners, Customs, and Religion*, London: Smith, Elder & Co., 1858.

Luhrmann, Tanya, *The Good Parsi: The Fate of a Colonial Elite in a Postcolonial Society*, Cambridge, MA: Harvard University Press, 1996.

Maguire, Joseph, *Global Sport: Identities, Societies, Civilizations*, Cambridge: Polity Press, 1999.

Majumdar, Boria, *Twenty-two Yards to Freedom*, New Delhi: Penguin, 2004.

—, *Lost Histories of Indian Cricket: Battles off the Pitch*, Abingdon: Routledge, 2006.

— ed., *Indian Cricket through the Ages: A Reader*, New Delhi: Oxford University Press, 2005.

—, 'When the Sepoys Batted: 1830-50 on the Playing Field', in Sharmistha

Gooptu and Boria Majumdar eds. *Revisiting 1857: Myth, Memory, History*, New Delhi: Roli, 2007, pp. 73-91.
—, 'Cricket in Colonial Bengal (1880-1947): A Lost History of Nationalism', *International Journal of the History of Sport* 23 (6), 2006, pp. 960-90.
—, 'Politics of Leisure in Colonial India, Lagaan: Invocation of a Lost History', *Economic and Political Weekly*, 36 (35), Sept 1, 2001, pp. 3399-3404.
Mandle, W.F., 'Cricket and Australian Nationalism in the Nineteenth Century', *Journal of the Royal Australian Historical Society* 59 (4), 1974, pp. 225-45.
Mangan, J.A., *The Games Ethic and Imperialism: Aspects of the Diffusion of an Ideal*, Viking: Harmondsworth, 1985.
—, 'Series Editor's Foreward' in Mike Cronin and David Mayall eds., *Sporting Nationalisms: Identity, Ethnicity, Immigration and Assimilation*, London: Frank Cass, 1998.
Mannathukkaren, Nissim, 'Reading Cricket Fiction in the Times of Hindu Nationalism and Farmer Suicides: Fallacies of Textual Interpretation', *International Journal of the History of Sport* 24 (9), 2007, pp. 1200-25.
—, 'Subalterns, Cricket and the "Nation": The Silences of "Lagaan'", *Economic and Political Weekly*, 36 (49), Dec 8, 2001, pp. 4580-88.
Mukharji, Projit B., 'The Early Cricketing Tours: Imperial Provenance and Radical Potential', *International Journal of the History of Sport* 21 (3-4), 2004, pp. 351-62.
Mushtaq Ali, *Cricket Delightful*, 2nd edn., New Delhi: Rupa, 1976.
Naha, Souvik, 'Adams and Eves at the Eden Gardens: Women Cricket Spectators and the Conflict of Feminine Subjectivity in Calcutta, 1920-70', *International Journal of the History of Sport* 29 (5), 2012, pp. 711-29.
—, 'Producing the First Indian Cricketing Superhero: Nationalism, Body Culture, Consumption and the C.K. Nayudu Phenomenon', *International Journal of the History of Sport* 29 (4), 2012, pp. 562-82.
Nandy, Ashis, *The Tao of Cricket: On Games of Destiny and the Destiny of Games*, 2nd Edn., New Delhi: Oxford University Press, 2000.
Patel, J.M. Framjee, *Stray Thoughts on Indian Cricket*, Bombay: The Times of India Press, 1905.
Rosselli, John, 'The Self-Image of Effeteness: Physical Education and Nationalism in Nineteenth-Century Bengal', *Past and Present* 86, Feb 1980, pp. 121-48.
Sandiford, Keith A.P., *Cricket and the Victorians*, Aldershot: Scholar Press, 1994.
Sarbadhikary, Berry, *Indian Cricket Uncovered*, Calcutta: Illustrated News,

1945.

—, *Presenting Indian Cricket*, Kolkata: A. Mukherjee & Co, 1946.

Sen, Satadru, 'History without a Past: Memory and Forgetting in Indian Cricket', in Stephen Wagg ed., *Cricket And National Identity in the Postcolonial Age: Following On, Abingdon: Routledge, 2005*, pp. 94-109.

Sorabjee, Shaporjee, *A Chronicle of Cricket Among Parsees and The Struggle: Eurpoean Polo versus Native Cricket*, Bombay, 1897.

Williams, John, *Cricket and England: A Cultural and Social History of the Inter-war Years*, London: Frank Cass, 1999.

Exploring Politics and Sports: Towards a Disaggregated Understanding

Jishnu Dasgupta

This paper is dedicated to the memory of two people. One, definitely the more famous in his life and thereafter is Saadat Hassan Manto, the famous advocate of communal amity and chronicler of disharmony. An avid cricket fan, he was eager to watch the Test match scheduled for Lahore during India's first cricket tour of Pakistan. But he died listening to AFS Talyarkhan's commentary of the preceding Bahwalpur Test. [1] The other, I most certainly would not have heard of but for the way he died and, then too, not without the research that I started on this topic. He was the Muslim youth who died in the violent clashes that took place as Hindu fanatics tried to stop Muslims from celebrating India's victory in the Johannesburg match between the two neighbours that forms such a prominent part of the following discussion. I could not find his name in any of the press reports that I went through. [2] Perhaps, I have not looked hard enough. Then again, it might be a deliberate, if not conscious, omission on my part. Nations always give great pride of place to the monuments honouring the Unknown Soldier. Let this be a tribute to all fighters against the processes that I seek to underline below.

It really does not require me to tell anyone that Indo-Pak matches are fraught with issues other than the 'cricketing'. As Boria Majumdar writes, only the naïve can regard sports as an avenue for entertainment alone. [3] It involves various processes.

This paper seeks to identify trends and histories marked by their coincidence in time and place, a coincidence that might be merely superficial in other terms. For they are truly disjointed, informed as they are by specific historical factors that are themselves determined contingently. Thus, broad similarities often mask more subtle differences that are crucial. By looking at these histories I seek to take a peek at the process of nation building around this 'game' as played out in the India-Pakistan matches, largely over a five-year period. Diplomacy, on whatever track, is not my focus here. It is not my intention to read how Indo-Pak diplomatic relations and cricket inform each other. Rather, I read this interaction as only one of several processes that inform the self-definition of the nation.

To Cut a Long Decade Short: A Brief Survey of the 1990s

In 1992, I was a twelve-year-old, watching excitedly as Pakistan took on England. I was watching the Final with a bunch of teenagers all seniors from school. Not one person in that room was against the 'old enemy'. That mine was not an isolated incident is borne out by various pieces of evidence. For instance, Ramchandra Guha cites that he was told by a Delhi chauffeur, "Akhir Cup Asia main hi raha" ('At least the trophy came to Asia'). Sunil Gavaskar, perhaps the greatest batsman produced by India, ignored the whip of the Shiv Sena supremo and the 'Lord' of Gavaskar's native Bombay, Bal Thackarey, and went to Lahore and Karachi to attend the celebrations there. [4]

But come 1999, the next time Pakistan was in the World Cup Final, the situation was very different. Then, Guha finds little evidence of any Indian looking more favourably at the other side of the border than just classifying them as enemies. [5] This observation, or rather the gaps in it, is however vulnerable to the Cardus statement he starts off the book with "It is a dreadful pity when a beautifully spacious generalisation is upset by one or two simple facts." [6] But like all such generalisations, it contains more than a grain of truth. India had already gone through the troubled decade of the 1990s through the Ram Janmbhoomi movement and the demolition of the Babri Masjid, Atal Behari Vajpayee's thirteen day government, the establishment of the National Democratic Alliance government that was led by the Bharatiya Janata Party, the nuclear tests at Pokhran, coupled with the Pakistani response at Chaghai and finally the World Cup coincided with the Kargil War. But it was not just the arena of what is conventionally understood as the political that was undergoing severe change. The game's own history was very much a party to the same process.

In 1992 itself, Guha had a conversation with a student of the Delhi School of Economics. This unnamed student of this bastion of Indian liberalism was quite unequivocal in his views. He attributed Pakistan's victory to the cohesion that Pakistan had due to the religious basis of her nationhood in this case, Islamic. He also felt that only the success of the Ram Janmabhoomi movement could lead to a similar success for India. The next edition of the World Cup, played in 1996, was held in the subcontinent. The Quarterfinal clash between India and Pakistan was played in Bangalore. During the match, Guha noted with shock the deafening silence that greeted the pyrotechnics of the Pakistani batsmen, particularly Aameer Sohail and Saeed Anwar and the total absence of the applause when Javed Miandad, the Pakistani great, left the field for what was to be his last innings. This was in obvious contrast to the standing ovation Asif Iqbal received when he retired from cricket at Calcutta's Eden Gardens. [7] But if there is room for pride for this performance at Calcutta, such pride was surely lost by the behaviour of the crowd at that very same ground in the semi-final match against Sri Lanka. When it was obvious that India was headed towards a humiliating defeat, the crowd threw projectiles on the field, making it impossible for the match to continue.

This was perhaps only to be expected in the situation in which the Cup was played. The media and the sponsors had played up the team as one of the, if not the, favourite to lift the coveted trophy. The triumphs in the Hero Cup and the Wills Cup in the preceding years had fuelled such expectation. The difficulty in defeating unfancied New Zealand did prove to be a hiccup. But it was brushed aside in the euphoria that was generated in the events preceding the tournament. Even former superstars like Gavaskar and B.S. Chandrashekhar leant their voice to the chorus as they featured prominently in the campaign to sign a giant-sized bat to wish the team luck. During the competition, too, press reports were provocative. In the press reports about the Bangalore clash, military jargon was freely in use. *The Telegraph* of Calcutta, thus, dubbed the batting display of Anwar and Sohail a "Blitzkrieg". [8] The following match was no different. Let me cite *The Telegraph* again. Under a headline, "Battlelines Drawn, City Bays for Blood", the report declared, "If there is one villain in Calcutta today, it is Sanath Jayasuriya." [9] But the press did not stop at dubbing the opposition's ace batsman a villain, or even at the fiasco at the Eden that it undoubtedly helped create. In it's match report, *Anandabazar Patrika,* the Calcutta daily with the largest circulation, denounced the Indian middle-order batsman, Ajay Jadeja for failing to provide what it saw as what the crowd wanted: "*Ektu moroder moto batting*" ('batting like a man'). [10]

The following years saw the further entrenchment of the same feelings of animosity. If anything, it saw a sharpening of the focus in naming the enemy. In a time when the forces of the Hindu right were steadily gaining ground, calls for boycotting Pakistan were also gaining ground. The question of boycott is one to which I will come back. But a few events of this period have to be mentioned. The first took place in Toronto, during the second edition of the

Sahara Cup. Inzamam-ul-Haq, the portly Pakistani batsman was not only called "alu"('potato') repeatedly by a fan on a megaphone, abuses were also hurled at his family, religion and county, provoking a heated response from Haq. [11] In the same year, India's short tour to Pakistan, the second match was almost abandoned due to crowd violence. [12]

The third and fourth instances took place during the full-fledged tour that Pakistan undertook of India in 1999. The attitudes of the crowd were marked by a stark difference. While the crowds of Chennai gave Pakistan a rousing reception when they beat India in a thriller, the scene in the Eden Gardens saw a sea change. When India's ace Sachin Tendulkar was given out in controversial circumstances, the crowd erupted. They stopped play by using the same methods used three years earlier. Abuses hurled at the Pakistani cricketers were clearly communal in tenor.

It would have been comfortable for me to subscribe to *The Telegraph*'s characterisation of the violent members as "the cellphone-toting yuppie, the sunscreen-lotioned Raybanned girls, the paan-masala-chewing, rotund businessman". [13] It would have sat well with my own 'identity' including class and language and even politics. I had a similar experience too at the Eden. When I tried to stop someone who clearly belonged to the last of the above categories, I was asked with a malice and threat that I had not encountered till then, "*Aap Hindu to hain na*?" ('Are you even a Hindu?') But the same article noted a college student's reaction, "We aren't pansies and this is not Chennai ... We have come to see India win or else we won't let them play." [14] A college student was what I was then. But I could still have ignored this as an aberration, as the class position of this student was left unclear in the article. But there were people around me, whom I knew to be otherwise 'liberal' and 'secular' who also showed similar trends. I was witness to communal and gendered slogans from such people that simply destroys the stereotype. A student politician, for instance, then leading an agitation to secularise Government Hostels, grabbed the collar of his friend when asked not to be parochial, and tried to punch him.[15]

Much Urdu About Nothing?[16]
Kargil and Old Trafford in 1999

As noted earlier, the World Cup match played at Old Trafford between India and Pakistan was played in the shadow of the Kargil war. It could hardly have been just another match, at least as far as the crowds, at the ground or otherwise, were concerned. This was however not the first time that Indian and Pakistani cricketers were interacting when the two countries were fighting a war. During the 1965 War, Hanif Muhammad and Mansur Ali Khan, then captains of their respective countries, were playing together for a Rest of the World side against England at Scarborough in Yorkshire. They sent a joint telegram to both governments: "We wish to express deep regrets at the war between India and Pakistan. We find unity on the cricket field by reaching for a common objective. We fervently hope both countries can meet and find an amicable solution."[17] During the Bangladesh War of 1971, some Indian and Pakistani cricketers were touring Australia for a Rest of the World side. They held a mock war with cricket gear, showing how untouched their life was by the war.[18] But by 1999, the history of the subcontinent and of the game had changed sufficiently for the atmosphere to be very different.

The growing communalisation of the society and polity, had as we have seen, already left its mark on cricket. Throughout the 1990s, through what has been called the dehumanising of the Muslims, the community was viewed as backward with medieval laws of marriage and divorce. If this was the 'soft' approach, then increasingly the hard-line thinking that was gaining ground was of seeing the Muslims as anti-national and as agents of Pakistan.

As far as cricket was concerned, this was reflected in the frequent assertion that Indian Muslims supported Pakistan against India. Bal Thackarey was the most vociferous in making these accusations, repeatedly casting doubts about patriotism of the Muslims, thereby strengthening the argument of seeing Muslims as something less than full citizens and therefore deserving less than the rights due to one.[19]

The liberals, of course, countered this, treating it as nothing less than slanderous. Let me just cite one such piece. Shashi Tharoor thus called this accusation "one of those 'urban legends' that acquires mythic proportions in the retelling, even though the evidence for the charge is both sparse and anecdotal. Certainly some Muslims may have behaved in this way, but the percentage of the community they represent is minuscule."[20] One must, of course, question why the liberal needed to disprove the allegation itself. Was it simply a desire to 'exonerate' a community of an unfair charge? Or was it that if the charge proved true then it would also prove that Muslims in India are as much second class citizens as people of subcontinental extract are in England and elsewhere? In any case, the allegations and the refutations continued unabated.

In, 1999, not only did the ordinary Muslim stand accused of disloyalty by supporting the Pakistan team, it was the Indian captain, Mohammad Azharuddin, who himself stood accused. Azhar was the only major Muslim player of his generation and had served as captain for close to a decade. Even the arch-communalist Bal Thackarey had to declare that he and the Shiv Sena were "not against patriotic Muslims like Azharuddin".[21] During the deeply troubled decade of the nineties, Azhar's presence at the helm and his often sublime batting and fielding did provide a balm to the situation. Campaigning for the 1998 general elections, the Sangh Parivar Hardliner, LK Advani asked Muslim youths to follow the example of patriotic Muslims like

Azharuddin and the musician AR Rahman. [22] But these classifications were clearly loyalty-based, and if performance deteriorated, they could very easily translate into from failures to deliberate sabotaging. Azhar, too, had his loyalty to the team and country repeatedly questioned. So much so, that it seems that some Indian supporters, at least, would have been happier to see Azhar fail to confirm their suspicions about the man and the community he came from. As the match-fixing scandal involved Azhar ever more deeply, many were only too eager to believe the allegations for the same reasons. As Ambarish K. Dewanji notes, this enabled them to continue propagating that Muslims were disloyal. They could now smirk and ask, "If even Azhar cannot be trusted, can anyone else?" [23] Sections of the press, too, were not unwilling to go along with this in order to get a saleable copy. Thus, Guha talks about two journalists from *India Today* and *Outlook*, disappointed at Azhar's sterling performance and India's victory as that deprived them of a best-selling story: 'Azhar Goes Out in Disgrace'. [24]

The match was itself played in what can only be described as an atmosphere surcharged by tension. The *Daily Express* noted its concern thus: "No cricket match in this country has ever witnessed such tight control but then, no cricket match in this country has ever attracted so much tension as this." [25] The reports published after the match are glaring in their portrayal of the match as war. "Pak falls to India's line of control," exulted The Pioneer. "India triumph in game of death," chimed The *Hindustan Times*. "Reborn India kill Pak," reported The Asian Age, which also observed: "India now wait for other pieces of the jigsaw puzzle to fall into place to win the war." The *Indian Express* urged readers to "Party away! Feel the warm glow. Wake up feeling good. Savour the moment to make it last." [26]

The martial imagery invoked by the press was only befitting the way in which the match was seen by a large section of the press and population. It was reported that Indian soldiers along the Himalayan front let loose round after round of "happy fire". "'These are the moments when a bit of indiscipline is OK",' an Indian army colonel explained, "'We just did not expect a result as awesome as this. This is a fantastic win and it will keep us going in Kargil.'" According to the Colonel, the fighting had intensified in the hours leading up to the crucial World Cup tie, but subsided during the match itself. [27] The *Manchester Guardian* published an equally poignant picture, that of an Indian soldier in Kashmir. He had a rifle in one hand, a radio in the other, his face "grim, his eyes crinkled up in fierce and worried concentration." [28]

Though India exited almost immediately after this victory, the display of hyper-nationalism and Pakistan-bashing did not end. When Pakistan were decimated by Australia in the FInal, *The Asian Age* came up with a (vulgar) headline: "Australia Turn Cocky Pakistan into Impotent Joke". [29] There were press reports of a victory procession along Mahatma Gandhi Road in Bangalore. One participant was quoted: "Pakistan has said Kargil or cricket we will win. Now they are defeated. This means they will be thrown out of Kargil also by India."' A government employee bursting firecrackers in Calcutta's maiden echoed the reasoning. "I am happy because Pakistan lost. They are always our enemy.... Look at what they are doing in Kashmir. This is one way how I can express myself with the Indian army.'" Even in the far eastern state of Assam, it was reported, hundreds of people danced in the streets and hoteliers distributed soft drinks and sweets. "'The Australian victory is definitely a cause for celebration", said a local college student, "I feel very happy as Pakistan, our arch enemy, has been defeated".' A retired professor added, "The pleasure of Pakistan losing the match is much more than India getting into the finals."' [30] In Calcutta's Budge Budge area, the celebrations turned into a riot as the participants stoned shops owned by Muslims. Three people died in the violence and the army had to be called in to restore order.[31]

The portrayal did not end with the World Cup or Kargil. The India-Pakistan one-day contests in Australia in early 2000, were marketed by ESPN-Star, the exclusive broadcasters, as "Qayamat" ('Apocalypse'), which could not, but evoke ominous feelings given the recent history of actual war and the threat of nuclear war.[32]

Johannesburg 2003
The Nation Advances?

The World Cup of 2003 was the edition of the tournament most fraught with problems regarding nationalism. While the organisers tried to play on national sentiments by introducing the playing of national anthems before a match, the national policies and sentiments tended to play havoc with the tournament. New Zealand refused to play in Kenya, citing security reasons. England did the same when it came to Zimbabwe, but it was rightly suspected that this was more in the nature of a denouncement of the racist policies of the Mobutu regime in that country.

India seemed to be the one bright spot for the sports nationalist. The nation seemed to become one as never before during the amazing run of 'Team India' between the two defeats at the hands of Australia. Motorbike processions, streets and parks decorated with festoons and banners, gates adorned with posters of cricketers, homes draped in the tricolour all were seen as signs of an unprecedented rallying around national fortunes as represented by 'Ganguly and his boys'. Even the 'Thackarey Test' seemed to have been cracked as there were no displays of support for Pakistan.[33] The students of the Madrase-e-Fazeelath-e-Quran, a co-educational madrasa of Bangalore, took leave on the day of the match. On the eve of the game, Muhammad Tuafil, a student, declared: "If India wins, I will distribute sweets to all my friends."[34] Kasshaf Ghani, a resident of the Muslim-dominated locality of Park Circus in Calcutta, pointed out that processions were taken out supporting India by local clubs of his area before the match and during the lunch break. "Some of these clubs", he said, "had earlier supported Pakistan. But now all of them support India." [35] In Mumbai, the heart of Shiv Sena power, the Muslim Council of India had special prayers held before the match at the Azad Maidan. In what is sometimes referred to derogatorily as mini-Pakistan, the South Mumbai area around Mohammad Ali Road, Muslim children saw the match on giant screens specially set up for the match with tricolours painted on their faces. Many houses of the area sported the Indian flag. A restaurant in Bhendi Bazaar even served a *firni* embossed in the colours of the flag. [36]

The tune seemed perfectly in unison everywhere. Immediately after the victory the team received congratulatory messages from the Prime Minister and, more surprisingly, the chief of the army. [37] On the day after the match, the Finance Minister, Jaswant Singh, announced a tax exemption for the prize-money given to the team, individually or otherwise. [38] That the match itself was seen in a different light was apparent from the statements issued by the cricketers themselves. Tendulkar, the architect of India's victory, said in an interview immediately after the match, "This has always been a special game for us and nothing means more to us than this." [39] The *Anandabazar Patrika*, in its stories on the match and the celebrations thereafter reported, with glee, the younger members of the team and the reserves indulging in hurling obscenities during the match and during the celebrations afterwards. [40] Even before the match, at least one report carried the story of the Indian captain, Sourav Ganguly, seeing this match as not quite just another match. [41] This direct involvement of the players in the charged atmosphere and their actual abetting of the situation stood in stark contrast with what had been the norm till then. Sanjay Manjrekar, who had an excellent record against Pakistan during his playing days (1987-96) had written in Wisden that the cricketers did not share the fans' perception of extra pressure during an Indo-Pak match. [42] But, this change in the players' attitude has to be contextualised in the hyper-nationalism surrounding cricket, and particularly that match. The messages of the Prime Minister and the army chief and the statement of the finance minister are clearly indicative of this. To underline the point, mention may be made of a photograph appearing in a leading Gujarati daily on the eve of the match. The computer-generated image portrayed the twenty-two players in military uniforms and holding guns. [43]

It was in this context that the much-celebrated show of Muslim support came. It must be remembered that India was the only country with a large Muslim community that did not see wide protests among the Muslims over the US attack on Afghanistan. As Irfan Habib put it, "A Hindu can criticise the US but if a Muslim does so, he is vulnerable to attack." [44] In this situation, it was naturally seen desirable by many Muslims to decry any claims for support of Pakistan on the cricket field. In another madrasa of Bangalore, a thirteen year old student whispered to a reporter, "*Inshallah, Pakistan hi jeetega is baar.*" ('God willing, Pakistn will win this time'). [45] Kasshaf Ghani debunked the shows of Indian support as a *dikhawa* (a show) and mentions the suggestion mooted by the local police station to clamp down on Pakistan supporters. Though the suggestion was rejected, it shows that such a possibility did genuinely exist and lends credence to Ghani's assertion that the display of support for India springs from a deeply felt insecurity among the Muslims. [46]

There is, of course, a more famous and established instance of the citizens of a country supporting another. Subcontinental teams and the West Indies enjoy vociferous support whenever they play in England. This generated the controversy of the Tebbit test, named after the Conservative politician who devised it. Norman Tebbit demanded a proof of loyalty from these West Indians and South Asians in form of their supporting England against such countries. [47] This support is however, something all subcontinental teams still receive without question. During Pakistan's tour of England in 2001, Nasser Hussain sparked off a huge controversy when he asked for support from the expatriate population against Pakistan. This plea came before the Second Test at Old Trafford and coming within days of race riots at Oldham, near the test match venue, sparked fear of further race riots surrounding the test match. [48] Even Englishmen of a different persuasion like the poet PJ Kavanagh, celebrated the instance of the thousands who "triumphantly failed the Tebbit test". [49] In the West Indies, the Indian tourists of 1953 drew large support from the expatriates in Trinidad. [50] In both cases, the support given to the touring parties was obviously a mark of cultural identity with and a yearning for the 'motherland'. It equally obviously marks an incomplete identification with the nation they adopt. In the case of Trinidad, for instance, the Indians suffered from cultural derision and economic deprivation. The performances of the Indian team on tour there, as Mihir Bose writes, came as a "culture shock" to both the oppressed and the oppressor as for the first time Indians were seen as physical equals of the Blacks of the West Indies. [51]

Another instance of the touring side getting local support from a particular group is cited by Jon Gemmel. He quotes Basil D'Oliveira to show that the Blacks, in the Apartheid era, used to support the touring teams against the home side. In the 1950 Durban Test, when Neil Harvey smashed 151 not out, he was cheered enthusiastically by black spectators, among whom was a young Nelson Mandela. [52]

It then becomes obvious that as sports become the signifiers of the nation, it can also be used by those suffering from its inequities as an arena of protest against that very apparatus. When an open lack of support for Pakistan was witnessed among the Muslims of India, it did not mean that such sentiments had ceased to exist, that Muslim disaffection had been successfully removed and economic inequities for the 'backward community' had suddenly disappeared. It did not mean that the project of nation-building and 'national integration had succeeded. It could hardly have been so when the NDA was steadily increasing its power and popularity as borne out by an *India Today* opinion poll that placed the government on its strongest wicket yet. [53] It could be even less so on the first anniversary of Godhra, when the victory celebrations in some Delhi localities were led by Nagaras of the Shiv Sena and other Sangh Parivar elements. The lack of reports of support for Pakistan simply meant what it was that such sentiments were not visible or audible. In an atmosphere where liberals were unable to voice their sentiments when the victory cry ran out: "*Oye Katue haar gaye*" from even a boy of six or seven, when the shouts of "*Bharat Maata ki jai*" merge happily with "*Mullon ko maar do*", [54] there were no other options but to tow the line. The magnificent chorus of unison that was heard was based on the voices that it submerged voices that would have leant a discordant note, whether of the Muslims or of Hindu liberals.

The Boycott Issue
War by Other Means?

> "Through sport, barriers are broken. Barriers are built through politics and religion. Sports is one vehicle through which people of all races can come together."
>
> Kim Hughes [55]

The preceding quote, given by the captain of the rebel Australian tours to South Africa during the Apartheid boycott years, perhaps sums up best the attitude of those who view sports as an avenue of people-to-people interaction. It was this view that was poised against the view of having nothing to do with the enemy the view voiced with increasing shrillness by the Hindu right through the nineties that became state policy by the end of the decade. This call for boycotting cricket with Pakistan was nothing new. As early as 1952, during Pakistan's first tour to this country, NB Khare, then president of the Hindu Mahasabha, called for such a boycott in view of what the Mahasabha saw as atrocities against Hindus and particularly "as a mark of respect for the honour of the women of the minority Hindus".[56] While there is no way to even imagine, let alone look back at an age when cricket was free of the 'poison' of politics, it is true that communalism was not strong enough in the India of the 1950s to allow for the success of this agitation. But between 1961 and 1978, no cricket was played between the two countries, given the bitterness generated by the wars of 1965 and 1978. The revival of bilateral cricket relations lasted a decade, but from the early nineties, India and Pakistan did not visit the other country for a full tour. By then the boycott rhetoric was firmly in place, though some one-day cricket was played.[57]

The rhetoric was actually further intensified and solidified during Pakistan's tour of India in 1999. For a long while, it was in grave doubt. In 1998, the two countries had already exploded nuclear devices, further vitiating the existing tense situation. In November that year, Bal Thackarey declared himself against the proposed tour. He directly attacked the then Board President, Raj Singh Dungarpur, saying that if he had "a modicum of national pride", the board "would have banned matches with Pakistan on its own. Pakistani terrorists are killing our people in Kashmir. Women and young children are mercilessly slaughtered every day." He went on to thunder, "The Pakistani team should not be allowed to set foot on Indian soil" and that "As staunch Hindus you must not see their faces and boycott them".[58] Note the similarities with Khare's programme. Hindu men were being asked to rise to protect their brothers, and more importantly, the masculine task of protecting their women. But there the similarity ends. Khare was a leader of a party of the 'lunatic fringe'. By 1999 the Shiv Sena and its like had moved far from the fringe, and if being on the fringe is the sign of lunacy, then surely the secularists were now there. It was the ruling party in Maharashtra, and controlled Bombay Maharashtra's and Indian cricket's capita (as well as that of the world of Indian finance). It was also a member of the BJP led coalition at the centre, and the shaky government was in no position to dispose of its 6 Mps.[59] On Sixth January, Shiv Sena goons dug up the pitch of the Kotla ground in Delhi.[60] Days afterwards, on the Seventeenth, the Minister of Sports in Maharashtra, Pratap Jadhav told the Indian players to boycott the series or "face the consequences". Earlier, the SS MLA, Vijay Loke, had threatened to vandalise hotels that took the teams in. Though the Union Government, which had already allowed the tour, did arrive at a face-saving compromise, the SS had achieved its objective of establishing its position as the more hardline party of the Hindu right. Even the RSS mouthpiece, the *Organiser*, voiced its apporval.

Over the next few years, what Kingshuk Chatterjee has called a "semi-consensus" was "manufactured".[62] Through an equation of governmental interest with national interest, a pervading opinion was created among cricketers, cricket-writers and the chattering classes that as far as playing Pakistan is concerned, 'the government knows best'. Thus, Kapil Dev, regarded by many as the greatest Indian cricketer ever, said, "Whatever the government decides, we must support ..."[54]. [63] Six days later, he said, "Government's policy should be more important. Let the relations improve and then let us play with friends",[64] obviously implying that the Pakistanis, players or otherwise, were not 'our' friends. Even Bishen Singh Bedi, a former captain and the most vocal advocate of resumption, admitted, "If playing Pakistan goes against the nation's interest, then I wouldn't press for an India-Pakistan match."[65] Other cricketers like Mohinder Amarnath and Yashpal Sharma lined up in favour of boycott, while even those like Bedi, Ajit Wadekar, Madan Lal and Kiran More, who favoured resumption, agreed that resumption should happen only when the *government* feels the atmosphere to be right.[66] Thus, as Chatterjee argues, a consensus was achieved by an equation of governmental view with natonal interest. The pervasiveness of this consensus is reflected in the fact that Chatterjee finds only sixty articles and seven editorials in his survey of five major English dailies and only one leading feature in the major sports journals that supported resumption over one year.[67]

In the history of sports, boycott is not a new feature. The Olympic Games themselves have been boycotted several times. In 1956, China, Switzerland, Spain, the Netherlands, Egypt, Iraq and Lebanon all boycotted the Games for various reasons. In 1980 and 1984 came the boycotts by first the Western Bloc and then the Soviet Bloc.[68] The most famous boycott in cricket's history is, of course, that of apartheid South Africa. Then, too, it was the liberal argument that sports should not mix with politics that was advanced by the advocates of continuing sporting relations with South Africa. They argued that a logical extension of such a policy would mean a commitment to boycotting all countries with differing policies, leading to a standstill in international sports. Mike Proctor thus argued: "For every Biko, there was a Sakharov and a Solzhenitsyn. We didn't want to penalise Russian sportsmen for the policies of their government, so why should our sports be subject to isolation for a policy we didn't support?"[69]

In order to understand the dilemma over boycott, the question that needs to be understood here is: Under what conditions does boycott become acceptable? Why is it that the boycott of South Africa in cricket and other sporting arenas has been lauded as a liberating manoeuvre, while boycotts protesting Soviet involvement in Hungary or Afghanistan have not? The answer could give us several clues to understanding our present problematic. The latter instance was steeped in Cold War rhetoric, one that despite its popularity in some quarters, does invoke an impression of suspicion of the motives of those claiming a higher moral ground in most. Aggression on the part of both sides seems more acceptable, or at least understandable to the modern mind. Writing on the Nazi extermination policies in the 1930s, Jawaharlal Nehru wrote that Hitler's massacres of the Jews would always draw more condemnation than that of his political rivals, for, to the modern mind, political violence is, at one level, passé. But killings on the basis of race is abhorrent as it is seen as 'medieval'. [70] Similarly, as Gemmel argues, the crucial difference in the South African case was that while inequities existed in every country, in South Africa, the inequalities were racial. [71] And, as Alister Sparks argues, a post world-war consensus found any public declaration of racism objectionable. [72]

What was essential to achieve the aim of boycott was then, to establish a discourse within which the Pakistani, and not just the Pakistan government, could be established as intractable enemies. The sustained campaign of a decade and more had established the Muslims (read Pakistanis) as something less than human being. They were not just backward or even just anti-India, they were such animals that desecrated religion by building mosques by taking down temples. Further, they 'even' killed children and 'worst of all', dishonoured Hindu women. This process of dehumanisation of the other, as it has been called, allows for such a stance as has been adopted in Apartheid South Africa and Nazi Germany, for instance. In India it was used to identify Pakistanis (and Muslims) as a category, with which no civilised contact, including the cricketing could be maintained.

But it was not as if all interactions were stopped. Diplomatic contacts were not broken off (as was the case with South Africa) nor were trade relations snapped. But then, as Gemmel points out, boycott of sports is relatively easy to enforce. [73] As Tertius Myburgh argued in reference to South Africa, "sports boycotts are ... a politically useful, but inexpensive way to demonstrate ... disapproval of apartheid without giving up something truly valuable like trade." [74] Schalk Pienaar put it even better: "Sports is a cheap way of boycotting. It is 'expendable'." [75]

This shows an amazing congruence with what the RSS had to say about the boycott as well. The *Organiser*, writing on the Government's efforts at going on with the Pakistan tour said, "the (Union) government should not stand on prestige in this endeavour ... After all, cricket is not an essential endeavour. We can live without it." [76]

In a situation where the politics of the dominant combine depended on hatred to what was imagined to be the other, [77] and yet either full-scale war or trade wars or the like were made impossible, cricket afforded an easy getaway. Cricket's greater visibility made it an easier target than other sports that suffered less disruption. It could also be that the tensions generated by such matches were seen by the rulers as a high-point of the expression of their version of nationalism, which the government didn't want to dilute by making such matches quotidian. As cricket relations became normal and matches became more frequent after 2004, ticket sales as well as public interest actually dropped rapidly. In any case, the government showed that the resumption of cricket had very little to do with anything other than the government's interests (as opposed to national interest, to follow Chatterjee's distinction) when it agreed to resume cricket in conjunction with a diplomatic manoeuvre. This, it has been convincingly argued, was largely due to US pressure. [78] The fact that this 'peace initiative' took place at the time of "an unprecedented rise in violence" only makes the point clearer. [79] Diplomacy is said to be war by other means. Track II Diplomacy, it seems, is no different.

The Revival Series, 2004
Feeling Good as India Shines?

What was called the 'Revival Series' when India went on its first full tour of Pakistan in fifteen years seems, at first glance, to be refreshingly different. Built up as a part of a renewal in the peace process, it seemed to be free of the jingoism evident on the cricket field on the earlier occasions. In what was Vajpayee's second dove avatar, he untied the Gordian knot to give the tour the necessary go-ahead, despite the reluctance of Advani. [80] The whole series has since been celebrated as a great display of bonhomie and neighbourly feelings.

The media reports generally showcased such a feeling reporting consistently about the remarkable amity around the matches. The traditional trouble spot in previous tours had been Karachi. In 1989, the Indian captain had been assaulted in the National Stadium there during the test match. In 1997, during India's next tour, the Second ODI played there was almost abandoned due to crowd violence. Therefore, there was much apprehension surrounding the 1st ODI scheduled there, as violence in the first match could throw the entire series into jeopardy. Instead, ABP carried headlines like "No Shadow of Kashmir & Kargil in Karachi", "Jingoism Vanishes". It went on to quote Ganguly, Manjrekar and the CEO of the Pakistan Board, Rameez Raja praising the crowd. [81] *Aajkaal,* another leading Bengali daily exclaimed in surprise, "There are no brickbats, only bouquets of friendship, what sort of Karachi is this?" [82] Throughout the series, there were many more such reports. The media thus described in detail the pleasant exchanges that occurred at the reception hosted by the Pakistan President, Pervez Musharraf. [83] *Aajkaal* went on to report a conversation that an unnamed English journalist had on the eve of the series with Imran Khan and Zaheer Abbas, two former Pakistan greats, asking them who they hoped would win. Imran answered, "The team that plays well", while Zaheer retorted, "Two teams of the subcontinent are playing. So why are you so bothered?" Ganguly, normally aggression personified at the start of a series, went on record saying that Pakistan's Wasim Akram was undoubtedly the best bowler he had faced. [84] So much so, that even Thackarey seemed to be revising his opinion. On the 1st day of the test series, he issued a statement to the effect that the SS would review its stand on Indo-Pak cricket.[85]

But here too, the rhetoric was not as uniform as it was supposed to be. The *Times of India* called the series "*Pakraman*" while the *Indian Express* called it "The Great Game", an obvious reference to the strategic confrontation between the British and the Russians in Central Asia and the North Western Frontier Province. Not surprisingly, the *Saamna* kept it simple: "Cricket War".[86] The spectre of violence loomed large over the initial part of the series. The press same media reported "A dark cloud of fear".[87] Similarly, *Anadabazar* reported on the 11th of March that when the team landed in Pakistan, the emotional euphoria evaporated in the security cordon.[88] India refused to play a test match in Karachi or even spend more than a night there.[89] Before the Peshawar ODI, fears surfaced about a terrorist attack in this city near the Afghanistan border. Due to the fear of the Al Qaida, the Indian team was not allowed to spend the extra night that they wanted to spend in that city.[90] The tour was preceded by an inspection by one of India's ace security agents, Yashovardhan Azad, who also supervised the team's security arrangements during the tour.[91]

But it was not merely the threat of terrorist attacks or even crowd violence, none of which eventually materialised, that was the only deterrent to the 'gay' atmosphere. There were incidents that seemed to be violations of the spirit of friendship. Even before the series started, Miandad, the Pakistan coach, started to apply pressure on Ganguly. On the same day, Ganguly declared that no special strategy was required to handle Pakistan's feared pace bowler Shoaib Akhtar. He declared that the Indian batsmen would pull the chain on the Rawalpindi Express, as Shoaib is known. More disconcertingly for the mandarins, he declared that he did not really agree about the goodwill issue in the series, which was, to him, a contest where both teams would compete to win.[92] The controversy over Shoaib's action kept recurring during the series, undermining the relations to some extent, as did Ganguly's repeated mind games. [93] The confrontationalrhetoric of previous matches was also not completely lost. The leading Bengali sports journal, *Khela* advertised its special issue on the tour as 'War' in bold print, followed by what looked surprisingly like a disclaimer on a cigarette packet: "This is not a border conflict with bullets and missiles. It is a war of bat and ball". [94] More glaring was the attempt of ARY Gold, the sponsors of the series, to have the series named "The LOC Series". Though they later clarified that they had a different connotation in mind, what they could not have ignored was the prevalent association of those initials with the Line of Control the cease fire line between India and Pakistan, the breach of which led directly to the Kargil War. [95]

More interesting was the way that the rhetoric of the nation appeared in the press reports. There were two reports on celebrations after India won the ODI seriesin *Anadabazar*. Both laid great stress on the attitudes of the Muslims. One started with a tongawallah who gave free rides to anyone who shouted pro-India slogans. There were other reports of Muslims and Hindus celebrating, or preparing to do so interspersed in the report. Surprisingly, or at least apparently so, it also spoke of a Pakistan supporter. The report ended with: "In Daryaganj, through the day, India & Pakistan supporters had differences of opinion. But there was no conflict." [96] Thus, it seemed to indicate the nation had now become secure enough to 'allow' such differences to exist. But the front-page report of celebrations in Calcutta betrayed the old nervousness. The two localities the report started off with were both Muslim ones. All names, even in other localities, of the exultant supporters were of Muslims, clearly seeking the same appropriation of the 'minority community. [97] *Anandabazar*, on 21st March, also featured a man who was the brother of former Pakistan captain Rashid Latif. It stressed that despite the relation with Rashid, this man, Shahid latif was an "Indian". It quoted Rashid as saying of the 1996 World Cup match, "Despite my playing in Pakistan, he supported India.... Though he is my brother, he is an Indian."[98] Another slippage occurred when the ABP referred to the Hindus of Multan as Indians.[99]

But this, if anything, were the milder assertions. Immediately after the victory in the 1st ODI, the President and the Prime Minister of India congratulated the team, though the army chief (understandably) did not bother this time.[100] That beating Pakistan was still extra-special came out in the words of Sunny Gavaskar. In an article titled "Proud and Silly with Happiness", written when India beat Pakistan in the first test, Gavaskar declared, "Today I understand what the phrase 'chest swelling with pride' means."[101] One must wonder why it took Gavaskar a victory against Pakistan to understand the meaning of pride. After all, he had played starring roles in Indian series victories abroad and a member of the World Cup winning team of 1983, and this was just one test.

On the other side of the border, or should one say the LOC, the reactions were equally vehement, dissipating the bubble of this series as different. Thus Imran remonstrated with the President of the Pakistan Board, Shahryar Khan, after the ODI Series loss, saying *"Intehaa ho gayi zillat ki"*.[102] After the test series was also lost, the media simply hit the roof. *The Nation*'s sports page carried the ominous headline: "Revisiting Kargil in Cricket".[103] Omar Kureishi's column in the *Dawn* freely used martial imageries of battles, wars and national pride under the headline "Pakistan Cricket's Blackest Day".[104] As a result of the defeats, a witch-hunt was launched against Shoaib Akhtar, as well as Board Officials and the team management, and even a number of suits were filed in the courts.[105]

Throughout the series, the press reports in Indian newspapers were marked by a remarkable congruence with the stated policies of the government and the ruling party. The smiling face of the two captains at the ritualistic photo session at the start of the series was dubbed 'Feel Good', referring to the NDA's chief electoral plank.[106] When India won the series, ABP ran a banner headline, '*Pakistane Bharat Uday*' ('India Shines in Pakistan'),[107] thus effectively echoing the NDA's electoral campaign. Press reports throughout the tour were replete with references to Vajpayee's farewell message to the team: "*Khel hi nahin, dil bhi jeetiye*" ('Don't just win matches. Win hearts as well.').[108] This too, like Feel Good and other slogans, was used freely in the reports. Even Sahara, the main sponsors of the cricket team, used this slogan of Vajpayee's in one of their advertisements.[109]

In a way, this series had more to do with electoral politics than anything else. A major reason of the government's reluctance to give the series a go-ahead just before the polls was that if India lost, it would deal a severe blow to the 'Feel Good' bubble. And even when the green signal was given in a meeting attended by top BJP leaders, it was argued that if this was not done, a negative impact would fall on the sports-lovers of the country, something they could not afford at poll-eve.[110] Moreover, to counter the indignation caused by the genocide in Gujarat, the BJP had made friendship with Pakistan an electoral issue. To further that, approving the tour became necessary. If the tour went well, it would naturally give a fillip to the BJP's campaign. But if an untoward incident occurred, they could always fall back upon the statement 'Now you understand, why we were not willing for so long?'[111]

The great fear of the BJP was that of India losing, thereby bursting the Feel Good bubble, as already noted. This perception was shared by others too. In two of the most liberal educational institutions of the campus, I encountered the feeling that secular Indians were quite prepared to concede the series as a series win would ensure the NDA's victory. I must confess here that I too was among these people.

The NDA left no stone unturned to take advantage of the cricket-generated hype. When the team visited Vajpayee on the eve of their departure, children greeted them with placards extolling the PM's contribution towards Indo-Pak peace by reviving cricket.[112] Cricket was generously used in the campaign. Narendra Modi, the '*Hindu-Hriday-Samrat*', asked how could a foreigner like Sonia Gandhi understand his 'feeling good' when India won.[113] Advani, too used the cricket imagery. He commented that unlike the Indo-Pak encounters, the electoral match was one "where we know the result even before taking the field."[114] The Congress, too, tried to take advantage of the cricket-politics. Members of its 'royal family' visited Pakistan and stole at least part of the limelight, decked as they were in blue the Indian team's colours. There were also SMSes circulating that read "*Bharat ki jai nischi thi, kyuki Priyanka-Rahul saath me thi*" and "*Bharat ko jeetne ki sahi aas thi*, Rahul *aur* Priyanka team *ke paas the*" as a counter to BJP's "Cricket *bhi jeeta, dil bhi jeeta, shabash* India".[115] When India won the match, Vajpayee called his party president, Venkaiah Naidu and asked "Feel Good?" to which Naidu replied, "Feel great Sir."[116]

The BJP were clearly runaway winners in this contest for claiming credit for the series and the victory. Mohammad Kaif, a hero of the ODI triumph, was granted tax exemptions.[117] Kaif, however, rejected overtures to campaign for the BJP.[118] But despite his refusal to campaign, the BJP sought to take advantage of Kaif's popularity by seeking to use him as the model it wished the minorities to emulate. After Kaif's star performance in the 4th ODI, he was referred to by Vajpayee to invoke the sentiments of both Uttar Pradesh and the Muslims.[119] But the BJP managed to claim a more prized scalp in Virendra Sehwag, the hero of the test series with his record-breaking 309 runs. Sehwag campaigned for the Union minister and his fellow Jat, Sahib Singh Verma.[120]

On the other side of the border, the hardline opposition, Jaamat-e-Ulema claimed that Pakistan had deliberately lost matches to facilitate Vajpayee's victory due to a secret pact between him and Musharraf.[121] Such allegations were also voiced by the Pakistan media and both Inzamam and Rahul Dravid were asked questions along these lines on the eve of the last ODI.[122] In

India, too, there were many takers for this theory. The exultation of the Parivar was clear in the issue of the *Organiser* on the 4th of April. Not only did it claim that the Indian victories were due to 'Captain Vajpayee', but that '*Bharat Uday*' had become '*Bharat Vijay*'. On the day when Sehwag got his record runs, the SMSes too ran wild, claiming that the BJP would also get 309 seats.[123]

How they arrived at such a number might be difficult to comprehend, but it is clear that the media and the chatterati were treating this cricket tour and the triumphs as an important factor, if not the most important factor in fashioning what they saw as an almost inevitable NDA victory. But, it seems no one told the voters this. When the NDA crashed at the hustings, all pollsters blamed the very India Shining campaign that they had predicted would lead the NDA to victory. It was claimed, both by these experts and politicians of what became the UPA-Left alliance, that the campaign, by focussing on urban India, had insulted the poverty-stricken villagers. A closer look reveals that the NDA, if anything, did worse in urban areas. Of the six major cities, it was only in Bangalore that it did well. In the other five, of a combined total of 23 seats, it won just three. In the erstwhile bastion of UP, of the six urban constituencies, only one returned a BJP candidate and that too, Vajpayee himself.[124]

So, if both rural and urban India rejected it, where was India Shining? Nowhere. And Indians were not voting depending on the results of a cricket tour.

Conclusion
Or Something Like That

> In 1984, riots spread across India after Indira Gandhi's assassination. Thousands of Sikhs were killed, and troops patrolled the streets to keep warring communities apart. Then the government remembered that India had won the World Cup, and sought the soothing power of cricket.

> Posters appeared with photographs of Kapil Dev, Mohammed Azharuddin, Roger Binny and Maninder Singh, captioned "Khelenge saath, jiyenge saath" (We'll play together, live together). Such faith in the ability of a multi-religious group of cricketers may seem naive, but within weeks, India returned to normality.[125]

This naiveté and poor historical memory demonstrated in this quote was not the sole preserve of its author, Salil Tripathi. The great Vijay Merchant recalled that in 1936 the Quadrangular and particularly the Hindus versus Muslims match stopped riots in Bombay.[126] Yet, as Ram Guha points out, history records something quite different. The riots had taken place in October, while the Quadrangular was played in mid-December, by which time peace had been long restored, though there might have been vestiges of tension.[127]

In a way, that has been the history of cricket in India. It creates a chimera of unity, of one nationhood. And that masks the real, tortuous, processes of nation-building, the deployment of both physical and ideological force. Thus, when we say the nation is cricket-crazy, we ignore the gendered statement we make (even if we kept aside how the entire 'North-East' is left out of the statement). Within this discourse, female viewership is seen in a quite specific manner. If we read the articles of Sudeshna Banerjee and Chandrima Chakraborty in *Sport in South Asian Society* together, certain stereotypes emerge about the role of females in cricket.[128] Women cricketers are ignored almost completely. Women are portrayed either as viewers of inane soap operas or unthinking viewers of a cricket match without an understanding of the game. They are either mothers and spouses encouraging (or obstructing) the players or sexualised objects still acting as encouragement (and a prize?). In fact the same woman could act as mother and object of sexual desire, as explicated in Mandira Bedi's portrayal. The trope of mother as the nation as well as the object of oedipal desires is of course a recurrent theme of Hindi films too.

These themes recur in press reports of the Friendship Tour too. When after the last match Irfan Pathan was edged out by VVS Laxman to become the Man of the Match award, the press reported Pathan's mother's reaction. To her remark that it was equally joyous to her that VVS had got the award, *Aajkal* added the comment, "She has become a true mother." [129] At the same time, Mandira was again portrayed as a sexual object, while another female celebrity flying over to support the national team was shown as unaware of who was the composer of India's national anthem. [130] The discourse around cricket was quite clear in the role it assigned women in the nation.

The dominant discourse of defining the nation in terms of the majority have also led to its own subversion by otherised areas of assertion & reconciliation. Irfan Pathan's rise is a case in point. There were numerous reports of how Irfan, a resident of the Jama Masjid in Vadodara that was attacked by crazed mobs during the Gujarat carnage. But he emerged as a hero of all communities with his success, particularly against Pakistan and Australia. It has been argued several times that his rise is a balm to communal tensions in the state. [131] But that is a throwback to the good Muslim-Bad Muslim dichotomy that the Sangh so successfully used throughout the nineties, particularly through contrasting the personages of Abul Kalam and Dawood Ibrahim. In that classification, the cricketer, in that case Azhar, could be a good (read loyal) Muslim only when he succeeded. Failures would lead to his becoming a traitor. [132] Moreover, it was patently unfair to put on the shoulders of Irfan the cross of maintaining communal amity through cricketing exploits alone.

In Gujarat itself, after the 'riots', Irfan and Zaheer Khan became repositories, perhaps unwittingly, of Muslim self-assertion & symbols of their 'full claim' to the nation, and were joined by Kaif in the national context. [133] Ashish Nandy has compared this search of sporting heroes by a community to counter allegations of disloyalty and criminalityto the black underclass's assertion through sports in the USA. [134]

What I have so far tried to do is to put together a range of events and histories residing in the same time and space. The underlined point here is that within the same discourse, no matter how dominant or hegemonic, there would be other notes, drowned as they might be in the resounding chorus. Cricket too, could serve several functions, none of which are 'given'. Some recent events in Gujarat might be cited to enumerate the open-endedness. Towards the end of 2003, there were two incidents of cricket-related violence. In Viramgam on 30th November three people were killed as violence erupted between Hindus and Muslims over a children's cricket match. [135] On the 1st riots broke out in Palanpur when a ball rolled into a temple during a match played by Muslims. [136] In February, contrastingly, cricket served as an agent of peace when teams made up of both communities played with each other in Godhra. [137]

To take another instance, it is easy to follow the 'yuppy nationalism' model of Guha to understand crowd violence in the nineties, but that does not explain the standing ovation in Chennai. While it is true that Chennai has no memory of partition violence, neither does Bangalore. And if Calcuttans are supposed to be "imbued with a gory love for militarism & violence", as Rudrangshu Mukherjee argued, [138] then, any student of Tamil nationalism will know of the volatile nature of crowds in Madras/Chennai. [139] These events, and the social history of the game are shaped by politics and the market, no doubt, but cannot escape the entrenched history of the game, which too, is made, unmade and remade with each event. It is easy to notice just the dominant note, but the task of a serious student of the game's history is to disaggregate the events and understand them separately. Identities, I agree with Kingshuk Chatterejee, are not permanent. [140] But they are not even the same within their own space-time position.

Notes

1. Hamid Jalal, 'Afterword' in Saadat Hasan Manto, *Kingdom's End and Other Stories*, translated from the Urdu by Khalid Hasan Penguin, New Delhi, 1989, pp. 249-250 cited in Ramchandra Guha, *A Corner of a Foreign Field: The Indian History of a British Sport*, Picador, London, 2002, p. 384.
2. See for instance *The Times of India*, 2 March, 2003.
3. Boria Majumdar, 'Prologue: Transcending National Boundaries' in Boria Majumdar and Fan Hong ed. The International Journal of the History of the History of Sport, Volume 22, Number 4, July 2005.
4. Guha, *A Corner of a Foreign Field*, p. 400.
5. This and the following account are based on Guha's work, unless otherwise cited. See, in particular, the chapter 'Kashmir Comes to the Pennines in *A Corner*, pp. 397-433.
6. Ibid, Back of Front Cover.
7. For how this continues to form a special place in the heart of the Pakistani cricket writer and fan, see, Qamar Ahmed, "Salim Malik classic will continue to illuminate Eden Gardens", http://archives.dawn.com/2007/12/04/spt7.htm, accessed on 07.07.2012. Ironically, this famous act of a sporting gesture from the fans has since been hounded as an act of treachery by netizens. See, for instance, the comments on http://www.cricketvoice.com/cricketforum2/index.php?topic=11651.5;wap2, accessed on 07.07.2012.
8. *The Telegraph*, 10 March, 1996.
9. *The Telegraph*, 13 March, 1996.
10. *Anandabazar Patrika*, 14 March, 1996.
11. http://www.espncricinfo.com/ci/content/story/74236.html, http://www.espncricinfo.com/magazine/content/story/245024.html, http://www.independent.co.uk/sport/cricket/article1220758.ece, all accessed on 07.07.2012.
12. http://static.espncricinfo.com/db/ARCHIVE/1997-98/IND_IN_PAK/IND_PAK_ODI2_30SEP1997_DAWN_MR.html, accessed on 07.07.212. For how the reputation of Karachi as a trouble-making site continued for years, see Rahul Bhattacharya, *Pundits from Pakistan: On Tour with India, 2003-2004*, Picador, London, 2005, Particularly pp. 49 and 54-56. Even in India's previous tour to Pakistan, the Test Match in Karachi saw K Srikkanth, the Indian captain, being assaulted, while the One-Dayer had to be abandoned.
13. *The Telegraph*, 21 February 1999.
14. Ibid.
15. Both the friends have gone on to become historians in their own right, the latter, incidentally, of cricket.
16. *The Sun*, 09 June, 1999.

17. Quoted in Mark Marquese, "Cricket, Politics and Peace in South Asia", http://ww5.thewicket.com/2001_05_24/main_story1.asp, accessed on 20.03.2004.
18. Sunil Manohar Gavaskar, *Sunny Days*
19. See any of the numerous press reports of Thackarey's inflaming statements on Muslims. For a sharp, concise framing, see anad Patwardhan's hard-hitting documentary, *Father Son and Holy War*, [Pitra, Putra and Dharmayuddha], 1994.
20. Shashi Tharoor, 'This Passion is a Six' in *The Hindu*, 30 March, 2003.
21. Ambarish K. Dewanji, 'The Fallen Icon', http://www.rediff.com/cricket/2000/nov/17azhar.htm, accessed on 07.07.2012.
22. *The Asian Age*, 5 December, 1997.
23. Dewanji, "The Fallen Icon".
24. Guha, *Corner of a Foreign Field*, p. 426.
25. *Daily Express*, 9 June 1999, quoted in Ibid, p, 419.
26. Quoted in Marquese, "Cricket, Politics and Peace".
27. Ibid.
28. Guha, *Corner of a Foreign Field*, p. 426.
29. *The Asian Age*, 21 June, 1999; quoted in Ibid, p. 427.
30. All of the above are taken from Marquese, "Cricket, Politics and Peace".
31. *The Telegraph*, 22 June 1999; quoted in Guha, *Corner of a Foreign Field*, p. 427.
32. Marquese, "Cricket, Politics and Peace".
33. For a more detailed analysis of the response to the Cup, particularly the Indo-Pak match, and its impact on communal relations and 'nation-building', see my "Manufacturing Unison: Muslims, Hindus and Indians during the India-Pakistan Match", in Boria Majumdar and JA Mangan (eds.), *Sport in South Asian Society: Past and Present*, Routledge, Oxon, England and New York, USA, 2005, pp. 239-248.
34. Debarshi Dasgupta and Nadeshda Zareen, "The View from Within", *rediff.com* news report, 28 February, 2003.
35. Interview with the author, 11 May, 2003.
36. Saba Naqvi Bhaumik and Priyanka Kakodkar, "Keeping the Faith" in Outlook, 31 March, 2003, pp. 32-33.
37. Gautam Bhattacharyya, "*Sampreetir Hawai Senadhakhyar...*", in *Anandabazar Patrika*, 15 March, 2004.
38. Reuters press release, 23 March, 2003.
39. "Tendulkar Battles Through Pain", BBC Sport, www.bbc.co.uk, 1 March, 2003. I am grateful to Prof. Subhash Ranjan Chakraborty for drawing my attention to this statement.
40. *Anandabazar Patrika*, 02 March, 2003.
41. Lokendra Pratap Sahi, "It's just another game, well, not quite", *The Telegraph*, 1 March, 2003.

42. Sanjay V Manjrekar, "Old Enemy", *Wisden Asia Cricket*, March 2003.
43. Cited in Lalitha Ramdas, "The Politics of cricket: Some Reflections", posted on the *South Asian Citizens Web*, 27-28 February 2003.
44. Quoted in Saba Naqvi Bhaumik, 'Pent-up and Silent', *Outlook*, 5 November 2001, pp. 40-50.
45. Dasgupta and Zareen, "The View from Within".
46. Interview with the author, 11 May, 2003.
47. For a brilliant, sarcastic take on what the Tebbit Test may or may not mean, see Raj Kaushal, "The Tebbit test is just not Cricket", http://www.guardian.co.uk/uk/2001/nov/25/race.world9, accessed on 07.07.2012.
48. Ibid.
49. Cited in Guha, *A Corner of a Foreign Field*, p. 427.
50. Mihir Bose, *A History of Indian Cricket*, Andre Deutsch Limited, London, Indian edition by Rupa & Co., Calcutta, 1990, p. 193.
51. Ibid. For the West Indians receiving similar support in England and its relations to race conditions in the 1970s, see Steven Riley's brilliant documentary, *Fire in Babylon*, 2010.
52. Jon Gemmel, *The Politics of South African Cricket*, Routledge, London and New York, 2004, p. 121.
53. Indeed, the opinion polls, right up to the elections themselves, continued to predict a massive win for the NDA. For the surge predicted, see Ajit Kr. Jha, "Atal Wave: NDA Rides on Vajpayee's Popularity, Appears set to sweep Elections 2004: India Today Poll", available on http://indiatoday.intoday.in/story/vajpayee-bjp-set-for-landslide-win-in-forthcoming-2004-elections/1/197000.html, retrieved on 10.07.2012.
54. Dhananjai Joshi "Hooligans of the Hindu Right Fan the Flames of Hate around India-Pakistan World Cup Match: An Account from Delhi", posted on the *South Asian Citizens Web*, 1 March, 2003, available on http://www.sacw.net/2002/DJoshiMarch03.html, accessed on 08.04.2004.
55. Gemmel, *The Politics of South African Cricket*, p. 128.
56. *Dawn*, 23 February, 1955, quoted in Guha, *A Corner of a Foreign Field*, p. 378.
57. There were tournaments in Sharjah, Singapore, Dhaka and Toronto. Pakistan also played in the Independence Cup to celebrate fifty years of India's independence, while India played three ODIs in Pakistan to celebrate their golden jubilee. The two countries also met in the World Cup.
58. *The Telegraph*, 4 January, 1998, *The Hindu*, 21 January, 1998; quoted in Guha, *A Corner of a Foreign Field*, pp. 408-409.
59. *Frontline*, Vol. 16, No. 3, Jan 30-Feb 12, 1999. See also Guha, *A Corner of a Foreign Field*, pp. 408-411.

60. Ibid, p. 411.
61. *Frontline*, Vol. 16, No. 3.
62. Kingshuk Chatterjee, "To Play Or Not TO Play: Fabricating Consent over the Indo-Pak Cricket Series", in Boria Majumdar and JA Mangan (eds.), *Sport in South Asian Society*, pp. 277-294.
54. Quoted in KC, 620.
63. *Deccan Herald*, 8 July, 2003, quoted in ibid, p. 284
64. *Indian Express*, 14 July, 2003, quoted in ibid.
65. Cited in Lokpally, "To Play or Not To is the Question", *The Sportstar*, 14 June 2003, cited in Chatterjee, p. 284. Other
66. Ibid, pp. 280-281.
67. Ibid, p. 280.
68. *Sahara Times*, 13 March 2004.
69. Quoted in Gemmel, *The Politics of South African Cricket*, p. 124.
70. Jawaharlal Nehru, *Glimpses of World History*.
71. Gemmel, *The Politics of South African Cricket*, p. 124.
72. Ibid.
73. Ibid.
74. *Sunday Times*, (Johannesburg), 13.5.1984. Quoted in Ibid.
75. Ibid.
76. The *Organiser*, 16 January 1999. Cited in Pravin Swami, "Battle for Hindutva Turf", *The Frontline*, Vol. 16, No. 3, Jan 30-Feb 12, 1999.
77. Here I used 'imagination' in the sense that Sudipta Kabiraj has used the word, so and it does not denote something that is not real, but rather, something that exists by having been imagined into being. See Kabiraj, *The Imaginary Institution of India: Politics and Ideas*, Columbia University Press, New York, 2010; particularly Chapter 5, "The Imaginary Institution of India", pp. 167-209.
78. CHatterjee, "To Play Or Not To Play", p. 285.
79. Syed Nazakat, "Valley Under Fire" in *Sahara Time*, 13 March 2004.
80. "*Jot Khullen Atal*", *Ananda Bazar Patrika*, 15 February, 2004.
81. *Ananda Bazar Patrika*, 13 and 14 March, 2004.
82. *Aajkal*, 14 March, 2004.
83. See for instance, "*Sachin Bina Katha Nei Musharrafer*", in *Ananda Bazar Patrika*, 18 March, 2004; "*Musharrafer Barite Bharatyo Dal*", *Aajkaal*, 18 March, 2004; "*Musharrafer Maitrir Balle Bowled Souravra*", *Pratidin*, 18 March, 2004.
84. "*Nepothyo Bhashon*", *Aajkaal*, 13 March, 2004.
85. *Aajkaal*, 29 March, 2004.
86. Rahul Bhattacharya, *Pundits from Pakistan: On Tour with India, 2003-2004*, Picador, London, 2005, p. 35.

87. *Ananda Bazar Patrika*, 12 March, 2004.
88. *Ananda Bazar Patrika*, 11 March, 2004.
89. For the diplomatic manoeuvres, administrative measures, security concerns and the constant perception of threat, see Bhattacharya, *Pundits from Pakistan*, chapter 2, "The Longest Day", pp. 39-84.
90. *Ananda Bazar Patrika*, 18 March, 2004 For the atmosphere of fear surrounding the Peshawar ODI, see Bhattacharya, *Pundits from Pakistan*, pp. 107-108.
91. Bhattacharya, *Pundits from Pakistan*, chapter 2, "The Longest Day".
92. Ibid, p. 35.
93. Ibid, pp. 109-112.
94. *Aajkaal*, 13 March, 2004. The leading light of both *Aajkal* and *Khela*, Asok Dasgupta, later apologised for this.
95. http://www.espncricinfo.com/magazine/content/story/137705.html; http://www.mid-day.com/news/2004/jan/74526.htm . For the public reaction to this, leading to the withdrawal of the nomenclature, see http://v4.sportnetwork.net/phorum/read.php?118,2615594 and http://www.sporttaco.com/uk.sport.cricket/guys_get_ready_2827.html; all accessed on 14.07.2012.
96. "*Musharrafer Janmabhitete*", *Ananda Bazar Patrika*, 25 March, 2004.
97. "*Anander Abir*", *Ananda Bazar Patrika*, 25 March, 2004.
98. *Ananda Bazar Patrika*, 21 March, 2004.
99. *Ananda Bazar Patrika*, 28 March, 2004.
100. *Aajkal*, 14 March, 2004; *Ananda Bazar Patrika*, 15 March, 2004.
101. *The Telegraph*, 02April, 2004.
102. Bhattacharya, *Pundits from Pakistan*, p. 167.
103. Ibid, p. 293.
104. Ibid.
105. Ibid, pp. 292-298.
106. *Ananda Bazar Patrika*, 13 March, 2004.
107. *Ananda Bazar Patrika*, 25 March, 2004.
108. See, for instance, *Ananda Bazar Patrika*, 11 March, 2004.
109. *Aajkal*, 13 March, 2004.
110. *Ananda Bazar Patrika*, 15 February 2004; Bhattacharya, *Pundits from Pakistan*, p. 09.
111. *Aajkal*, 13 March, 2004.
112. *Ananda Bazar Patrika*, 11 March, 2004.
113. *Pratidin*, 14 March, 2004.

96. *Pratidin*, 14.3.

114. *Aajkal*, 15 March, 2004.
115. *Pratidin*, 14 March, 2004; and Bhattacharya, *Pundits from Pakistan*, p. 71.
116. *Pratidin*, 14 March, 2004.

117. *Ananda Bazar Patrika*, 31 March, 2004.
118. *Aajkal*, 31 March, 2004.
119. *Aajkal*, 22 March, 2004.
120. http://www.rediff.com/cricket/2004/apr/18sehwag.htm, accessed on 11 July, 2012.
121. *Aajkal*, 30 March, 2004.
122. Bhattacharya, *Pundits from Pakistan*, p. 141. Though both the cricketers reacted violently, perhaps Dravid more so, the association of Lahore sports journalists demanded an apology only from Inzamam, and actually got an apology from Haroon Rashid, the Pakistan manager, on behalf of the team.
123. *Aajkal*, 30 March, 2004.
124. See http://eci.nic.in/eci_main1/ElectionStatistics.aspx, accessed on 14.07.2012.
125. Salil Tripathi, "Every six a nail in the coffin of the Empire", http://saliltripathi.com/articles/25,07,02IndependantCricketIndia.html, accessed on 25.08.2004.
126. "Get Ready. We Are Playing" (transcript of an interview given by Vijay Merchant to Mridula Mukherjee, Aditya Mukherjee and Bipan Chandra in 1987), *The* Telegraph, 7 February, 1988; quoted in Guha, *A Corner of a Foreign* Field, pp. 310-311.
127. Ibid, p. 311.
128. Sudeshna Banerjee, "Fleshing Out Mandira: Hemming in the Women's Constituency in Cricket"; Chandrima Chakraborty, "Bollywood Motifs: Cricket Fiction and Fictional Cricket", in Majumdar and Mangan (eds.), *Sport in South Asian Society*, pp. 166-196 and 213-238 respectively.
129. *Aajkal*, 3 March, 2004.
130. Ibid.
131. *Ananda Bazar Patrika*, 27 March, 2004.
132. Guha, *A Corner of a Foreign Field*, p. 413.
133. For a fuller exposition of this theme, see my "Manufacturing Unison".
134. Quoted in Bhaumik and Kakodkar, "Keeping the Faith", p. 32.
135. http://gujaratfiles.net/news/violence_palanpur_after_cricket_match.html, accessed on 20.11.2003.
136. *Times of India*, 02 December 2003. See also ibid.
137. *Times of India*, 01 February, 2003.
138. *The Telegraph*, 15 June, 1996, quoted in Guha, *A Corner of a Foreign Field*, p. 404.
139. For a detailed study on the theme, see Sumathi Ramaswamy, *Passions of the Tongue: Language Devotion in Tamil India, 1891-1970*, University of California Press, Berkeley and Los Angeles, 1997.
140. Chatterjee, "To Play Or Not To Play".

Sporting Nationalism in the Global Era: The Case of Football

Avipsu Halder

Introduction

Nationalism manifests itself in various facets political, economic [1] and cultural. [2] The present study focuses on its cultural and the political dimension by examining its links with sport, since the latter is integral to the culture of a community. It significantly underpins integration of a community into a single cohesive bond. Nevertheless, before extrapolating the role of sport as a representative of national identity it is essential to grapple with the theoretical aspect of nationalism. The article studies football in establishing its case for sporting nationalism. It aims to serve three broad purposes. First, it underlines the conceptual dichotomy in theories of the state and the nation. Secondly, it tries to answer the debate whether sport represents the cultural nation or its political counterpart. Thirdly, it seeks to demonstrate that theorizing nationalism in the sporting arena needs to obliterate the 'civic' versus 'ethnic' understanding of nationalism. Finally, the article focuses on the relevance of national identity in the context of globalization. In this connection, it traces the extent to which the fervor of national identity reinforces or transcends itself due to the impact of global forces on the game of football.

Defining Nationalism: The Theoretical Parameters

Let us begin our discussion by unraveling the theoretical

premises of nationalism. As a concept, it has been largely viewed through the lenses of culture. Therefore, the politico-administrative dimension of a nation fails to receive sufficient attention. The article argues that sport constitutes a part of national identity both politically as well as culturally. The argument gains strength when we analyze the existing literature on nationalism. The dominant school of thought on the subject has categorized nationalism under two broad headings - the *perennialist* and the *modernist.* [3] However, even these schools could not contribute a great deal in addressing the rift between the political and the cultural explanations of nationalism. In this context, is it is necessary to examine their respective viewpoints on nationalism. The *Perennialists* support the *Primordialists* [4] line or argument in theorizing nationalism. They envisage the nation as an ancient and immemorial entity. The Perennialists focus on the ethno-cultural sphere in envisioning a nation, stressing shared ancestry, history and a common homeland. [5] Besides, the Perennialists visualize nation as a popular and demotic community of people which embody their needs and aspirations. The arguments of the Modernists stand in sharp contrast to the Perennialisits in theorizing nationalism. The Modernists perceives the nation as a civic community of legally equal citizens. They do not accord much importance to factors such as shared ancestry, history in the making of nations. On the contrary, they argue that the nation is a recent occurrence and a novel product of the modernizing process.

These two schools of thought only manage to produce two differing views of nationalism. They are not successful in making any major breakthroughs in resolving the politico-cultural dichotomy in theorizing nation. The article finds certain anomalies in the arguments of this categorization. First, it fails to produce any answer regarding the definition of a nation and national identity. Are nation/ national identity solely cultural? Secondly, or, can there be a political understanding of a nation/nationalism? Thirdly, or, is it possible to co-opt both in defining nation/nationalism /national identity? The article intends to answer these questions by contextualizing theoretical parameters of nationalism in the domain of sport.

Sport and National Identity

Sporting nationalism has often been seen in terms of ethnic nationalism. This is evident from the case of Basque football.[6] Also, Benedict Anderson's [7] concept of 'imagined community' gets manifested by perceiving the nationalist phenomenon through the lenses of sport. In this context, we can cite the case of the development of Gaelic Games in Ireland and countries with a sizeable Irish Diaspora. The football clubs certainly provides a platform for the people to meet and develop a common consciousness.[8] Thus, the Gaelic Games contributed in instilling a feeling of Irishness among the migrant population of Ireland in Europe, United States and Latin America. The case of sporting nationalism in the Irish context reveals the importance of shared culture and history in creating a nationalist consciousness.Thus, the concept of national identity is defined from the paradigm of culture. To put it differently, this explanation emphasizes the perennialist[9] line of thinking on the subject. As a response to such an understanding, the study urges to forward an argument of sporting nationalism that is mindful of considering both the political and the cultural factors while theorizing nationalism in sport. The rationality of this argument lies in the fact that although attempts have been made to theorize nationalism by focusing on the political angle, not much aspect has been explored in determining the process through which the notion of national identity becomes a political entity. In this connection, the article explores the process through which national identity in the domain of sport is explicated by throwing light on the politico-administrative aspect of identity. Hence, it delves into the debate concerning the literature of sporting nationalism in considerable detail.

In the context of sporting nationalism, the 'state' and the

'nation' are treated as coterminous. It provides a simplistic definition of national identity. However, conceptualizing nationalism and national identity is not as simple as it has been done in the case of sport. Alain Bairner takes recourse to the case study of Europe and North America in locating the link between sport and nationalism. [10] In their study, the nation and national identity has been defined solely in terms of shared cultural traits. To put it differently, sport reveals national identity as people belonging to the same cultural group represents their nation in the international sporting forum. As a corollary to this statement, we can also define sporting nationalism in terms of its resistance to alien cultural practices. Let us explain the ontological meaning embedded in this statement by illustrations both from the European and the North American context. The dissemination of football in Sweden is conceived as 'Americanization' of Swedish sport. [11] Similarly, the Americans introduced the game of baseball and soccer as a response to Britain's introduction to cricket and football respectively.

In the cases mentioned above, sport has been identified with the national culture of a country. This paves the way for the development of a collective consciousness which pivots around sport. [12] As a consequence, people of a country begin to identify themselves with the sport. Sport becomes instrumental in drawing the lines of 'us' versus 'them'. Joseph Maguire posits a similar view in his analysis of sport and nationalism. The lines of inclusion and exclusion become clearer when we observe that members of a national team sings national anthem before the start of a game as a symbol of national unity. The Berlin Olympics of 1936 gave the world the first chance to witness such a practice.

The factors of race and descent also play a defining role in determining identity in sport. In this case, the practice of assimilation becomes critical. Naomi Chiba, Osamu Ebihara Shinji Morino [13] cites the case of Canadian born players of Japanese descent in their hockey team. These authors envisage that the administrators of the Japanese ice-hockey association decided to include the players of 'relevant social descent' in order to achieve success. The article takes recourse to Y. Fukuoka's thesis of superiority of blood to establish the concept of 'relevant social descent'. Fukuoka reminds us of the distinction between blood and descent. [14] He advocates that the former transcends national border while the latter does not. However, it is hard to argue with Fukuoka on the view that blood transcends national boundaries. The rationale for such an argument is the context in which Fukuoka is locating his argument. We will have to remember that Fukuoka is not arguing in the context of natural science but in terms of culture. Had it been the former, we would have accepted Fukuoka's argument. However, in the context of sporting nationalism, 'blood' is perceived through the lenses of shared myth, histories and ethnicity. Thus, the article places both blood and descent in the same pedestal.

Thus far, the article has only examined the political and the cultural dimensions of nationalism. However, it must also be remembered that nationalism is multidimensional in character. This aspect gets manifested in the works of Kamenka. [15] He argues that nationalism has 'both a positive and a negative side: it can be democratic or authoritarian, backward looking or forward looking, socialist or conservative, secular or religious, generous or chauvinist'. As a response to this statement, we can argue that sporting nationalism often fails to consider the negative aspect. The case of Germany during the Third Reich provides a classic illustration of an oppressive and authoritarian nation which effectively used sport as a medium to motivate its people.

Another interesting aspect that we unravel while theorizing nationalism through football is that sporting nationalism does not invest much effort in differentiating between the ethnic and civic dimension of nationalism. The former came in with the artificial creation of nation during the nineteenth century. J. G. Kellas opines that this variant of nationalism came in due to the sense of shared identity, community and culture. [16] On the other hand, civic nationalism traces its roots to the ideas of citizenship and rule of law. [17] An important rationale for not distinguishing between the two forms of nationalism is that a nation is as much a political entity as it is a cultural one. In this case, we cannot agree more with the views of Anthony D. Smith who envisages that it is incorrect to separate the two. [18] Also, the development of national identity through football in Ireland, Canada, United States and Britain often obliterates this distinction. The writings of two authors, Alan Guttmann [19] and Jack Donnelly [20] reveal the logic of this statement. The development of sport and national identity in the United States seems quite interesting. In their quest of resisting the influence of British sports, the Americans preformed acts such as replacing the word 'football' with 'soccer' and initiating baseball as against the spread of cricket. Here again, we notice that national identity has always been conceived from the cultural realm. Sport has been treated as an integral part of national culture. David Miller cites the case of the dressing of the sports fans into their respective national costumes, painting themselves in the colors of their national flags to reveal a sense of oneness. [21] Nevertheless, in all these illustrations, an important question is left unanswered. Which aspect of the nation gets precedence? Whether the cultural paradigm subsumes the political realm or does the reverse take place? The article envisages that a peaceful coexistence of the two occurs in the sphere of sporting nationalism.

To enunciate the coexistence of these two distinct aspects, the article takes recourse to the concept of imagined community. [22] As a concept, imagined community portrays that people within a definite territorial demarcation share a common national consciousness despite hardly knowing each other. In this connection, is must be notified that the territorial community is governed by a politico-administrative apparatus. Thus, people residing within a given territorial demarcation share a common government alongside an identical history, culture and memories. [23] Let us conceptualize imagined community in the context of sporting nationalism. Bairner opines that apart from war, it is during international sporting competitions such as the World Cup Football tournaments that the communion between the members of a nation are felt who are otherwise regarded as total strangers. [24] The vigour that sport accords to national identity can be realized when we examine the view of Bairner more closely. Bairner finds nothing extravagant or glorious about writing an individual's nationality in a hotel register book. In addition, Bairner also enunciates the rationality for this claim. He believes that action of this sort is essentially solitary and fails bring one another with ones compatriot except in an abstract sense. But sporting events unite members of a nation in highly emotional circumstances. [25] Grant Jarvie goes a step further by stating that the imagined community or the nation becomes more active in the athletic tracks. It is evident that sport plays a pivotal role in binding a nation. [26] Arguing the case of South African nationalism, John Nauright illustrates the role played by sport which eventually paves the way for the emergence of a 'rainbow nation'. [27] Therefore, explicating sporting nationalism through imagined community serves an important purpose. It reveals that although national identity in sports may have a cultural angle, nevertheless, it also possesses a strong political connotation.

However, the article aims at correcting the politico-cultural dichotomy rather than deepening the fault line between them. In this connection, an illustration from the domain of sporting nationalism is worth mentioning. Sport not only unites the nation but also plays as instrumental role in uniting different nations. During the 2002 World Cup Football which was co-hosted by Japan and Korea, the Emperor of Japan declared that the royal family of Japan had its origins from the Korean civilization. Therefore, it can be easily argued that sports not only accord a sense of unity to the national citizens but also the essence of unity is felt across nations. [28]

If we perceive this analysis from the theoretical parameter of nationalism, we can claim that the two nations in questions are conceived as two distinct political units. Therefore, the civic and the ethnic dimension of nationalism must not be viewed as conflicting yardstick that explain nationalism. In a similar fashion, when we define nationalism/national identity in the context of sport, the civic and the ethnic notions of nations are treated as coterminous entities. To elaborate this point more vividly, the article takes recourse to the views of Anthony King [29] on the relationship between national identity and sport. King elucidates that during the 2004 European Cup Championship held in Athens, the cars on all the English highways were carrying flags of the Union Jack as a means for depicting their support to the English National Football side. There is hardly any debate over the fact that national flag is a symbol of national solidarity. Nonetheless, which aspect of nationalism (civic or ethnic) does it highlight? This is an issue worth pondering over. Flags reveal both. A possible counter argument to this statement may be that a flag symbolizes the cultural traits of a nation and not always the political ones. However, is must be to be remembered that the flag of nation is officially sanctioned and approved by the administrative wings of the state. Hence, it becomes a representative of the political aspect of a state. Therefore, a flag resemble the nation both in its cultural as well as political connotation.

Thus far, the article has defined national identity by referring to the nation-state. In this context, national identity in sport manifests itself when a team represents a group of people who share similar historical, cultural traits, belongs to the same territory and government. Now, the article explores another interesting aspect of national identity in the sporting arena- the sense of national identity among the diaspora of several countries. The game of cricket bears a classic illustration of this statement. Very often, it has been observed that when any South Asian (India, Pakistan, Sri Lanka and Bangladesh) nation plays in any part of the world, the nationals from these countries turn up in huge numbers to cheer for their team. The intensity of support has been so great that at times it is hard to distinguish between the home team and the tourist. The literature on sporting nationalism also reveals important cases as a testimony of this fact. Roy Hay traces the development of a Croatian football team among the migrant population of Croatians in Australia. [30] Hay argues that the football team played a critical role in developing a sense of solidarity among the Croatians living in Australia. According to Hay, Joe Radojevic, a Croat migrant to Australia was a major influence behind the emergence of a 'Croatian Melbourne Football Club'. Moreover, to highlight the role of sport in binding a distinct section of a population, Hay refers to the Presidential speech of the Melbourne Football Club. The speech stressed on the fact that a football tournament has the potential for the development of a Croatian community.

Earlier, we have already mentioned two distinct features of sporting nationalism. First, it does not differentiate between civic forms of nationalism and its ethnic counterpart. Besides, distinguishing the two would not lead us to traverse any new dimension of sporting nationalism. The case of sporting nationalism among the diaspora does not confirm this fact. Most importantly, it gives impetus in traversing new terrains of the theoretical dimension of nationalism. How this is done? This is a pertinent question which is encountered. The population of country's diaspora resides outside the territorial frontiers of their home country. Yet, they convey their support to their home team during international sporting competitions. In this case, one can argue that a disjuncture takes place between civic and ethnic conceptualization of nationalism. To put it differently, the two variants does not always seem to reconcile as it has been portrayed in the case of sporting nationalism among the non-diasporic section of a nation's population. The ethnic dimension of sporting nationalism can be explicated through case of diaspora but certain hardships are encountered while manifesting them through the paradigm of civic nationalism. There are two rationales for such an argument. First, the diaspora are not governed by the rule of law of their home country. Secondly, it must be remembered that not every people of a country's diaspora are citizens of their home country. The civic basis of nationalistic consciousness does not seem to fit in this case. Nevertheless, despite these differences, perceiving the issue from an optimist's perspective, we can still pose the argument that sporting nationalism acts to heal such contentious matters.

National Identity and Sport in the Global Era

The preceding section has been successful to a considerable extent in establishing the fact that sports is a representative of national identity. However, an aspect which national identity and the ontology of identity at large have to encounter in this post-modern era is the impact of the globalizing forces. The phenomenon of globalization and its ramifications raises important queries regarding the relevance of national identity. The probable queries are? Is national identity still relevant in the global era? Does globalization pave the way for the emergence of a transnational incarnation of identity? These questions also seem relevant in the realm of sport. This section seeks to grapple with an important question. Does national identity in sports retains its importance in the midst of globalizing forces in world sport? In this coming section, the article tries to examine these questions.

Let us begin our discussion with an important concept of nationalism, the imagined community. In the previous section, we have observed the process through which sporting nationalism manifest this concept. Similarly, proponents of globalization would argue that Anderson's concept can also be in the transnational sense. David Mato introduced the concept of a 'transnational imagined community'. [31] The emerging fandom for the football clubs all over the world provides a classic illustration of this concept. The argument cannot be refuted completely. The twin forces of the market and communication technology have created a network society.[32] It has facilitated the development of horizontal networks worldwide.[33] Fans from across the continents get a chance to watch their premier club in action. These fans share a common identity of being a supporter of a certain football club despite not knowing each other and residing within a common territorial boundary. Eric Hobsbawm[34] uses the example of sports and envisages that the vigor of nationalism and national identity is on the decline in the global era. Hobsbawm argues that the monolithic dimension of nationalism have been breached due to the impact of the global forces. He claims that when a football player from a different nationality represents a club in the transnational football league, he is being cheered by the supporters/fans of that club whose nationality differs from that of the player. It is true that the rise of global capitalism has ushered in a global culture which is instrumental in transforming identity into a commodifiable entity.[35]

Nevertheless, all these arguments are far from ringing the death bell that would signal the demise of the relevance of national identity in sport in this globalized era. In this light, the article will try to point out the instances of sporting nationalism in the existing literatures of transnational sporting cultures and fandom. The fact which needs to be remembered is that even when any argument is posed in favor of trans-nationalism, it is nationalism that becomes the point of departure. In other words, methodological nationalism[36] becomes the take-off point. Let us now explore some of the dominant literatures on sporting trans-nationalism and try to carve out a place for national identity. Amin Ben-Porat[37] argues the case of migration of foreign players in the Israeli football league to underline the impact of the global capitalism. It can be argued that the intermingling of the national and the foreign players project a sense of transnational character to the Israeli league. However, this is only side of the coin. We can easily get an alternative perspective by perceiving this case from a different angle. It can be easily argued that it is the national identities of the foreign players that have attracted transnational attention to the league. Viewers from different parts of the world take interest in these competitions mainly because of the presence of their national sporting stars. As a consequence, the importance of national identity in sports does not get eroded with the emergences of the global forces.

Any argument in favor of transnational identity must delineate the process through which it developed. The Hyperglobalists [38] proclaims that the development of communication technology have created a 'borderless world'. [39] Hence, people can interact globally and a transnational identity is formed caring little for territorial boundaries. However, if this argument is viewed from a reverse angle, it never loses its rationality. If we argue that a transnational fandom for global sport comes into vogue only when supporters from different nationalities share a common identity alongside their national identity. Similarly, the football clubs which forms the cornerstone of this sort of identity comprises of soccer players who are nationals of a certain country. Therefore, we would be making an extravagant claim if we argue that national identity in sports is replaced by its transnational incarnation.

In order to substantiate the presence of national identity in global sports, let us delve into the literature of global sporting in further detail. In this regard, Tom Gibbons and Kevin Dixon [40] make an interesting differentiation between two categories of supporters the real and the virtual. Besides, the real and the virtual are sub-categorized into online and offline supporters. The real/offline supporters are those who view the match from the stadium. On the other hand, the virtual/online supporters follow the proceedings through the internet. The authors argue that internet followers have greater reach than gallery spectators. Tim Edensor and Steven Millington [41] echo a similar sort of argument. They say that that football culture has become an important theater of exploring contemporary dimensions of identity. These authors also refer to the role of the internet which enables fans from different parts of the globe to interact with another. Furthermore, the viewpoint of Wagner Wilson [42] is no different from the arguments that have already been extrapolated earlier in this paragraph. Commenting on the fan following of the of the major soccer leagues in the United States, Wagner opines that the development and the availability of information technologies such as the internet will certainly facilitate both development and consolidation of the virtual communities of fans who want to follow specific teams and leagues. The point which must be kept in mind is that these authors never mention the sort of football supporters they are referring to. In other words, they does not explicate whether they are arguing about club football supporters or supporters of the national football teams of various countries.

In addition, these authors fail to consider an important thing. Merely following the match through the internet and the website does not always confirm the creation of a transnational identity in sport. It may very well be the case that the online supporters follow the match of their respective national team through the internet. Although the increasing popularization of televised sport has created a new category of arm chair audience, [43] such an innovation does not run counter to the idea of sporting nationalism. On the contrary, it may reinforce the national consciousness in the sporting field. It is true that television and the internet have increased the viewership of sport. Supporters living within their country as well those in distant territories get an opportunity to follow their national sporting team. Similarly, the premier football clubs may equally be source of sporting nationalism. In this connection, the argument of Liz Crolley [44] deserves some elaboration. Crolley attempts to showcase the process through which a Spanish football club, Villarreal tries to tries to attain a global stature through the internet. It may seem that in its quest to become a global brand, it loses some of its national character. However, it is not always the case. Global means of communication can also be used for extending the nationalistic feelings alongside the club's endeavor to increase its global appeal. The Presidential address bears evidence to this statement. In his opening address, the Club president urges its supporters to use the website of their football club for gathering information which the fans feels are essential for them. A nuanced interpretation of the Presidential address enables us to visualize the definition of supporters in an open-ended fashion. In other words, supporters refer not only to those whose nationality is identical club's home country but also who support the club despite being a foreign national. It is to be remembered that supporters follow club matches for two reasons. First, it features some of their national star players. Secondly, the club has its origin in their home country. Let us illustrate this point with an example. When clubs of England and Spain compete in a transnational football league (for example, the UEFA Champions League), the nationals of these two countries will tend to support their respective domestic clubs.

The debate whether national identity in sport retains its relevance in global era or is it on the decline is encapsulated in the famous 'club versus country' debate by Richard Giulianotti.[45] He cites two cases that underline the relevance of national identity in sports in the midst of growing popularity of transnational club football leagues. Giulianotti mentions that during the 1990 Football World Cup held in Italy, the Argentinian football genius Maradona asked the people of Italy to support his team during their match against Italy as he played for an Italian club during that period. However, his request was turned down by the Italian fans even though his statement attracted great media attention. Giulianotti also cites a similar incident which occurred during the during a quarter final match between England and Portugal in the 2006 World Cup Football in Germany. Christiano Ronaldo, the star player from Portugal used his gamesmanship effectively in succeeding to get his English opponent Wayne Rooney sent off despite the fact that both these players represented the same football club (Manchester United) in the English Premier League. [46] Thus, these instances contribute a great deal in establishing the fact that national identity in sports has been successful in weathering the storms of the globalizing tendencies in sport. A similar vein of argument is posited by David Rowe. [47] In his opinion, the relevance of the nation/ national identity in sport does not get marginalized with the increasing circulation of sportsmen throughout the world. Rowe stresses the importance of playing for the country as compared to the clubs. This becomes prominent when he envisages that the clubs retain a national brand irrespective of the cosmopolitan character of its players and officials. The rationale for such a claim lies in the fact lies in the fact it is obligatory for the players to serve their national teams in their respective countries for peak international sporting events such as World Cup Football. [48] In other words, if there is a clash between the international schedule and the club matches, the former is prioritized ahead of the latter.

The two preceding illustrations share a commonality. Both refer to the international Competition such as the World Cup soccer to emphasize the importance of national identity in sport in an age of growing popularity of the transnational club football leagues. Hans Hogenstad [49] takes a different approach as compared to his fellow scholars. He chooses the case of club football to elucidate the importance of national identity in sport. He cites the case of a friendly football match between two English clubs, Arsenal and Barnet to drive home his argument. Some Ghanian supporters of Barnet football club were observed wearing Arsenal jersey with the name of their favorite footballer 'Owusu-Abeyie' on their back in support of both the player and the club. The point which is to be noted is that the Ghanians were cheering for an English club especially because Owusu-Abeyie happened to be a citizen of Ghana. Thus, this instance only strengthens the argument that the article has already discussed. National identity becomes the main driving force for extending support to a particular football club. Moreover, through sporting nationalism, we perceive a considerable understanding of not only the phenomenon of inclusion and exclusion but also a greater understanding of the yardsticks/criterion of inclusion.

A brief understanding of the subtle differences between supporting the national side during an international competition and supporting a club side in a transnational football league is essential. During an international football competition such as the World Cup Football or the European Championship the 'us' versus 'them' difference becomes clear. In these tournaments, two distinct national sides compete with one another on the football field. In contrast, in the global/transnational football leagues, the support for the clubs is mostly based on the criteria of nationalism. Interestingly enough, the clubs consists of players from diverse nationalities. Therefore, support for the club is mainly based on the criteria of inclusion. Supporters from the across the globe seeks to figure out which of their favorite national footballer is representing a definite club. Thus, the feeling of 'us' receives precedence. The factors of exclusion do not play a major role in this case. In their quest of extending support to their premier national sportsman, the supporters ends up supporting an entity (the club), which in some cases has its origin in an alien territory and comprising of players and support staffs from various countries. Nevertheless, in the midst of all these factors, national identity still remains a potent factor in building the support base for the clubs. As a result, whenever any investigation of the literatures grappling with the transnational aspect of sport is to be unearthed; we will have to do so with a pinch of salt.

The literature on global sport portrays that the multinational companies producing sporting merchandize product has played a key role in transforming notions of national identity and have eventually converted them into a global brand. The proponent of this line of argument proclaims that global sport developed into a new commodity of signs. [50] However, exceptions are there. A renowned sporting multinational Umbro, produced the official jerseys for the English National Football team. The company earned huge profit through it as the English both in the United Kingdom and abroad purchased these branded England Jerseys in support of their national side. [51] This illustration helps us to unravel the role of sporting nationalism from a different angle. The article has already mentioned that transnational identity in sport that emerges as a consequence of the global forces transforms itself into a brand. This occurs mainly due to its association with several sporting MNCs. This does not imply that national identity in sport either gets eroded or it fails to acquire the brand value similar to its transnational counterpart. On the contrary, it signifies that even the MNCs utilize the nationalist emotions attached to national sporting teams for promoting their products. Such an action on the part of the sporting multinationals helps in exemplifying two things. First, it shows that the MNC uses national sporting teams and international sporting as a medium for the global dissemination of their products. Secondly, even national identity possesses the potential to become a brand.

Conclusion

Although the article reflects on the theoretical underpinnings of two variants of nationalism, it tries to resolve the politico-cultural dichotomy that exists in theories of nationalism. As the article observes, the nation must be conceived both from the political and cultural angle. These two forms may be different but are not conflicting entities. The form of national identity as depicted in the sporting fields is both civic and ethnic. Forging these two factors, sporting nationalism becomes a major force in integrating the nation. The rationale for such an argument is that the ethnic dimension of nationalism at times may produce sub-national tendencies. Sporting nationalism acts as a bulwark against such phenomenon. Acts of flag-waving and painting of faces with national colors is a testimony to this fact. The article has also discussed the ways through which national flags carry both civic and ethnic connotations.

Besides, .the article has also discussed that nationalist philosophy does not remain confined to the territorial boundaries of a nation, but also plays a critical role in raising the nationalist consciousness of the diaspora. The article has examined the instance of the sporting nationalism among the migrant Irish population in Australia, in which playing football generated a sense of oneness among them. This case reveals that although the diaspora neither resides within their national territory nor are governed by the rule of law of their home country, they share the national consciousness of their homeland. Therefore, the article has showcased that nationalist spirit in sport is not hindered even if one the aspect does not manifest itself properly. In the case of diasporic sporting nationalism, ethnic nationalism manifests itself more vividly than its civic counterparts. Despite this, it does not affect the sense of integrity among the nationals of a country during any international sporting events.

Finally, the article has also dealt the resilience of national identity in the global era. It admits that the impact of the globalizing phenomenon in sports has given birth to a transnational version of identity. Nevertheless, the article points out that centrality of national identity in the formation of transnational identity, by examining the club versus country paradox in the context of football. [52] The support base for football clubs often takes a national outlook. Besides, the article has also countered the view that only transnational identity eventually succeeds in attaining the stature of a global brand. It has forwarded an alternative explanation that national identity also transforms into a brand with the assistance of the market forces.

In this era of globalized sports, the sporting multinationals invest resources to become official sponsors of several national football teams. Thus, the national jersey of the football playing nations becomes a popular merchandize product which is worn by their fans in solidarity of their national team.

Notes

1. Robert Gilpin, *The Challenges of Global Capitalism: The World Economy in the 21st Century*, New York: Princeton University Press, 2000.
2. Ramon Llopis Goig, Identity, nation-state and football in Spain: The evolution of nationalist feelings in Spanish Football, *Soccer and Society*, 9:I (2008), 56-63.
3. Anthony D. Smith, *Nationalism and Modernism*, London and New York: Routledge, 1998, pp. 18, 19, 20.
4. Anthony D. Smith, *Ethnic Origin of Nations*, London: Blackwell, 1986.
5. Ibid.
6. Goig, opcit. 2008.
7. Benedict Anderson, *Imagined Community: Reflections on the Origin and Spread of Nationalism*, London: Verso, 1983.
8. Paul Darby & David Hassan, 'Introduction: Locating Sport in the study of Irish Diaspora', *Sport in Society*, 10:3 (2006), 333-346.
9. Smith, opcit.1998, pp. 18, 19.
10. Alan Bairner, *Sport, Nationalism and Globalization: European and North American Perspectives*, State University of New York Press: Albany, 2001.
11. Ibid. p.118.
12. David Rowe *et al. Globalization and Sport: Playing the World*, London, Thousand Oaks and New Delhi: Sage Publications, 2001.
13. N. Chiba, Morino Shinji and O. Ebihara, 'Globalization, Naturalization and Identity: The Case of Borderless Elite Atheltes in Japan', *International Review of the Sociology of Sports*, 36:2 (2001), 203-221.
14. Y. Fukuoka, *Koreans in Japan*, Tokyo: Chuko Shinsho, 1993.
15. K. Kamneka, *Nationalism: The Nature and Evolution of an Idea*, Canberra: Australian University Press, 1976, p. 85.
16. J.G. Kellas, *The Politics of Nationalism and Ethnicity*, United Kingdom: Macmillan, 1991.
17. R.Brubaker, *Citizenship and Nationhood in France and Germany*, Boston MA: Harvard University Press, 1992.
18. Smith, opcit, 1998.
19. Guttman, opcit, 1994.

20. P. Donnelly, 'The Local and the Global: Globalization in the Sociology of Sport', *Journal of Sport and Social Issues*, 20:3, 239-257, 1996.
21. David Miller, *On Nationality*, Oxford: Clarendon Press, 1995, p. 27.
22. Anderson,opcit, 1983.
23. Steven Elliot Grosby, *Nationalism: A Very Short Introduction*, Oxford University Press: London, 2005.
24. Bairner, opcit, 2001.
25. Gilpin, opcit, 2000.
26. Grant Jarvie, *Sport, Culture and Society: An Introduction*, London and New York, Routledge, 2006.
27. J. Nauright, *Sport, Cultures and Identities*, London: Leicester University Press, 1997, pages. 152,187,188.
28. Cornell Sandvoss, *A Game of Two Halves: Football Fandom, Television and Globalization*, London and New York: Routledge, 2003.
29. Anthony King, 'Nationalism and Sport', in Gerard Delanty and Krishan Kumar (eds.), *The Sage Handbook of Nations and Nationalism*, London, Thousand Oaks and New Delhi: Sage Publications,2006, pp. 249-259.
30. Roy Hay, 'Croatia: Community, Conflict and Culture: The Role of Soccer Clubs in Migrant identity', *Immigrants and Minorities*, 17:1: 49-66, 1998.
31. D. Mato, "On the making of Transnational Identities in age of Globalization: The US- Latinian/o 'Latin'American Case", *Cultural Studies*, 12:4, 598-620, 1998.
32. M. Castells, *The Rise of the Network Society*, Oxford: Blackwell, 1996.
33. M. Castells, *The Power of Identity: The Information Age, Economy, Society and Culture*, London, Wiley Blackwell, 2009.
34. Eric Hobsbawm, *Globalisation, Democracy and Terrorism*, Abacus: London, 2008.
35. S. Bridgewater, *Football Brands*, United Kingdom: Palgrave Macmillan, 2010.
36. U.Beck, *What is Globalization?*, Cambridge: Polity Press, 1999.
37. Amin Ben-Porat, 'The Political Economy of Soccer: The Importation of Foreign Soccer Players in the Israeli League', *Soccer and Society*, 16:2, 54-68.
38. David held & Anthony McGrew, *The Global Transformation Reader: An Introduction to the Globalization Debate*, London: Blackwell, 1999.
39. Kenichi Ohmae, *The Next Global Stage: Challenges and Opportunities Our Borderless World*, New Jersey: Wharton School Publishing, 2005.
40. Tom Gibbons & Kevin Dixon, 'Surfs-up! A Call to Take the English Soccer fan on the internet more seriously', *Soccer and Society*, 11:5 (2010), 599-613.
41. Tim Edensor & Steve Millington, 'This is our City: Branding Football Local Embededness', *Global Networks*, 8:2, (2008), 172-193.
42. Wagner Wilson, "Alltogether Now, 'Click': MLS Soccer Fans in

Cyberspace", *Soccer and Society*, 8:3, (2007), 381-391.

43. Gerry P.T. Finn & Richard Giulianotti, (eds.), *Football Culture: Local Contests, Global Vision*, USA: Frank Cass Publishers, 2000, p. 273.
44. Liz Crolley, 'Playing the identity Card: Stereotypes in European Football', *Soccer and Society*, 1:2 (2006), 107-128.
45. Richard Giulianotti and Roland Robertson, *Football and Globalization*, London: Sage Publications,2009, pp.107,108.
46. Ibid.
47. David Rowe, 'Sport and the Repudiation of the Global', *International Review for the Sociology of Sports*, 38:3 (2003), 281-294.
48. David Rowe et al., *Globalization and Sport: Playing the World*, London, Thousand Oaks and New Delhi: Sage Publications, 2001.
49. Hans, Hogenstad, 'Transglobal Scandinavian? Globalization and the Contestation of Identities in Football', *Soccer and Society*,10 (3): 358-373.
50. Ellis Cashmore, *Making Sense of Sports*, USA and Canada: Routledge, 2000.
51. King, opcit., p 255, 2006.
52. Giulianotti and Robertson,opcit., p.107. 2009.

Sporting Nationalism in Twentieth Century Bengal: The Gendered Perpective

Suparna Ghosh

Sport and its values are a microcosm of society itself. Over the years, Indian sports have become major vehicles of nationalist self-expression. In the colonial period, it was the patriotism of a colonized people resisting an imperial power. In the post-colonial period, it represents the hopes, ambition, fears and anxieties of a nation, collectively the national identity in international sport.[1]

The present paper seeks to plot the gendered nature of nationalism and the ways they can be transformed through the participation of women in sport. The scope of this paper will be from the 1920s to the 1950s. It is an established fact that nationalism is a part of the public sphere while women have been relegated to the private domain. Traditionally, women had participated in nation building process primarily as biological reproducers of the nation. From that perspective, nationalism is gendered. Sport has always been considered a masculine domain where conceptions of hegemonic masculinity as well as the nation are developed and also reinforced. It was traditionally believed that fighting was the responsibility of males thereby automatically leading to the exclusion of females from the gladiator's arena. This was translated into the banishment of women from the playing fields, a training ground for war.

National Movement and Physical Culture: Locating the Link

The anti-colonial nationalist movement started emerging in Bengal by the turn of the nineteenth century. However, the anti-partition movement during 1905 sparked the fire of protest throughout Bengal. In this changed socio-political context, the nationalist leaders wanted women to participate in the struggle who for centuries had been denied any public space. At this critical juncture the question arises that why women were called to get involved in the exclusively male sphere of politics? It can be argued that the nationalist leaders converted their socio-economic struggle against the British into a worship of the motherland. [2] The nationalist requirement constructed the model of a 'new woman' who would retain the basic values of the traditional domestic system and the inner spirituality of indigenous social life. The home came to be considered as the principal site for the expression and retention of the spiritual quality of the national culture. Partha Chatterjee advocates that the Indian nationalists, many of whom had received western education, accepted the superiority of the west in the public sphere of rationality, progress, impersonal bureaucracy, and modernization but maintained their cultural superiority in the private, spiritual sphere, traditionally the domain of Indian women. The nationalists sought a specific site of resistance for Indian cultural identity while at the same time fighting for an independent nation-state. This constituted dichotomy of the world/home or the spiritual/material lay at the heart of the nationalist project. [3] Hence, the new woman was valorized as 'grihalakshmi' (goddess of the home), a combination of old and the new to suit men intellectually colonized but emotionally rooted to the Indian tradition.

When the nationalist movement and the nationalist ideology began to take shape motherhood became central to maintaining an orderly home for the new woman. [4] She was now assigned a specific and crucial role in rearing a special breed of men who will be brave, patriotic and nationalistic. The nation needed strong sons to fight against the colonial rule and to infuse the sense of self-respect among the people. Similarly, the nation needed daughters to lend support to their nationalistic men and mother nationalistic heroes. [5] Thus, the ideal woman was now given additional social responsibilities to give birth to brave and courageous progeny who could fight the might of the colonial power. As a consequence, in the twentieth century, tracts, manuals and articles in journals began to appear on how to look after the health and well-being of children and redefining motherhood at the same time. In fact, Mrinalini Sinha argued that in the second half of the nineteenth century, middle class Bengalis made several efforts to combat the problem of the emasculation of the Bengali male. [6] There was a revival of the *akhra* culture/gymnasium in order to cultivate and instil a sense of pride in the physical powers of the Bengalis. It was also believed that the future of any nation and its people depends upon the child (progeny) and the bearer of that child, the mother. In this context, womanhood was often equated with motherhood. Therefore, it can be argued that the growth of 'new woman' and her 'womanhood' can be understood under the light of effeminate babu of the nineteenth century Bengal who was quite weak and fragile; hence the revival of his strength was needed. [7]

Sports and Indian Women: An Attempt to Rewrite History

Against such an outset, one is also reminded of Sarala Devi, one of the foremost Indian women in our nationalist movement who also believed that improvement in the health and physique of the youth was an essential step for the success of the freedom movement. In her quest for the fulfilment of this cause, she established an *akhra* (club) and a *byayam samiti* (gymnasium) which also served as linkages with the revolutionaries. In fact, the first and third decades of the twentieth century covered the phase of revolutionary movement in Bengal. But prior to 1920s, women were restricted from direct operations in the organisations. Their relegation to the private, domestic sphere prohibited them from public life and thus from equal access to social, economic and political resources. This exclusion was the primary basis for their subordination.[8] However, the situation became favourable for the women revolutionaries from the 1920s. The impact of contact with the foreigners, new ideas through the journals and books, the emergence of *mahila samities* (women's associations) both in the metropolis as well as the districts, Gandhiji's constructive programme and the Montague and Chelmsford reforms that had granted limited franchise to women enabled women to cross the threshold of their traditional sphere of home. According to Chatterjee, once the essential femininity of the modern Hindu Bengali woman was fixed in terms of certain culturally visible spiritual qualities, they could go to schools, travel in public conveyances, watch public entertainment programs and in time, even take up public employment outside the home.[9]

Therefore, by toeing Griffin's argument we can enunciate that women's integral participation in nationalist struggles was not necessarily more peaceful than men.[10] Cynthia Enloe was quite justified in her claims while advocating that women's participation in such movements against the colonizers represents a new era wherein they play active roles in defining feminism and nationalism.[11] The first female revolutionary to be recruited as member of Dacca Sri Sangha was Lila Nag in 1924.[12] After her, many revolutionaries like Kamala Dasgupta, Preetilata Waddedar, Kalpana Dutta joined the different revolutionary organizations. Most of these women were below thirty years of age, which is the active age for sports participation.[13] The socio-political forces in the 1920s brought about changes in the sphere of physical education for women. Physical fitness was the important pre-requisite for participation in revolutionary movement and its foundation was laid in their school and college days. For instance, both Kalpana Dutta and Preetilata Waddedar associated with Chittagong Armoury Raid used to play badminton together in the Khastagir Girls High School in Chittagong.[14] They continued their sporting activities as students of Bethune College. Even Leela Nag was associated with Sri Sangha and founded the Deepali Sangha for playing tennis, badminton, hadudu everyday in the Bethune College premises. [15] With a view to train up young girls and to culture physical strength, lathi and dagger play, jujutsu, cycling, swimming, shooting, jumping, long distance run and other free hand exercises along with various other sporting events were arranged on the day of Janmashtami at Dacca town, Mymensingh and other places of Dacca district. [16] Thus, the physical culture movement which developed around the akhras fulfilled the duel objective of revolutionary work and the entire gamut of physical fitness followed by sports.

The establishment of All India Women's Congress in 1918 further opened the doors for women's suffrage and emancipation. Due to this movement, issues such as sport gained currency among the Indian women. The contemporary journals were also instrumental in highlighting the relevance of sports among women and opined that participation in sports would further stimulate the movement for women's emancipation. The report of the 'Deepali Patrika' in Calcutta provides a classic illustration of this statement. The report enunciated stressed that if the Bengali women would concentrate more on physical exercise than dance and song then they would be really considered moving towards progress. It is only in Bengal, that the mothers are called Abala. This criticism for Bengali mothers can be removed if the Bengali girls follow Bani's footsteps. [17] "During this period, (1934) Bani Ghosh broke Miss Lucy's (an English woman) record in the national swimming clubsports. She also became the Triple All India Olympic Champion in 1936. [18] In 1934, the journal Meye Mahal conveyed the idea that earlier sport for women was an extremely limited enterprise. Sport was primarily perceived as playing of cards or other indoor games. By the 1930s, things had changed. Women had started taking a keen interest in cricket, football and hockey. Women expressed: If we are to rise from ignominy, we must take sports more seriously. When the Mohun Bagan Football Club had won the IFA shield in 1911, Indian males had made a huge issue out of it. We should also equip ourselves to achieve similar victory. Such a victory is only possible in sport.[19]

Sport upholds hegemonic masculinity. This includes reinforcing the idea that men are strong, competitive and weak. Since nationalism is gendered, it prescribes certain sets of roles for both women and men within the nation. The contemporary vernacular journals are full of details with respect to revival of all the powers of women for inspiring the men to fight against the British.[20] At the same time, women should engage in physical exercise and sports for developing physical and moral strength.[21] A few articles also highlighted the fact that the girls and women needed physical exercises and sports not just for their own physical fitness but to procure healthy children.[22] It can be argued here that a strange dichotomy existed among the male intelligentsia about women sports participation. On one hand, they wanted that the women should walk away from traditional gender expectations and challenge the male dominated status quo in the field of sports. On the other hand, women's quests for equal opportunity, physical empowerment and respect were being resisted by many men and institutional forces. These articles revealed that the future of any nation and its people depended upon the child (progeny) and the bearer of that child, the mother.[23] Hence, the mother through regular exercise should enhance her beauty, strength and power.[24] The bhadrolok allowed the women to participate in sports not for their own recreation or enjoyment. On the contrary, they were brought in an atmosphere of physical culture for the respectful qualities of motherhood which are inherent in them and are capable of transforming weakness to strength, frailty to fortitude.

It was also specifically mentioned that women need exercise which are not strenuous and rigorous but would facilitate them to retain their femininity.[25] Femininity urged women to only participate in sports that involved graceful movement because women were considered frail, and therefore unable to take the contact delivered in traditional men's sports. For instance, *Prabartak* strongly recommended slow-cycling for women because fast cycling was considered harmful for the physical build of women. [26] As a result, from the 1920s the Bengali women became conscious of the importance of sports. But physical activities were mostly confined to the so-called feminine sports. Cricket and soccer both remained a male monopoly because of their more masculine character as envisaged by the colonial male. Perhaps, they believed that involvement in these masculine games would lead to a conscious challenge to their hegemony. Even the educated women as heads of educational institutions were opposed to further such masculine sports in their institutes for its corrupting influence on the students. [27] They were not opposed to women's recreation in the sporting arena but it remained confined to badminton, table tennis, basketball, track and field games in their institutes. Hence, women's physical activity was controlled by an ideological system of gender roles and values that dictated what a woman can and cannot do with her physicality.In the process, however quite a few Hindu-Bengali women had come out of the threshold of their houses breaking the shackles of century old tradition and not abiding with the so called culturally visible spiritual qualities of being a woman.

Participation in Sporting Event by Indian Women: A Categorical Analysis

Golf

It was viewed primarily as a leisured pastime for the ladies of elite families. It could be pursued without violating the cult of true womanhood. Most of the players were either English or Anglo-Indian ladies as evident from the names of the participants such as, Mrs. Allan Harvey, Mrs. Downe Leslie, Miss Cobbold, Mrs. T. Swan, Miss Stewart, Mrs. H. Bennett, Mrs. Hope Stewart, Miss D.

Baker, Mrs. Lamond Walker, Mrs. Le Messurier, Mrs. Clyden, Mrs. Evers, Mrs. Firminger, Mrs. Elcock, Mrs. Bairin and others. [29] These competitions were held mostly in the golf clubs of Calcutta like the Tollygunge Club or the Royal Calcutta Golf Club. Mrs. Reid Kay and Mrs. Hope Stewart among other were efficient women golf players in those days. [30] Thus, golf could not penetrate the Bengali households who were not yet socialized into the club life of the British.

Lawn Tennis

Lawn tennis was also played extensively by the women during this time because this game also conformed to middle class notions of femininity minimizing body contact, exertion, and the display of female flesh. [31] Here again, most of the participants in the 1920s were either English or Anglo-Indian ladies like Mrs. Cobbald, Mrs. Keays, Mrs. Berthoud etc. [32] They played ladies singles and mixed doubles as well in competition like Bengal Lawn Tennis Championship. [33] In the 1930s, women participated in various types of competitions like the North Indian Lawn Tennis Championship, East Indian Tennis Championship, All India Tennis Championship, Delhi Tennis Championship, Oudh Gymkhana Tennis Championship and the like. Within Calcutta, Ballygunge Tennis Championship, Calcutta, Gymkhana Lawn Tennis Tournament, Calcutta South Club Tennis Championship were organised. Miss Dubash, Miss M.G. Dinshaw, Miss Leela Row, Miss Mcleod, Miss Moir, Miss Footit, Miss Woodbridge, Mrs. Boland were quite prominent, players of that period. Like Golf, Calcutta was the pride of lawn tennis.

Hockey

As far as hockey is concerned again the English and Anglo-Indian ladies displayed their skills in this game from the 1920s to the 1940s. Mention can be made of a few prominent players like Miss. D. Wollocombe, Miss E. McGrath, Miss J. Michael, Miss P. Anderson, Miss. L. Brown, Mrs. Boland etc. Inter club, inter-district and all-India women's hockey [34] league matches were held during this time. For instance, clubs like Hornets, Hai Girls, Wanderers, Blue Birds, Grass hoppers, Grail Club organised such events. [35]

Basketball

The participants of basketball in the early 1920s were confined to the English and Anglo-Indian communities. Basketball is more popular than hockey among the Calcutta girls possibly because it is easier to play and its rules do not confuse the feminine mind as much as the hockey rules. Matches in Calcutta attracted great crowds and they got their share of recognition from the applauding spectators. Likewise, hockey league matches and inter-club matches were arranged for basketball as well. Clubs like Wanderers, [36] Rangers, Grail Club and the like [37] participated in all the competitions. Schools and colleges like Loreto House, La Martiniere for girls and others also participated in the above mentioned competitions. In fact Loreto girls used to become the champion in senior basketball league matches. [38] It was in 1929 that men or rather the Bengal Basketball Association sponsored women basketball and soon after, the Women's Basketball Association of Bengal came into being. They developed their own panel of women referees and solved the "referee problem" They grew from strength to strength and secured an alteration on the Maidan just before the war. Gradually, Bengali girls started playing basketball in the post-independent period in the Rakhi Sangha Club.

Swimming

Swimming is considered to be one of the beneficial forms of exercise and attracts people with a wide range of abilities from all age groups. It is enjoyed by millions of people both as a popular recreational activity and as a competitive sport. During this time, quite a number of Bengali girls participated in swimming competitions. Aquatic marathons attracted small girls like nine year old Miss Manu Mukherjee swam continuously for sixteen hours at College Square in 1934.[39] In the same year eight year old Kumari Sabitri Rani Khandelwala swam for fifteen hours in Hedua swimming club. The same girl had won gold medal at Rangoon, the previous year with her hands and feet tied together. She had other medals as well to her credit.[40] Thus, the girl reflected great patience, potential, grace and strength required in marathon swimming. There were many other examples of small Bengali girls participating in marathon swimming.

Apart from marathon swimming, Bengali girls also participated in different events of swimming at the All India level competition. For instance, in All India Swimming Competition in 1938 in 100 metres first, second and third rank holders were all from Bengal. Kumari Leela, Kumari Rama and Kumari Sukhalata came first, second and third respectively.[41] Then again, the Bengali girls not only participated with European girls in swimming but also secured first rank. For instance, Kumari Leela Chattopadhyay came first in the 100 meters event of Central Swimming Club. She was followed by two European[42] girls (names not mentioned in the source) in the same competition. But the European girls still maintained their stand in swimming as is evident from the contemporary newspapers and journals. Miss Avelino Saunders came first in the 100 meters free style at the South Calcutta Swimming Association.[43]

Athletics

Clubs like Wanderers, Victoria Institution, Blue Triangle, Calcutta West Club and the like organised athletic competition. Despite the emergence of Bengali girls, the Anglo-Indian and English girls still dominated the scene. Miss L.Carew, Miss S. Isac, Miss P. Cook, Miss Satyabati Biswas were a few noted athletes prior to independence. Bengali girls were also attracted towards athletics. During this time, there were various institutions like girls' school, colleges, private clubs etc. which organised sporting activities for women. The Victoria Institution had organised its first annual sports meet at the college compound in 1937. The college had a cosmopolitan character comprising of girls from different communities' viz. Bengali-Hindu, Bengali-Muslim, Christians, and Marwari etc. They all participated in sporting activities as well. For instance, in 100 yards flat race Miss Sovana Gupta came first and was followed by Miss Hussenara Haque and Rajkumar Singh respectively. [44] The Mohan Bagan Athletic Club sports also in its 48th Annual sports meet had kept certain events open to Indian girls along with other club members and amateurs thereby encouraging the Bengali girls to participate in sports like activities. [45]

Despite the emergence of Bengali girls, the Anglo-Indian and the English girls still dominated the scene. For instance, at the Kalighat Sports Annual Meet winners of 200 yards run, 86 yards low hurdle, 150 yards run, one mile cycle race were Miss. L. Carew, Miss S. Isac, Miss. P. Cook, and Miss D. Smythe respectively. [46] It's because there was a lot of difference in the standard of performance between the Anglo-Indian and Bengali girls so the latter in most cases did not participate in the Kalighat Club sporting events. However, in the districts unlike Calcutta, the Bengali Hindu and Muslim girls did quite well in athletic sports. Evidently, Miss Satyabati Biswas became the individual champion for second year in succession in the third annual sports of the Jalpaiguri district. [47] Quite a few Muslim girls like Rezia Khatoon, Ashrafan Nessa also did credit to their community by participating in the above mentioned sport meet. [48]

Alongside carom, billiards, table tennis and badminton were also quite popular sporting activities among Bengali women prior to1947. Intra-College and inter- college carom competitions were held regularly. In 1940, Anila Sen of Ashutosh College became the winner in inter-college carom competition. [49] In inter college table tennis championship Nirmali Puri of Ashutosh College became the champion in 1940. [50] By 1940s Bengali girls had earned great applauds in this sport. Significantly, Kumari Banni Sen participated for the first time in Bengal table tennis championship and by defeating Miss S. La Didd became the champion in 1938. [51] Billiards being a costly sophisticated game was still prevalent among the English and Anglo-Indian ladies during this time. Evidently, Miss Mary Jacob became the Calcutta billiard champion in 1941. [52]

Badminton

During 1935 and thereafter, badminton competition had started for women The All India Badminton Association was formed in Bengal in the year 1934, due to the co-operation and enterprise of the local clubs of Bengal. [53] However, there wasn't a single winner at the national level who could represent the Bengali community. In 1945-46 and in 1955-56 two Bengali girls, Priti Basu and Meera Das respectively won state championship. In doubles event, during 1946-47, Purbi Basu and Kana Basu became champion. Similarly, Meera Das and Nilima Ghosh became champion in 1954-55 doubles event. Except for these Bengali girls, most of the girls who participated and became champions in badminton were either Anglo-Indian or resident non-Bengali's girls. For instance Pearl Goss, Betty Catchik, Mrs. Boland, Phyllis Cook, Sheela Burma, Prem Parashar, Doreen Stevens etc. [54] Amidst Anglo-Indian girls, the presence of one Bengali girl Peeti Basu was really exemplary in those days. [55]

Soccer

From the 1920s onwards, the Bengali women were fast catching up with their European counterpart in sports. Nevertheless, rigorous sporting activity among women was still discouraged by the society. Therefore, when Brajaranjan Ray attempted to start an annual soccer tournament for women under the aegis of the Women's Sports Association, established in 1929, he was met with severe opposition from the educated stratum of the society. [56] The decision to start an annual soccer tournament for the girls' colleges of the city was treated as an attempt to promote vulgarities. Consequently, only Victoria College and

Ashutosh College consented to participate in the tournament. Due to parental opposition, the Bethune College was not ready to field a team with men referees, linesmen and male spectators..[57] Despite considerable opposition this soccer tournament for the women continued for four years and eventually the Women's Sports Federation was formed in 1938. However, women's soccer in Bengal had declined by the early 1940s.[58]

Apart from the college girls, the women members of the National Youth Association formed by Brajaranjan Ray in 1928 in Calcutta were also interested in soccer. One of its members Purna Ghosh[59] attempted to play soccer and became the subject of ridicule in many sections of the society.[60] Her rejection of the traditional attire to play the sport seriously created further hostility towards women's football. From 1932-1935 Purna Ghosh was the fastest schoolgirl, (an excellent athlete of Oriental Seminary School). Besides, she was the winner of fifty, seventy five, hundred yards race organised by Mohan Bagan Sports, Crown sports, Bengal Athletic Sports, Boys Union Sports, Sreerampur, Chinsurah etc.

Cricket

In Calcutta, women cricket was yet to achieve a considerable degree of popularity like it did in Bombay,[61] Delhi and Rawalpindi where this game had stated gaining ground among women. In Delhi, the women team was being defeated by the men team; however the women team at Rawalpindi had defeated the team of military officers.[62] In Bengal, the European and Anglo-Indian ladies used to play cricket.[63] The vernacular journal Prabartak expressed the opinion that soon Bengali girls will also start playing cricket.[64] In the colonial period particularly from1920s till independence, an interest was thus generated towards sports among women in Bengal. It was not simply an act of mimicry. It served as a mirror in which female identity assessed itself.[65] Several historical empirics reveal this claim. During the phase from 1935 to 42, Ila Sen had established herself as an excellent sports woman who was equally proficient in athletics, basketball, badminton and tenniquoit. [66] She represented India in Olympic Games in 1940 thereby proving the worth of Bengali girls in sports. She was the only Indian girl in an all white athletic team.

Women's sport was thus certainly part of a nationalist enterprise. The British colonizers in an effort to naturalize British patriarchy emphasised on the effeminisation and hyper sexualisation of Hindu Bengali men. The status of Indian women in Indian tradition served as the key issue in this process of effeminisation. [67] The British colonizers drew a parallel between the characteristics of British women and Bengali men on the grounds that both were incapable of public, political participation. Mrinalini Sinha states, that the benevolent protection of both native and British women became the heart of British colonial masculinity, a mythology in that the "manly physique" and "manly character" of the "sport-loving" British male made him a natural and justified ruler. The Bengali reacted to this charge of effeminacy by pursuing neo-traditional physical culture and indigenous games in the akhras.The middle class cultural nationalists like Rajnarayan Basu, Bankim Chandra Chatterjee, Krishna Kumar Mitra, Sarala Debi, Nabagopal Mitra and Swami Vivekananda all strongly emphasised on the needs of physical culture against the British charge of the Bengali's supposed racial effeminacy.

Yuval Davis also seems to argue that women participate in nationalism in five major ways- as biological reproducers of the nation, transmitters of culture and markers of citizenship, participants in nationalist struggles and as symbols of the nation. [68] Joanne Nagel agrees with Nira Yuval Davis on the roles available to women within nationalist projects. [69] In this respect, McClintock claims, that "all nationalisms are gendered, all are invented, and all are dangerous dangerous in the sense of representing relations to political power and to the technologies of violence." [70] Nationalism thus is gendered, and as such it prescribes certain sets of roles for both women and men within the nation. Simultaneously, sport also upholds hegemonic masculinity which includes reinforcing the idea that men are strong, competitive and aggressive while women are more passive, cooperative and weak. At the same time as Griffin added that women's sexuality is also important to nationalists because it is a matter of masculine honour and is necessary to reproduce the nation.[71] Thus in the case of Bengal also the nationalists used sport to cultivate nationalism in their nation building processes.

In the post-independence era, the Bengali girls continued their sporting prowess in swimming, athletics, table tennis, badminton, lawn tennis and also team sports like hockey, basketball and the like. Independence was achieved in 1947 after great turmoil and struggle. The entire world was hard hit due to the Second World War and its aftermath. In India, independence was followed by partition and communal riots. During this period, rehabilitation of the refugees, reconstruction, settlement and general welfare of the people were the primary tasks before the government. Under such a situation the government was not able to concentrate systematically on the affairs of physical education and sports. As such, government formulated policies with respect to these two vistas from the mid-fifties. During such troubled times, women's bodies and sexuality become sites of vulnerable activity, so further restrictions were imposed on women by the society for security reasons. Consequently, a women sport which requires outdoor activities was affected. In ordinary peaceful times, women are seen as icons of the honour of the community. So, the easiest way to assail a community, therefore, is to define the sexual purity of its women. The refugee girls had to survive in the new situation undergoing a lot of struggle. They had to sacrifice their own dreams and wishes and pursue the real role of women being caring and nurturing. As such, sports as part of their leisure and recreation were removed from their social landscape.

Despite such problems, women sports continued to some extent. From 1948-1958, Nilima Ghosh, a famous athlete from Bengal dominated the world of women sports. Her outstanding performance in the Asian Games, 1951 and national championship in 1952 paved the way for participation in Helsinki Olympic Games in 1952. She had also shown her prowess in badminton by winning applauds in state badminton championship. Throughout the 1950s, the tall, well-built Bengali girl, Kalyani Bose surprised everyone with her terrific swimming skills. [72] Bharati Shah, the sister of Arati Shah was also an excellent swimmer from Bengal in the 1930s. Her specialisation was in free style swimming and she represented India in 1952 Helsinki Olympics as well. But she didn't receive the same opportunity as her sister despite the fact that in inter-school competition she used to come second after her sister in all the competitions. The contemporary vernacular tract wrote that these swimmers will remain as guides to future swimmers of Bengal. [73]

Other eminent sporting personalities during the 1950s were that of Dr. Tapati Mitra, Shakuntala Sen, Usha Iyengar. Tapati Mitra was proficient in athletics, cycling and table tennis. Her name featured in the newspapers for all these sports from 1949-1959. From 1945-1951 she was number one in cycling. Same was evident in athletics as well. Her entry to the world of table tennis was in 1954. [75] Arpita Das (Ghosh) was another Bengali girl who excelled in sports during the late 1930s and 1940s. At that time she became the college badminton champion and also won the state table tennis championship for three times respectively. From early childhood she used to play cricket, practice cycling along with jump and race with neighbourhood friends. She was not associated with sports while she studied in Loreto House. It was only at the Ashutosh College that she became college champion. From 1940-48 she was at the peak of her sporting career representing Bengal in table tennis championship. [75] Anuradha Guhathakurta also participated in international athletics at Helsinki Olympics in 1952.

However, despite a few measures undertaken by the central and state government, there wasn't much progress of physical education as an essential requirement in educational institutions. Despite the theoretical provision as per the Youth Welfare Scheme, there wasn't in reality, proper arrangements available for playgrounds, nevertheless, inter-school, inter-district and inter-college competitions in selected sports and games were usually conducted. In the post-independence era, the feminists did not project sports as a means to emancipate women as in the colonial period. It's because during the freedom struggle, in order to fight the might of the white race (the British imperialists) the strength of the women were extremely required. Hence, women were oriented towards physical culture and sports. Since the common enemy, the colonisers were no longer visible after the independence, so the feminists were quite fragmented and they did not focus specifically on gender relations. In the colonial period, the women themselves believed that sporting prowess would help them to challenge the forces of imperialism and patriarchy. In the process they crossed the threshold of their houses forgetting the conservatism of centuries. But after independence, they went back to the safe shelter of their homes believing that their mission was accomplished.

What seems clear is that with some notable exceptions, there has been an extraordinary neglect of women sports in Bengal more particularly during the post- independence period. It's probably as Griffin suggests that women frequently end up in subordinate positions once the goal is achieved. So after independence they are again forced to continue serving as the reproducers of the nation. [76] Besides, hegemonic masculinity in the post-colonial period is also manifested through the amounts of media coverage for women's sports compared to men's sports. For instance, Ananya Sen, a swimmer from Bengal reported to Chiranjeeb in an interview in 1970. She said that the newspapers are not interested in sports news related to swimming and that too achievements of sportswomen. So much so, inter-state and national records are sometimes not published and even if published they are full of mistakes. It seems that masculine games like cricket and football are the only games worth mentioning.[77]

Concluding Observations

In the final analysis following Patricia Clasen, it can be said that the dualistic definition of masculine and feminine created a paradox for the female athlete.[78] It is because femininity is defined in contrast to masculinity, and sport is classified as a masculine domain, a female athlete or sportswoman is thus a contradiction in itself. The evolution of women sports in Bengal took place at a time when Bengal was caught in a surge of the nationalist movement the battle between the 'colonisers' and the 'colonised', had crossed the boundaries of political arena and entered the world of sports, the social sphere. Sports had thus become a symbol around which anti-colonial consciousness developed. The same consciousness stimulated the feminists to demand sporting activities for women. To a considerable extent, the emancipation of women was possible via the medium of sports. But in the absence of such consciousness after independence there was a lull in the sporting activities of women of Bengal for some time. The society demanded higher moral standard for women than men in sports in an effort to enforce 'ladylike behaviour' which would fit societal norms. However, this paper tried to demonstrate that sport can provide women with an opportunity to challenge traditional gender ideals.

Notes

1. For. details see, Caldwell Geoffrey, '*International Sport and National Identity*', International Social Science Journal, 1982, 34
2. Ray, Bharati: *Early Feminists of Colonial India: Sarala Devi Chaudhurani and Rokeya Sakhawat Hossain*,(New Delhi:OUP,2002),pp.38-40
3. Chatterjee, Partha: *The Nation and its fragments: Colonial and Postcolonial Histories*, (Princeton, New Jersey: Princeton University Press, 1993), pp. 35-157.

4. Ray, *Bharati*, op.cit
5. Ibid
6. Sinha, Mrinalini,, *Colonial Masculinity : The Manly Englishman and the Effeminate Bengali in the Late Nineteenth Century,* (Manchester : Manchester University Press, 1995) op.cit.,p.21
7. Bharati, Aasar 1320 B.S(1913) ; *Prabartak* Aasar 1329 B.S(1922)
8. Anderson, Margaret, L.: *Thinking About Women: Sociological Perspective on Sex and Gender,* (U.S.A.Pearson Education Inc., 1983), p. 390
9. Chatterjee, Partha, op. cit., p. 130
10. Griffin, Michele McHugh: As a woman I have no country. *Peace Review* 10, (2), 1998, p. 253
11. Enloe, Cynthia, *Bananas, beaches and bases: Making feminist sense of International Politics*. Berkeley, (CA: University of California Press, 1989), p. 62
12. For details see, Mondal, Tirtha: *The Women Revolutionaries of Bengal 1905-1939*,(Calcutta:Minerva Associates Publications Pvt Ltd.,1991)
13. Ibid,p.27
14. Dutta, Kalpana: *Chittagong Armoury Raiders: Reminiscences*,(New Delhi: People's Publishing House,1979), p. 49
15. Chattopadhyay, Preeti:"Leela", Jayasree, Bhadra,1375 B.S(1968); Mohanti , Dipankar: Leela Roy O Banglar Nari Jagoran, (Calcutta:Sahitya Prakashani, 1999), p. 20
16. De, Amalendu, (ed.) *Amar Jiban Kahini: Pulin Behari Das,* (Calcutta: Anushilan Samiti, 1987), pp. 170-172
17. Deepali Patrika, Baisakh 1341 B.S(1934)
18. Prabartak, Poush 1349 B.S(1942-43); Bhadra 1348 B.S (1941) ,pp.445-7
19. Mazumdar, Boria and Bandyapadhyay, Kaushik , *Goalless: The Story of a Unique Footballing Nation,* (Delhi:Penguin Books, 2006), p. 181.
20. Prabartak, Kartick 1341 B.S (1934)
21. Baithak, Ashwin 1329 B.S(1922)
22. Panja, Mohan Lal, 'Why Women Need Physical Exercise?', Nirmalya Vyayam Patrika, Jaiyastha 1364BS (1957).
23. *Prabartak,* Jaiyastha1340 BS (1933),p.185
24. Ibid.,Jaiyastha 1330BS(1923), p.308
25. *Nirmalya Vyayam Patrika,* Ashwin,1364 BS(1957),p.66
26. *Prabartak,* Kartik, Chaitra, 1341 BS(1934), pp.698-9
27. Majumdar and Bandyopadhyay, op.cit., p.182
28. Greeta L.Cohen(ed.): *Women in Sport: Issues and Controversies* (Newbury Park, London,Delhi:Sage,1993), p 3
29. *The Statesman,* 4th January, 1920
30. *The Statesman,* 15th January, 1920 and 4th July 1920

31. Christensen, Karen, Guttmann, Allen, Fister, Gertrud P., (Eds.), *International Encyclopaedia of Women and Sports*, (U.S.A.: Macmillan Reference, 2001), Volume -1, p. 1215.
32. *The Statesman* 13th January 1920
33. Ibid.
34. The *Amrita Bazar*, 13th January, 17th January, 1934; *Amrita Bazar Patrika*, 7th January 1940, *Amtira Bazar Patrika*, 23rd January, 1940
35. The Amrita Bazar, 13th January, 18th January, 1934; Amrita Bazar Patrika, 4th January 1940.
36. *Bharat Varsha*, Kartick 1343 BS, (1936)
37. *Bharat Varsha*, Agrahayan 1346 BS, (1939)
38. *Bharat Varsha*, Kartick 1344 BS (1937)
39. *Prabartak*, Ashwin 1341 BS(1934), p. 672.
40. *Prabartak*, Aasar 1341 BS(1934), p 335.
41. *Bharatvarsha*, Aashar 1345 BS(1938), p.155
42. Ibid., Kartick, 1344 BS(1937), p.818
43. Ibid., Agrahayan 1346 BS(1939), p.989
44. *Hindustan Standard*, 24th December, 1937.
45. Ibid.,19th January, 1938
46. Ibid., 21st January, 1938
47. Ibid., 2nd February. 1938
48. Ibid.
49. Ibid., Chaitra 1347 BS(1940)
50. Ibid.
51. Ibid., Agrayahan 1345 BS(1938)
52. Ibid., Kartick 1348 BS(1941)
53. Official Souvenir, *All India Badminton Championships Tournament*: 7th Annual, 1940, Calcutta.
54. Mukul: *Kheladhulaye Banglar Meye*,(Calcutta: Anandadhara Prakashan, 1976), p. 132
55. Ibid.
56. Ibid., p. 183
57. Ibid., p. 184
58. Ibid.,p. 185
59. Ibid.; Also see *Mukul*, op.cit., pp. 125-129
60. Ibid., p. 183
61. *Prabartak*, Jaistha 1346BS(1939), p. 190
62. Ibid., Baisakh 1346 BS(1939), p. 91
63. Ibid., Jaistha 1346 BS(1939), p. 190
64. Ibid., Baisakh 1346BS(1939), p. 91
65. Mazumdar and Bandyopadhyay, op. cit., p. 191
66. *Mukul*, op.cit., p. 93

67. Sinha, Mrinalini , op.cit., pp. 33-68; For details see, Roselli, John., *The self image of effeteness : physical education and nationalism in nineteenth century Bengal*, Past and Present 86 February 1980
68. For details see Yuval-Davis, *Nira: Gender and Nation*, (London, U.K.; Thousand Oaks, CA: Sage Publications: 1997)
69. Nagel, Joane: Masculinity and nationalism: gender and sexuality in the making of nations, Ethnic and Racial Studies 21, (2), 1998, p. 242
70. McClintock, Anne: Family feuds: *Gender, nationalism and the family, Feminist* Review 44, Summer , 1993 p.61
71. Griffin, Michele McHugh, op. cit., pp.255-256
72. *Nirmalya Vyayam Patrika*, Ashin, 1356 B.S(1949)
73. Ibid
74. *Mukul*,op. cit.,pp.74-78
75. Ibid, p p.149-153
76. Griffin, Michele McHugh, op. cit.,p. 255
77. Chiranjeeb, *Khelarmathe Meyera*, (Calcutta: Purna Prakashan, 1383BS 1976), p.59
78. Clasen, Patricia: *The female athlete: Dualisms and paradox. Women and Language*, 24, 2001, p. 37

Male Body in the Making: Physical Culture Movement in Colonial Bengal

Amitava Chatterjee

Imperial masculinity was the normative or hegemonic masculinity in nineteenth-century Britain. This is evident in John Ruskin's inaugural lecture at Oxford (1870), where he affirms the responsibility of Britain's "energetic and worthiest" sons to found colonies and pleads with British men to "Reign or Die", [1] and in Kipling's call in "The White Man's Burden" to "Send forth the best ye breed". [2] Scholars view the remaking of British identity through its remasculinization in the latter half of the nineteenth century as intimately connected to the institutions and ideology of empire. [3] Roland Hyam describes the nineteenth century's idealizing of the physically strong British man when he notes "[a] shift from the ideals of moral strenuousness, a Christian manliness, to the culture of the emphatically physical ... a shift from serious earnestness to robust virility, from integrity to hardness, from the ideals of goodness and good learning to those of clean manliness and good form ..." [4]

Ascetic nationalist discourse takes religion and its associated practices out of the private realm and into the body politic, opening up possibilities for exploring how traditions and histories are disrupted not just by the consciousnesses of dissident subjects, but also by representational practices. It comes to function as a "technology of the self," which, as Michel Foucault explains, implies "certain modes of training and modification of individuals" that allow people to transform "their own bodies and souls, thoughts, conduct, and way of being". [5] Almost without exception the first generation of Indian Nationalists emerged from the upper classes and the growing English-educated middle classes in Calcutta, Bombay, and Madras. John Rosselli notes, "In the myth of physical downfall and resurgence the educated elite appeared as sole actors". [6] Their self-perception of effeminacy made them the targets of their remasculinizing endeavours as they competed for dominance and struggled for hegemony. [7] Even within the educated Hindu elite, wrestling with the allegation of effeminacy, the experience, interpretation and enactment of masculinity varied enormously, based on caste, education and geographical location.

Seeking to affect a synthesis of the values of the East and the West in the contemporary philosophy of education, Sri Aurobindo insisted that a healthy body is a necessary condition for intellectual or spiritual attainment. For him physical education means not only the proper functioning of the various organs of the body but also the development of strength, balance, and a sense of beauty. According to him, beauty is the ideal which physical life has to realise. 'If our seeking is for a total perfection of the being', says Aurobindo, 'the physical part of it cannot be left aside: for the body is the material basis, the body is the instrument which we have to use. [...] The perfection of the body, as great a perfection as we can bring about by means at our disposal' must be the ultimate aim of physical culture'. Therefore, 'a development of the physical consciousness must always be a considerable part of our aim, but for that the right development of the body itself is an essential element: health, strength, fitness are the first needs, but the physical frame itself must be the best possible'. [8]

The colonial binary of the "manly British" and the "effeminate Indian" provoked the Hindu elite to search for indigenous masculinities that would enable them to recuperate their "lost" or "forgotten" manhood. In *The Intimate Enemy*, the work that initiated the study of colonialism and masculinity in India, Ashis Nandy argues that the nineteenth-century Indian elite saw the British as agents of change and progress, and accepted the masculinized ethos of aggressive imperialism. They held themselves responsible for their subject status and chose the Kshatriya or warrior model of manliness as an equivalent to the imperial model of masculinity. Kshatriyahood, Nandy asserts, functioned as the normative model of Indian manhood, until Gandhi's grounding of nationalist politics in a feminized semiotic. [9] Other influential studies on Indian masculinity also reiterate this structure. [10]

The Proliferation of Physical Culture Associations

As Indians strove to decolonize the male body by remasculinizing it and thereby build national character, the colonized body emerged as an object of nationalist reform. [11] Bodily reform, both personal and collective, offered the possibility of purging the colonizer and rejuvenating the national body politic. Emphasizing the virtue underlying collective will and action against the individualist quest for moksha, Vivekananda is said to have told Hindu youth: "You will be nearer to God through football than through the Bhagawad Gita". [12] Sports were encouraged to make men healthy and instill the necessary moral virtues. In 1866, the Nationality Promotion Society began its campaign for the revival of "national gymnastic exercises". [13] In 1867, the Tagores organized the first Hindu Mela (fair) to promote cultural arts and sporting events, particularly wrestling, gymnastics, and traditional sports, to re-establish Indian manliness in a "space 'unconstrained' by colonial interference". [14] The Anusilan Samiti, which began in 1901, was one of the first in a series of such societies that were set up all over Bengal as sites of both bodily reform and political instruction. [15] In the early decades of the twentieth century, similar societies and akharas proliferated allover India and became a space of refuge from an increasingly interventionist colonial state, as well as the locus for secret revolutionary groups that deployed violence against colonial rule.

In the last two decades of the nineteenth century, the struggle to free the motherland from British rule was gaining gradual acceptance among the people. Early twentieth century saw the resurrection of thc nationalist spirit. A number *of akhras/clubs/ samities* developed during this period. The motto of these *akhras/samities* was twofold- i) to make the youths conscious about the necessity of freedom and to make them devote themselves to the freedom struggle ii) to develop the moral and physique of the youths so that they may take active role in violent movement. In these clubs, physical exercises and training with various weapons was an essential part of the activities along with careful study of European and nationalist and revolutionary literature. In the second half of the nineteenth century middle class Bengalis made several efforts to combat the problem of perceived emasculation of the Bengali male. Rosseli has demonstrated the various efforts in the second half of the nineteenth century in Bengal to revive the culture of akharas or gymnasiums in order to cultivate and instill a sense of pride in the physical prowess of the Bengalis.

Endeavours of Sarala Debi

Sarala Debi, a prominent woman among mostly male nineteenth- century Bengali nationalist leaders played an important part in the 1890s in arousing Bengali youth to the pursuit of a militant and nationalistic culture. By the turn of the century, Roselli notes that the physical culture movement in Bengal had become a base for terrorist organizations against the British. Sarala Debi insisted that *vyayam* (exercise) is a mechanism by which the dynamic energy of food is converted in to potential energy of stamina and physical strength. She masterminded the formation of an organization called '*Bharat Uddhar*' with active support from Jatindranath Tagore who trained the youths with the lesson of dagger and sword, horse riding, boxing and physical culture. Members of the Dacca Anushilan Samity actively participated in the training programe of this organization. She also took leading role in organizing '*Birastami Utsav*' (1902) and '*Pratapaditya Utsav*' in order to eradicate the false notion of effeminacy imposed upon the Bengalis by the colonizers.

Happy with the success of her experiment, Sarala Devi introduced many such celebrations in memory of the national heroes with a view to inspiring the youth of Bengal with the legacy of the heroism of their own Bengali leaders. In May 1903, she initiated the Pratapad*itya Utsav* in memory of Pratapaditya, the last independent Bengali zamindar of Jessore who dared to resist the Mughals. The celebration made immediate impact. Sarala Devi then introduced the *Udayaditya Utsav* to commemorate the death of Prince Udayaditya of Jessore, who at the age of nineteen died bravely fighting for the country. On these occasions, young Bengali men displayed their skill in sword play and worshipped heroic ancestors.

Pratapaditya Utsab

The newly started festival gained momentum in the cities as well as the fringes of Bengal and it continued almost on a regular basis. A newspaper report reveals that the young men of Baranagar celebrated Pratapaditya Utsav on 26th May, 1907. Largely attended meeting was held under the presidency of Rai Yatindra Nath Choudhury. Babus Khirod Prasad Vidyabinode, Lalit Mohan Ghosal and Rajani Kanto Sanadhyayee of Barishal addressed the meeting. Lathi play, sword play etc were displayed by the local boys and young men. Interestingly, both Hindus and Mohamedans participated in this show. Three medals (one gold and two silver) were presented by Babu Narayan Chandra Sengupta of Baranagar to three young players. Two special prizes of One rupee each were awarded to two Mohammedan boys by the Utsav Samiti. [16] Here we can raise a question that whether the Mohammedans were kept aside the main competition? But since the report does not mention the specific names of the medalists, the question remains unanswered. The Suhridi Samiti arranged to celebrate the Pratapaditya ustab in Maymansingha on second and third Jaistha 1315 B.S. Babu Bipin Chandra Pal presided the whole event. Many Calcutta and mufussil leaders were invited on this occasion and samities in different districts were also invited to depute delegates. A strong reception committee with Babu Anath Bandhu Guha, as president was formed. The people of the town anxiously waited for the gala event. The members of local and mufussil Surhid Samities arranged for the exhibition of lathi play, fencing with sword on the occasion. In an appeal in a newspaper they mentioned...

> Since the samity underwent plenty of calamities, one of which caused the loss of important papers including the address of many of our surhids we regret that for this reason we cannot invite them much though we wish to ask them to join us.[17]

Birastami Utsab

Physical culture movement in India is often linked with nationalist discourse. Birastami became a part and parcel of the Bengali society during the pujas. The effect of anti partition movement was reflected in the physical culture movement of Bengal. Englishman reports that people who attended the Birastami festival at the house of a retired district judge at Padmapukur road greatly enjoyed themselves. There was a fair gathering and a mofussil zaminder was proposed to chair. After the installation the Babu introduced a few 'Lathials', whom he called stick-fighters. Then he announced that the chairman had offered a gold medal for wrestling and Babu P.C. Dube, a star wrestler of Bengal, was ready to engage any competitor in single contest. At first no one responded to the challenge; however one accepter was soon found in the shape of a pigmy and both accepter and the challenger were soon found doing active work on the mat.[18] The same incident was reported more elaborately in *Bengalee* where it stated that Raja Bahadur of Mahisadal chaired the ceremony. In spite of bad weather there was a fair attendance of ladies and gentlemen. From the very beginning of the contest, Babu P.C. Dube had the better of his opponent and was about to lay him down when a hue and cry was raised by the party of his opponent and a great rush was made towards the wrestling arena which very much interrupted the bout. Thus the game was left undecided. Then there was sword and dagger play. The meeting ended with singing some national songs. [19] Another celebration of Birastami was reported as, "A wrestling match was organized on 10th of this month. Mr. and Ms. J. Ghosal gave an afternoon party at their residence No 26 Ballygunge Circular Road to celebrate Birastami otherwise known as 'Mahaastami'. It is called Birastami because it is on this day the older used to bless the young men by saying "may you be heroes and warriors" and woman by saying "may you be mother of heroes and warriors". Miss Ghosal must belong to the credit of having the initiative in establishment of what we all should like to see as a popular institution all over the country namely the celebration of Birastami by sword fencing, lathi play and by display of skill in arms of all sorts and kinds as was witnessed in the house of Miss Ghosal on the 10th instant. She asked a large number of young man to witness the celebration of Birastami and we note with pleasure there was large gathering of them and justify by enthusiasm displayed on the occasion we have every reason to suppress that Birastami will become a recognized institution in the land. At the end of the fest of arms by the performers, a young zaminder was requested by some of the ladies and gentleman to address a few words to the young spectators present there."

Bangiya Pradesik Jatiya Krira O Shakti Sangha made an earnest effort to organise Birastami Utsab in almost all the important hubs of Bengal as well as in the important cities all over India. Bharatvarsha writes that this effort needs to be materialised for the betterment of the physique of the youth force of the newly constructed independent India. [20] An advertisement of Birastami festival to be organised by Bengal Gymnasium of Ballygunge was published in *Indian Mirror* inviting participants, both amateur and professionals as well as clubs from any part of India, wishing to display athletic feats. The events include boxing, wrestling, fencing, shooting and riding. The competition was open to all, irrespective of caste or creed. Further the Birastami Championship medal of Bengal for fencing (amateur) was announced which was a distinction of championship to be contested for year after year. [21]

Similar Endeavours

The anniversary of Shivaji Utsab was celebrated in Kustia with great éclat under the auspices of the local Sebak Samiti. Wrestling and lathi playing were displayed by the members of the Samiti and the feats of the young boys excited great admiration of the spectators. [22] Shakti puja became a very important aspect of Bengali physical culture. The celebration of Shakti Puja commenced on Saturday 25th and came to a close on Monday 27th after surmounting to a good many difficulties that stood on the way. On Saturday a meeting was held with Raja Jotindranath Chowdhury in the chair. The house was crowded almost to suffocation. Every inch of the spacious courtyard was taken up. The subject selected for the day was 'what is Shakti and how it can be attained'. Babu Amrita Lal Basu began by saying that we lacked three things viz. *Dharmabal, Annayabal* and *Arthabal.* These three were all that we received to make our lives happy and without which we could not but be miserable and wretched. He extorted the audience to try to gain *Dharmabal,* which was Shakti in its true sense. He was followed by Babu Bipin Chandra Pal. Some Madrasi gentleman present asked him to speak in English but he said that he would much prefer to speak in his mother tongue, when in the midst of his own countrymen. He said that for over a fortnight he had been silent and had determined to remain unless and until we should choose some one to be our spokesman. He then treated the subject from a purely religious point of view. In the second day two plays was staged .In the third day from the morning Chandipuja and Chandipath. In the evening *Pratapaditya* was performed by students and young men's reciting club on the stage of star Theatre. Amongst those present noticed Babu Bipin Chandra Pal, Pasupati Nath Basu, Amrita Lal Basu, Dr. Sundari Mohan Das, Manmotho Nath Basu and other well known persons of the town. The play was a great success.

Hindu Mela

The importance of physical culture was well realized by the patrons of Hindu Mela and it was included in the regular proceeding. The first assembly of Hindu Mela was held on 12th April, 1867. It was decided there to invite and felicitate the renowned wrestlers of the town in the Mela and to spread the consciousness about physical exercise among the fellow Indians. In the following year (1868) the performers showed their feats in indigenous style. Then there was demonstration of lathi-play and wrestling which was thoroughly enjoyed by both native and European spectators. In the eighth session of 1874 tickets were sold at the rate of 50 paise for muscle posing shows. Competitions of physical feats were arranged for young enthusiasts in the Mela. The champions were presented with medals. [23]

The movement started by the Hindu Mela and National Society for the widespread consciousness about the value of physical prowess among the youth compelled the government to introduce physical education in the schools and it was also included in the syllabus of Civil Service Examination. There are instances where students from government as well as local schools demonstrated their physical feats in the Mela. [24] *Amrita Bazar Patrika* reported that National Society was the pioneer in fostering physical education among the school students. Moreover most of the trainers of physical exercise department set up by the government in schools and colleges were the students of National School founded by Nabagopal Mitra, chief patron of Hindu Mela. [25] Nabagopal Mitra founded National School on 1st April, 1872 for the cultivation of arts, music and for physical training. In the following years horse riding was also introduced as a part of physical exercise. Some of the eminent students of this school were Jitendranath Bandopadhyay, Bipin Chandra Pal, Dr. Sundari Mohan Das etc. Shyama Charan Ghosh after successfully graduating from this institute joined Civil Service Institution as a physical trainer. [26] Prior to the establishment of National School, Nabagopal imparted horse riding training in his stable and Satyendra Nath Tagore and few of his peers were trained there. [27]

The Drive for Physical Education

In an appeal in *Amrita Bazar Patrika* one Prof. M.V. Krishna Rao wrote:

> The importance of Physical culture have not been receiving due attention from all parts of India. Nor has it been recognised that it is one of the essentials for the building up of a healthy and prosperous nation. With this end in view, I with the able assistance and support of Mr. Piyush Kanti Ghosh, the managing editor and proprietor of Amrita Baazar Patrika wish to organise an all-India physical culture movement, the objects of which will be set put in a scheme ... As a means of propaganda and in order to bring home to the minds of our people all over India the necessity for such an organisation. [28]

Sometimes respectable social persons blamed the teachers for the students' apathy towards sports. Hon. Khwaja Sir Nizamuddin while presiding the annual general meeting of the Indian Schools Sports Association deplored the lack of interest taken by schools in Bengal in sports generally and in the Association in particular. He further opined that if the teachers would had taken sufficient interest in sports, they could have prevented some of the youths from taking the misguided path, as they had done. [29]

Prof. S Goswami in an article on 'Physical Education and Man-making' wrote that the main aim of physical education is to maintain the normality of the physico-chemical process and develop both body and mind to a high standard and maintain a balance condition between them so that proper inner reactions may take place between the body and mind. According to him, a philosopher's mind in a Herculean body properly tempered and brightened with emotions is the ideal of modern physical education. Exercise develops maximum health and strength, brightens the mind and stabilises emotions. The correct expression of emotions through physical activities is essential for avoiding complexes. He further goes on to say child's mind should not be cramped by stereotyped educational systems but allowed to develop freely and normally. Its emotions should be allowed to express through normal channels without repression. The author emphasises on the following exercises like running, walking combined with running, jumping, throwing, swimming, dancing, and stretching etc. as correct physical practices for a human body.[30]

Everybody will agree that all work and no play makes jack a dull boy, that sports have their value in building up character and even acquiesce in that old copy book dictum that Waterloo was won on the playground of Eton. But subject to one reservation football and cricket, hockey and tennis are to us, Indians, rather expensive game and the propensity on the part of the boys to indulge in these games means a larger hole-already capacious due to spending on books and college fees and private tutors-in the pockets of their guardians. It is well and good that students should take to athletic games, that they should not be mere intellectual fossils but grow up to be physically strong men. *Hindoo Patriot* puts up the proposition: could not inexpensive games substituted for expensive ones? Is a Kapati shield match altogether an old-fashioned and queer idea, too grotesque to be worthy of serious consideration by serious people?[31]

Moreover, the revolutionaries adopted the theory that physical culture is the foundation on which tire structure of political regeneration can be raised. As a matter of fact, the rules and regulations formed in 1922 by the great revolutionary leader Bipin Behari Ganguli of the Jugantar party, in consultation with other revolutionists, laid down the establishment of societies for physical culture by means of regular exercises in gymnasium, sports, boxing, wrestling, lathi play etc., find a prominent place in the building up organisation. In 1930, the reports by the Inspector of Schools revealed that there were about 280 'Akhras' in Bengal, 42 of these were characterized as quasi-political organization and objectionable in character. After the Chittagong Armoury Raid, the Education Department started taking steps against the schools and colleges, which indulged in undesirable political activities in the guise of physical culture. The most important suggestion to combat forces of terrorism in schools was to introduce more extra-academic activities, out of school activities, like evening games and sports for both boys and girls.

Bande Mataram Sampraday of Ditch Lane, Shyambazar organized a *byam pradarshani* (physical culture show) to infuse the spirit of physical culture among the youth of Bengal. This sort of activities became a common feature for the local nationalist organizations who carried on with these programmes on a regular basis. [32] Bengal Hindu Sabha in its executive committee meeting proposed to hold provincial tournament in wrestling, lathi, sword and dagger play in Calcutta. It was also decided that the district Hindu Sabhas would hold district tournaments with a view to find out best experts of the district in the above mentioned sports. [33] Swadeshi Mela of 1912 witnessed a wrestling competition where more than 25 wrestlers participated. [34]

Prof. B. Ghosh's School on Indian acrobats of 9, Bosepara Lane was unique of its kind. Within a very short time span of establishment it proved its standard. An acrobatic performance was given at Sovabazar Rajbati in the presence of a large and respectable assembly. The performance began at 9:30 p.m. and lasted till midnight. It opened with excellent performance on triple horizontal bar. Wire dancing of Monmatha, balancing of trapeze by Bidhu, boneless play by Sanathan, wonderful performance of Ramen, a boy of eight, on trapeze, Prof. Bose's canon ball play exhibited Herculean strength. He also showed barrel play and jugglery which was applauded by all. Maharaja of Sovabazar was highly pleased with the performance and awarded a gold medal along with a purse of Rs.100. The reporter mentioned that this kind of institution needs patronage and support from the elites as well as ordinary people of the society.[35] The same institution under the able guidance of Prof. Ghosh displayed their performance at the Calcutta orphanage. All the items were so skillfully displayed that the gentlemen of the locality highly appreciated them.[36]

On 11th April, 1873 a grand demonstration of physical feats was arranged by National Society. On 7th January, 1875 a similar event was arranged exclusively for the students of government schools to inspect the progress of their physical competence after imparting physical education in schools. Students from Hooghly, Patna, Dacca, Baharampur College, Madrasha College, Normal School, Habra School, Barackpore School gathered to prove their physical proficiency. Events include acrobatic feats with parallel bar, trapezium, ring, wrestling etc. Students of Dacca University stood champion. It is worth mentioning that majority of the competitors were Bengali, among the students only three were Muslim and one European.[37]

But the decision of not to include the students of National School in this competition raised huge criticism. Amritabazar wrote:

> ... to hold a gymnastic tournament without the students of the National [School] is to perform the act of Hamlet without the hero. We do not think that without the trained students of the school the tournament cannot be made worth seeing.[38]

On 25th December a physical training school was established in Upper Circular Road for promotion of practice of physical exercise among Bengali youth. Rev. Macdonald, Lady

Macdonald, Dr. Krishna Mohan Bandopadhyay, Babu Keshab Chandra Sen, Babu Surendra Nath Bandopadhyay graced the occasion. Physical instructor of the institute Babu Haricharan Mukhopadhyay's exercise display got great applause. Afterwards the students present there engaged themselves in the games of cricket, badminton etc. [39] The National Y.M.C.A School of physical training which began its pioneering work in Madras in 1920 achieved grand success in sector of physical culture. The Bengal Government while trying to imitate the above mentioned physical training programme announced its intention of employing physical instructor in schools whenever a suitable opportunity comes. But the main hindrance of the government was a financial crunch which they intended to overcome soon. [40]

Calcutta Corporation stalwart Babu Sarat Kumar Roy Choudhuri took steps to provide facilities for selected Indian outdoor games in the Corporation squares and to provide funds for the purpose. This was a move to become westernized even in the matter of games. On the motion of Mr. Puller the Corporation passed a resolution recording the need for an immediate extension of playground facilities for children in the squares and parks of the city. [41] Swadeshi movement in Burdwan was in its full swing. Local students resolved to use home-made articles and they were rigorously engaged in physical feats. [42] The boys of the Uttarpara Universal Gymnastic Club held their performance on the Sri Panchami Day. More than 500 gentlemen were present and the play was a grand success. The young boys who appeared were mostly under teens and were highly appreciated for their skilfulness in their parts. Above all a youngster named Manmohan Chakraborty showed excellent feats in balancing which were met with loud applause. [43]

Games and physical feats were displayed even in the Fifteenth Annual Session of the Congress. Bengali periodical *Desh* commented that it is really important to note that the supreme institution of the nation, Congress has at last realized the profound association between sports and nationalism. [44] Pulinbehari Das was the first to train lathi-play to the educated Bengali youth using a disciplined and scientific technique. In 1905 Advocate P. Mitra, Bipin Pal and other nationalist leaders set up various physical culture institutes. Pulinbabu was selected one of the trainers and went to Dacca. His mock fight training imbibed the fighter spirit among the youth. But his most notable contribution was perhaps the book 'Lathi-khela o Asi-khela'. It was the most illustrated and methodical description of the discipline which was a path-breaking example in sports literature. In the review of the above-mentioned book in Amrita Bazar Patrika it has been stated "... it gives us the lessons in the skilful handling of the lathi and the sword sports which are India's own and which till the outlandish games took their place were most popular in this country. Sri Pulinbehari Das published these essays in 'Probashi'." The review further states, "we fully agree with the introductory remarks of the author that there is a close connection between physical strength and moral force. Many of us are cowards and cannot take, when we should, a tooth for a tooth and an eye for an eye because we have not the physical power. It is easier, the author says, to acquire the skill, say in the use of the sword and the lathi than to be a Sandow or a Bhim."

The Senate of University of Calcutta adopted a resolution to appeal to the Government of Bengal to formulate a scheme for extending facilities for military training to college students. Earlier the Senate appointed a physical education committee who recommended that physical training (some form of physical drill or physical exercise or some organized scheme of games for example football and hockey as well as Indian games such as wrestling, club exercise, playing with sticks etc) for at least one year at the rate of three days a week during the school terms at any period of school life should be made obligatory on every student and a certificate to the effect that he has undergone the training. [45]

A similar view was expressed by Dr. Ramesh Chandra Roy in his article titled 'Physical Culture conference' published in *Amrita Bazar Patrika* where he mentioned that,

> I am of the opinion that every child's promotion from one inferior stage to the higher throughout his or her entire period of education should be made dependent on simultaneous progress physically and academically. For this purpose, it is necessary to lay down age by age, the minimum amount of physical development that every pupil should satisfy his examiner about, before he or she is eligible for promotion to the next higher class. [46]

In an article titled 'Bangalir Swastha Samashya O Tar Samadhan' in *Bharatvarsha,* Sanat Kumar Ghosh wrote that the Bengalis are becoming feeble day by day. He lamented that the Bengalis lost their physical vigour only due to their lack of interest in the physical culture. He gave a detailed account of diet chart and exercise regime to be followed regularly to gain the physical prowess. He also emphasised on the proper mental set up which according to him was extremely essential for carrying on with physical vigour. [47] With the initiative of the local youths a gymnasium named 'Young Sabita' was set up in the residence of Sri Kishori Mohan Bandopadyay of Shibtola. Sri Amarendra Nath Sur was appointed as the secretary of the Club. Apart from regular free-hand exercise, the members also practised lathi and dagger play. In order to imbibe more spirit among the youth force the plan to establish a rowing club was in their cards. [48]

Master Jagat Kanta Sil, one of the greatest Bengali boxers of his time wrote 'Byam O Anushilan Path' in order to imbibe regular practice of physical exercise among the Bengalis. The exercises demonstrated in his book along with pictures were easy to follow and perform. He insisted that this kind of exercises can be performed even at home within a small span of time. [49] Even 'My Scientific System of Graduated Physical Culture' by Prof. M.V. Krishna Rao of Bangalore gained market in Bengal and the book was advertised in the pages of *Amrita Bazar Patrika.* [50] Several photographs along with articles for the development of Bengali physique were featured in the contemporary periodicals like *Bharatvarsha* and *Desh* with the view of enhancing the interest of the Bengalis in the sector of sports and gymnastics. Master gymnast Mani Dhar's unique physical feats were featured in *Bangabani* to draw public attention. In some of those pictures he can be seen pulling a loaded cart with his hair. Even he pulled a motor car in its full pick up with the help of his teeth. [51]

Capt. J.N. B nerjee, Bar at Law, secretary of All Bengal Physical Culture Association appealed to the Bengali students for the development of physique. According to him, the physique of the Bengali race of 150 years ago drew the admiration of even the foreigners then residing in Bengal. But the condition became deplorable. He mentioned the main cause of this present physical degeneration of the Bengali people is due to the lack of proper assimilation of food we take. He also mentioned the urgency of fun required for the building of the association with necessary equipments. [52]

In an article titled 'Physical Culture and its importance' Basanta Kumar Banerjee, Director of Physical Culture and Gymnastics, B.M.A.A Association wrote about the importance of physical culture among the youths of Bengal. He mentioned that health in the body produces health in the mind i.e. a powerful mind must have a body built with strong muscles. He appealed to the young friends not to idle away their time any more. Physical exercise strengthens the muscle and quickens digestive function and enables the organs to perform their functions with great effort. To preserve and to maintain good physique the youths of our country must take up regular exercises of 'dan-baithak', parallel bar and light barbell. He further wrote:

> there are various systems of physical culture such as gymnastics, free hand exercises, running, swimming, muscular feats, acrobatics etc. in my opinion as a practical

> man I say that to secure a super human strength and a good control over the muscles of all the parts of the body, the Herculean exercises viz. gymnastics, muscular feats and the systematic methods of practicing the uniform contraction and relaxation of the muscles are best to practice.[53]

Several well-known residents of Calcutta interested in Boxing and physical culture formed an association which was called The Calcutta Sporting Club. After months of labour they have succeeded in acquiring a really first class gymnasium in Indian Mirror Street which has been fitted up at a cost of Rs. 7500. The gymnasium was placed at the disposal of the soldiers taking part in the recent Boxing Tournament and General Strange at the prize distribution thanked the committee for their action. An officer who was up in Calcutta for the tournament, who has had considerable experience and knowledge at Home remarked that it was one of the best fitted Gymnasia he had seen. The idea of the Club is to run Boxing on sound lines under National Sporting Club Rules and to improve the physique of the young men of Calcutta by teaching them physical exercises, boxing etc. The Hon'ble Sir Henry Wheeler, K.C.I.E, C.S.I, is the President of the club and the Hon'ble Mr. F.W. Carter, Vice-President, supported by a strong committee.[54]

Physical Culture in Eastern Bengal

The physical culture movement in Bengal actually started in its eastern fringes. Dacca, Jessore, Mymensingh were the hubs of this movement where men like Shyamakanta Bandopadhyay, Paresh Nath Ghosh indulged in the development of gymnastics and wrestling. Gour Hari Mukhopadhyay and Krishna Lal Basak of north Calcutta showed tremendous enthusiasm for nurturing physical activities from 1870s onwards. Krishna Lal completed his training under the supervision of Boshtom Basak and joined a circus team where he earned a lot. Gour Hari established Aheeritola Model Amateur Athletic Association. This institution gained huge popularity under Gour Hari's able disciple Rash Behari Mukhopadhyay. Gour Babu stressed on the importance of gymnastics as a best medium of developing physique among the youth force of Bengal. He even emphasised the importance of gymnastics for the theatre as well as bioscope actors. Some of the contemporary actors became inclined towards his training academy for gaining popularity in their professional spheres. [55] The New Year celebration in Dacca included a felicitation programme in honour of the sports persons. The reputed lathials of the city were invited and duly recognised for their competence. [56]

Amrita Bazar Patrika reported one Kartik Baruni's fair held every year near Dhuleswari River in Munshirgunj in the district of Dacca. The report also mentioned that........ "this year the mela saw more and more swadeshi goods and swadeshi men showed their physical strengths in different events." [57] As the swadeshi movement gained its momentum from 1905 onwards the physical culture of the Bengalis were somewhat brushed up. The political supremos of the provincial as well as local levels wanted to modify the physical culture ethos from the grass-root level. Thus students were targeted. Lathi play became popularised as a part of indigenous game. Newspaper report reveals that every Sunday evening beginning about 4 o' clock, gangs of school boys, teachers and students assembled at a place known as Simdie Akhara to receive instruction in lathi play in order to be prepared. [58] In another report it is mentioned that in Khandarpara (Faridpur) swadeshi sabha was inaugurated for encouraging the use of indigenous products. A lathi play was organized on this occasion where local lathials participated with full vigour and strength. [59]

Students of Comilla clashed with police with lathis. Here it may be noted that it was a regular practice among the students to groom themselves in the art of lathi play. [60] *Bengal Times* reports that one student was hurled down and another or others horse whipped by an employee of Messers Ralli Brothers for reasons that have not transpired. A mob of trained athletes went down to

Narayangunj after this incident to wreck a blood curdling vengeance and thus repair injured honour. [61]

Conclusion

The class structure of this physical culture movement in colonial Bengal is somewhat contrary to Bourdieu's formulation on body habitus. Bourdieu's work stresses the role of the body in the creation and reproduction of social difference by bearing the imprint of social class. The working class supposedly visualise their body as an instrument to earn subsistence. They tend to characterise their body as a machine in relation to health, illness, exercise and lifestyle which should always be kept working properly. On the contrary, the dominant classes purportedly view the body as a project and have available resources to choose the course of action and modes of functioning of the body. Again in comparison to working-class groups, the middle-class is deemed to have more control over their health which can be exercised by choosing an appropriate lifestyle. [62] In the case of Bengal, such class distinction could not be made since physical culture, initially an upper middle class undertaking, was permeated among all classes across regions.

Notes

1. Elleka Boehmer, *Colonial and Post-colonial Literature: Migrant Metaphors*; Oxford University Press, 1995
2. Rudyard Kipling, *Selected Poetry*; Cambridge: Chadwyck-Healey, 2000
3. A Mangan, *The Game, Ethic and Imperialism*; London-Viking, 1985
4. Ronald Hyam, *Empire and Sexuality: The British Experience*; Manchester, 1990
5. Michel Foucault, "*Technologies of the Self*", *Ethics Subjectivity and Truth*, Ed. Paul Rabinow, New York Press, 1997
6. John Rosselli, *The Self-Image of Effeteness: Physical Education and Nationalism in Nineteenth Century Bengal*; Past and Present 86, 1980
7. Mrinalini Sinha, *Colonial Musculinity: The Manly Englishman and the Effeminate Bengali in the Late Nineteenth Century*; Manchester University Press, 1995

8. Aurobindo, S., 1990 reprint, *On education,* Pondicherry, Aurobindo Ashram, p. 68-69.
9. Ashis Nandy, *The Intimate Enemy: Loss and Recovery of Self under Colonialism, Delhi: Oxford University Press, 1994.*
10. John Rosselli, *The Self-Image of Effeteness: Physical Education and Nationalism in Nineteenth Century Bengal;* Past and Present 86, 1980
11. Joseph S. Alter; Celibacy, Sexuality and Nationalism in North India in *Bodies in Contact* edited by Tony Ballantyne and Antoinette Burton; Duke University Press, London 2005.
12. For details see Mrinalini Sinha
13. John Rosselli, *The Self-Image of Effeteness: Physical Education and Nationalism in Nineteenth Century Bengal;* Past and Present 86, 1980
14. Indira *Chowdhury, The Frail Hero and Virile History: Gender and the Politics of Culture in Colonial Bengal; Delhi, Oxford University Press*
15. John Rosselli, *The Self-Image of Effeteness: Physical Education and Nationalism in Nineteenth Century Bengal;* Past and Present 86, 1980
16. *Bengalee,* May 29, 1907
17. *Amrita Bazar Patrika,* May 5, 1908
18. *Englishman,* September 28, 1906
19. *Bengalee,* September 29, 1906
20. *Bharatvarsha,* September 8, 1947
21. *Indian Mirror,* August 17, 1905
22. *Bengalee,* May 30,1907
23. *Hindu Melar Itibrittwa,* Jogesh Chandra Bagol; 2009
24. Ibid
25. *Amrita Bazar Patrika,* February 14, 1875
26. *Hindu Melar Itibrittwa,* Jogesh Chandra Bagol; 2009
27. Satyendra Nath Tagore, *Amar Balya Kotha O Amar Bombay Probash*
28. *Amrita Bazar Patrika*
29. *The Statesman,*
30. *Amrita Bazar Patrika,* April 22, 1922
31. *Hindoo Patriot,* June 11, 1919
32. *Bengalee,* February 16, 1906.
33. *Bengalee,* July 20, 1910.
34. *Hindu Patriot,* October 28, 1912.
35. *Amrita Bazar Patrika,* October 21, 1907
36. *Amrita Bazar Patrika,* November 6, 1907
37. *Sulabh Samachar,* January 12, 1875.
38. *Amrita Bazar Patrika,* December 17, 1874
39. *Sambad Prabhakar,* December 30, 1878
40. *Amrita Bazar Patrika,* May 23, 1933
41. *Englishman,* July 26, 1926

42. *Indian Mirror*, October 20, 1905
43. *Bengalee*, February 20, 1910
44. *Desh*, December 28, 1935
45. *Englishman*, May 2, 1927
46. *Amrita Bazar Patrika*, March 15, 1936
47. *Bharatvarsha*, Magh BS 1344.
48. *Bangabani*, Baisakh 15, BS 1337
49. *Bangabani*, October 19, 1932
50. *Amrita Bazar Patrika*, July 27, 1927.
51. *Bangabani*, September 28, 1932.
52. *Amrita Bazar Patrika*, September 14, 1927
53. *Amrita Bazar Patrika*, July 25, 1928
54. *Indian Planters Gazette*, 1918
55. *Bharatvarsha*, Shraban BS 1343.
56. *Bengal Times*, Dacca, January 6, 1900
57. *Amrita Bazar Patrika*, December 19, 1905
58. *Bengal Times*, Dacca, September 12, 1906
59. *Amrita Bazar Patrika*, October 16, 1905
60. *Amrita Bazar Patrika*, December 7, 1905.
61. *Bengal Times*, Dacca, October 11, 1905
62. Bourdieu, 'Sport and Social Class', *Social Science Information* 17 (6), 1978, pp. 819-40.

Constructing Colonial Masculinity through Everyday Life:
Narrating the Practice of Game as Sports among European Officers in the North-East India

Binayak Dutta

Colonialism represents a unique combination of ideology and practice presenting its own justification, expressed in diverse fields. One such practice is games and sports. The transformation of sports into a platform to justify colonialism is today well researched. But what is lacking in such narratives are the stories of North East of India. This paper tries to bridge this absence. The purpose of this study is to trace the construction of colonial masculinity in North East India. This region has had a rich tradition of games and sports which found place in old Assamese scriptures and medieval texts. [1] This perception had been passed down to the colonial administrators as well. Col. Wilson, the author of the text Sports and Service in Assam and Elsewhere, and an officer based in this region, referred to his commandant making a reference to this region as, "Assam is a first rate place for all kinds of sports ..." [2] This perception was reinforced over time when other colonial officers like John Butler recorded their notes of their posting in this region. These notes of Colonial military officers who recorded their experience in this region is the clay that has helped to make this narrative.

Of the many practices that is in vogue in the re-writing of History today is the use of private papers and memoirs in the narration. This movement to move away from the statist archives has made the narratives more inclusive and incisive. With the historical scholarship of Thompson, Ladurie and Ginsburg, and their like, the use of diaries and memoirs have gained legitimacy today more than ever before. Assam has been central to the construction of colonialism in what was considered the region north east of the Bengal Presidency. The name has stuck for this region till today in official and administrative parlance, which is being adopted here as well. Though these narratives were intended to contribute towards reinforcing both colonialism and colonial masculinity their unconscious reference to the native gaming practices in these texts also help to challenge ideas of difference between the west and the East and western claims of superiority, which are foundational to the construction of colonialism itself.

While there could be no doubt that the military machine was the iron structure that made colonial rule possible, it was a complex web of stereotypical practices which justified it. Therefore, if colonial military service was only for the fearless and the manly, meaning the British, gaming added lusture to it. This construction of colonial masculinity had varied dimensions and multiple meanings. The construction of a sporting complex within military garrisons and the regular engagement of the colonial military officers with the practice of hunting or game, as it was referred to, were not an end in itself but were all part of a well-crafted colonial strategy to inscribe in native minds the awe of the colonial, represented as virile, manly and fearless. This construction was a picture of contrasts. The European was pitted against the native who was pictured as effeminate and incapable of masculine practice or tradition. Scholars engaged in the study of colonialism have identified colonial constructions of stereotypical distinctions between the British and the native which helped to justified colonial rule. Games and sports was a part of it. One such account from this region is of David Scott who was the Agent of the Governor General in Assam since 1826 to his death in 1831 and in that sense the first European colonial administrator of the region. Major Adam White, the author of a Memoir on Scott wrote in 1831, "His favourite sport was hunting the wild bear; this amusement, when at Goruckpore, before his appointment to Assam, He would follow in the hottest season, on horseback, and sometimes unaccompanied." [4] Probably for Scott's biographer this information about his hunting habits added to his picture of the robust administrator of region described as a "stout man weighing about fourteen stones marching across the heights between Gowhatty and Nunclow." [5] This narration of a part of the everyday life of the colonial military officers was a deliberate attempt at creating a larger than life image of the European colonist. The intention of colonial biographies and memoirs were to construct hierarchies between the colonizer and the colonized- an encounter between a higher civilization and a lower one. [6]

But unlike other areas of India, for both sports and game in north east India was a case of difference. It was a region which could prove that such practices were not exclusively western and in the practice of which the image of masculine and brave European often faced a beating. Colonial officers who visited the distant parts of the north east often ran away from the hunt when faced with an animal charge and resistance and were surprised at the discovery of natives also indulging in gaming with as much enthusiasm as the Europeans. "I was surprised to see many people in canoes, hunting a group of young wild boar that the torrents had pushed into the river ..." [7] And yet hunting continued to form a part of European attempts at mythicizing colonial masculinity in North East India as well through their everyday accounts.

The three diaries which are our concern here belong to European officers who had come to the north East guided by the demands of their colonial duty. All the three officers vividly describe European indulgence in Game as sport in the eighteenth and nineteenth century. Uncontained European excitement at the prospect of indulging in game in the region can be seen in the account of Scott who in as early as mid-1820s says, "Imagination can scarce conceive wilder scene than are introduced by the sporting in Assam." [8] Though few Europeans had had the opportunity of visiting this distant land, [9] till the fifteenth century, it was not unknown to them. A Dutch traveler had visited Assam along with the Mughals which was followed by the French. [10] Of the Europeans, the French were the first European Company to make a formal request to establish a Factory in Assam. The French ambassador was Jean- Baptiste Chevalier, [11] whose account, *Historical Memoir and Journal of Travels in Assam Bengal and Tibet* is one of the Texts used to construct this narrative. British engagements with this region were post-Plassey. The English East India Company victory at Bauxar created an opportunity for the Company officials to engage commercially with this region that lay proximate to their holding in Bengal. But the real opportunity came with Company engagement with the Anglo Burmese War 1824-1826. Victory of the company in the war gave them access to and control over Assam, which became a foothold for their expansion in this region. The entry of military officers into this region was part of the Company plan to administer Assam as a Non-Regulated Province, which was closely connected with the entrustment of military officers with administrative duties. [12] Both Major John Butler and Lieutenant Colonel Alban Wilson were appointed in this region as part of this system. The other texts, in chronological terms is Major John Butler's Travels and Adventures in the Province of Assam originally published in 1855 and Lieutenant Colonel Alban Wilson's Sports and Service in Assam and Elsewhere first published in 1873.

Though till the second half of the twentieth century, hunting and killing of wildlife as indiscriminate killing of wild animals for pleasure and recreation was officially called sports, such activities in North East India have not received much scholarly attention from historians writing Sports history or history of Gender. Fewer still have attempted to link the two. Constructing masculinity was often in the context of man-women relations or division of labour and authority between them. Construction of the same by narrativizing the practice of sports and games indulged by the colonial officers is few and far between. Separated by a century and more these narratives offer interesting entry ports for revisiting the colonial practice of sports and games in this colonial periphery along with the ideas of masculinity itself both from the perspective of the British and the French. Chevalier's visit to Assam is in a sense one of the earliest European account of European gaming practices in this region. Sent on a mission to Assam to set up a factory by the French Governor at Chandernagore, Chevalier discussed in great detail his hunting expeditions in the Assam Bengal border. His description was vivid." In the evening, I was hunting on a mountain two hours away from Jouguigoupat towards the south, namely Pangeroten ..." [13] In another part of his memoir he wrote that, " I saw a number of peacocks and killed many. I was chasing these animals when I was interrupted by a rather large herd of elephants that I saw on the edge of the mountain. I did not want to run against them and took the prudent decision to return to my bazra promptly." [14] Chevalier's account was often interspersed with detailed accounts of his hunt which was also related to the respect that such practices brought for him from the local people. One such account was his report on his visit to Goalpara. "In the evening I hunted in the mountains of Gualpara which are filled with an amazing number of various kinds of game, especially peacocks and stag. Wild boar are also found in abundance, besides bears, but they are not dangerous. We saw many running away in front of us. Our hunt ended with the death of 50 peacocks, a stag and a wild boar. The people of the country brought me two wild boar as present. Hence the distribution I made to the soldiers of my detachment was ample. Upon my return from the hunt, the Jamadar of Gualpara came to pay me a visit abroad my Bazra. He brought some amounts of practically everything that his country could produce in terms of rice, other grains and fruits ..." [15] These narratives of game were not just descriptive accounts of recreational activities of these colonial officials but were also signposts to prove western practice of equity as "... the distribution I made to the soldiers of my detachment was ample" and the idea of European hegemony over the non-European natives, as "upon my return from the hunt, the jamadar of gualpara came to pay me a visit ..." [16] Game was an activity that was mediated by the European understanding of their colonial duty and these accounts were records for an intended audience- the colonial governments and their immediate sponsors.

Separated by more than a century from Chevalier is Major John Butler whose Travels and Adventures in the Province of Assam is my next account. Butler was an officer of the English East India Company who came to Assam in 1837 to serve the Company and was appointed as the Principal Assistant to the Commissioner to the Nagaon District. [17] From the inception of colonial intervention in Assam, military officers played an important role in the Administration of Assam. [18] The administration of Assam was governed by the Non-Regulation system which facilitated the wide spread employment of military officers in civilian administration. [19] Butler was one of such military officers who came to Assam in the initial years of Colonial Company rule and played a vigorous role in the expansion of the Company domains in Assam, the Naga Hills and Cachar. [20] Butler provides a comprehensive account of colonial hunting practices in Assam. To the colonial officers Assam with its vast jungles was a natural sports field. In his language, "From the vast extent of waste or jungle land everywhere met with in Assam, there are, perhaps few countries that can be compared with it for affording diversion, of all kinds for the English sportsman." [21] To the Englishman who had come to this distant land to conquer and subdue the native, sports was a spectacle. It was one of the many arenas where the European would mentally and physically jostle with the native and prove his supremacy and assert his right to rule. For the colonial officer the true quality was to be fearless and the duty was to overcome all challenges. The hunt or Shikar was the miniature version of the world that he was expected to experience overcome and dominate. Butler was in this sense candid. For the Englishmen who had been trained in the school of European masculinity, Manliness was indispensible from his love for sports. For British officers, trained in the habits of Fox Hunting, Assam was an irresistible tract for keen sportsmen "who enjoy excellent sport". [22]

By the 19th century game had firmly entrenched itself within the colonial lexicon of power, in true English tradition. Perhaps, the gradual rise of the Company consciousness of its role as rulers of India, replacing the Mughals also helped to integrate the royal practice of shikar [23] into the lives of its officers to give their dominance in India a regal legitimacy. Therefore all steps were taken by the English men to cover their weakness and construct an image of themselves which justified their hegemony. Unlike the accounts of Chevalier, written a hundred years before Butler, when the European colonial ambition had not been properly conceived and far from realization, Butler was much more cautious. If Chevalier could candidly write of his fears and admit that he would run and climb the trees to save himself on being charged by wild animals, butler's admission of his latent fears and apprehensions were couched in the language of a general advisory for his fellow Englishmen. The contrasts between the two accounts were obvious. If Chevalier wrote, "[b]othered by the fact that these ferocious animals happened to be on our path every day, and having had to give up the place several times, I asked some soldiers who were with me to shoot them and immediately climb the trees; as for me I did the same," [24] Butler wrote ..."the reader must not imagine a field day in Assam un attended with danger, or less exciting than fox-hunting ..." and "... all wild animals of the forest may be fearlessly encountered and overcome."[25] The account of Butler is interesting. It not only listed the hunting methods but also presented a moderately comprehensive list of hunted animals in the jungles of Assam. Tigers, buffaloes, rhinoceroses, deer and hogs were the favoured animals. For a colonial officer of the Company, in the 19th century hunting had become part of his life and shooting wild animals, his favourite sport. Butler therefore mentions," the most pleasant sport in Assam is deer shooting ... and in open plains many may be killed in a day ..."[26] Both Butler and White, the author of the Memoir of David Scott, shared a striking similarity. Both glorified of colonial officers indulging in solitary hunting excursions. Often these accounts were deliberate which helped to highlight the fearless quality of the English officers and legitimize their position as natural rulers. White's account of Scott as Magistrate and Registrar at Goruckpore was part of his attempts to mystify his subject and make him into a hero ... "His favourite sport was hunting the wild bear; this amusement, when at Gorukhpore, before his appointment to Assam, He would follow in the hottest season, on horseback, and sometimes unaccompanied" surely added to Scott's glory. It added Scott's name to a rare brand of reckless, enthusiastic Colonial officer sportsmen who ventured alone on a hunt and "enjoyed excellent sports".[27] These accounts of game continued to be written all along the nineteenth century who came to Assam.

The third account that is used to construct this narrative is an account of Lt. Col. Alban Wilson, entitled Sports and Service in Assam and Elsewhere, published in 1873. Wilson was initially in the Punjab but had opted to a service in Assam in the Gurkha Regiment, then engaged in an expedition in Assam. Wilson's account is a unique text replete with anecdotes and helps to justify an account of Assam as indispensible to construct Colonial history of Sports. But in it one can also see descriptive accounts of native tradition of games and sports and fearlessness which runs counter to the ideas of sports and game being an exclusively

European activity.

An interesting part of Wilson's account is the story of the Manipuri sport of native polo or Sagol Kangjai as it is locally referred to. Wilson's account of the game of polo is not only revealing of a complex native sport played by men but is an account of reverse colonialism as well. In Wilson's words, "the game of polo was originally brought from Manipur to Calcutta by an officer of my regiment named Sherer, who died a Major General ... From Calcutta it soon spread all over India and to England. It is said to have been started in the state about 1600 A.D ..." [28] Another interesting account of Wilson that exalts the native is about the Leopard kills in Shillong, which in his time abound the area in which he was stationed. The first story was about a leopard that had been sighted near the station in which he was based was in a way uninteresting because it was a regular account of around fifty men led by the author ganging together for a leopard hunt. But what was interesting was his account of another tribal native who walked up to the author within minutes of author killing his leopard with another leopard carcass. "before the skin was pegged out, a Khasia (an inhabitant of those parts) appeared with a rusty old musket and behind him were some others, bearing a leopard slung on a pole. We looked at it and asked where he got it, and we were told it was the one I had fired at first, which was hit and had crawled through the ferns into the bed of the stream. He had noticed this and when we went away, fetched his gun and finished it off. He now brought me the beast in the hope of reward, which he speedily got. The first shot had smashed its hind leg and raked its belly, so it couldn't spring , or it undoubtedly would have attacked some of us, who must have been quite close to it when the men came up to the second one on the road." [29] Wilson's accounts are vivid accounts of the encounter between colonial and native masculinity and the grudging respect of the European for the native. If game and sports were indices to construct the masculine, the native in colonial north east would not fare worse than the Europeans who had colonized him.

By the nineteenth century when Wilson's Commandant in Punjab told him that Assam was a great place for all kinds of sport, and as a man who was fond of sports he could go there, the idea of sports had acquired several deeper meanings. Sports and Game had become synonymous with the performance of colonialism itself. A great part of the land in Assam was "waste or jungle" in colonial perception and the colonial flag had to negotiate and subdue this wilderness to establish itself in the true sense of the term. Therefore colonial engagement with the wilderness in this colonial periphery made game a legitimate part of colonialism in practice. As Colonialism began to be reinterpreted in recent times, this growing realization of sports and games as part of the colonial contest has found popular expressions as well. *Lagaan*, the celebrated movie by Ashutosh Gowarikar is one of its finest expressions. But nothing similar has come on this peripheral region of the Indian Empire. But there is no denial that beyond these symbolical attempts to integrate colonialism and sports for popular minds, the connectivity between the two is today more academically established than ever before. In establishing this link, in this colonial periphery, the relevance of these colonial memoirs is something that we are only gradually beginning to discover.

Notes

1. Pradyumna Sharma, *Social Contexts of Traditional games of Assam*, in Proceedings of North East India history Association, Goalpara Session 2007
2. Alban Wilson, *Sports and Service in Assam and Elsewhere*, Guwahati, 1987
3. See John Mac Kenzie's introduction to Mrinalini Sinha's *Colonial Masculinity The 'manly' Englishman and the 'effeminate Bengali' in the late Nineteenth Century*, p. vii
4. Major Adam White, *A Memoir of The Late David Scott*, p. 217
5. Major Adam White, *A Memoir of The Late David Scott*, p. 216

6. See Major Adam White 's memoirs of Scott where in a description of an interaction between the Europeans and the people of this region, he quotes Scott in saying," the treating with people of lower civilization requires the use of increased vigilance...",p. 228
7. Jean Deloche, *Adventures of Jean Baptiste Chevalier in Eastern India,* p. 149
8. Major Adam White, *A Memoir of The Late David Scott*, pp. 228-229
9. Here distant is used bothin the context of geographical distance from Europe and the psychological barrier imposed on Western entry into Assam by the Ahom rulers, for details see S. K. Bhuyan, *Anglo Assamese Relations,*
10. Jean Deloche, *Adventures of Jean Baptiste Chevalier in Eastern India,* p. 12
11. Chevalier was sent as the French Ambasador to Assam by the French Governor of Chandernagore Renault de Saint Germain to acquire land for the establishment of a factory in Assam.
12. H.K. Barpujari, *Comprehensive History of Assam,* Vol. IV, p. 27
13. Jean Deloche, *Adventures of Jean Baptiste Chevalier in Eastern India,* p. 138
14. Ibid,p. 143
15. Ibid, p. 148
16. Ibid
17. L.N.Tamuly (ed) *Travels and Adventures in the Province of Assam* by John Butler, See editor's note
18. H.K.Barpujari, *Comprehensive History of Assam,* Vol.IV, p. 25
19. Ibid, p. 27
20. Tamuly, opcit, Editor's Note.
21. Ibid, p. 160.
22. Ibid
23. It is today an acknowledged position that Hunting was an element of Kingship in Mughal era and Mughal kings like Akbar and Jahangir led elaborate hunting expeditions, which were not an end in itself but an exercise at image building and reconescence mission before launching a military expedition
24. Jean Deloche, *Adventures of Jean Baptiste Chevalier in Eastern India,* p. 149
25. *Travels and Adventures in the Province of Assam by John Butler,* p. 159
26. Ibid, p. 162
27. Ibid, p. 159
28. Alban Wilson, *Sports and Service in Assam and Elsewhere,* Guwahati, 1987, p. 128
29. Ibid, p. 28

Footballing Nationalism in Colonial Bengal: a Comparative Analysis

Debashis Majumder

Introduction

During the second half of 19th century as an inseparable part of the new emerging colonial culture certain new sporting activities were also introduced in Bengali society. From this period the physical sporting activities started to become popular among the native masses. To destroy the colonial myth of the physical weakness of Bengali people the physical exercises and sporting activities became more regular in practice. One section of Bengali society also tried to prove that they were equally competent with the Europeans in all sorts of physical challenges. Bengali entrepreneurs of aristocrat families also involved themselves in certain activities. Nabogopal Mitra and Priyanath Bose introduced modern circus in Bengali society. Priyanath Bose gave prior importance to the physical performances like trapeze and gymnastics in his circus. Colonel Suresh Biswas; the famous Bengali adventurer was also a person of this period. [1] The adventurous Bengali novels like *Chander Pahar* of Bibhutibhushan Bandyopadhyay and *Jokher Dhon* and *Abar Jokher Dhon* of Hemendra Kumar Roy are also set on the background of this particular time period. During this phase the colonial sports like football, cricket and hockey were introduced to the Bengali society. These sports gave birth to a new sporting culture in Bengal. Along with the native sports these new sporting activities started to popularize during this time among the common masses. Though at first these colonial sports were generally limited within the Europeans and Anglo Indian communities but gradually the local peoples started to participate in these sporta and with this their popularities started to increase massively. As a result of that soon competitive measures were introduced in these sporting activities. The Indian Football Association (IFA) is founded in 1893 in Calcutta as the first ever football association in India. [2] The Bengal Hockey Association (BHA) and Cricket Association of Bengal (CAB) are founded in the same year of 1908. [3] So towards the end of the 19th century and in the beginning of the 20th century a completely new sporting platform was emerged in Bengal. These sporting activities played a great role behind the emergence and spread of nationalist zeal among the common masses. But in case of Bengal gradually the nationalist expressions became more connected with the game of football than any other sports.

The Great Successes of Local Football Clubs

The European masters enjoyed the early superiority in all these colonial sports. In Bengal the football clubs gradually turned into the representatives of the popular identities. Clubs like Calcutta Football Club, Hastings, Dalhousie Athletic Club, Rangers and many other army teams represented the European identity, [4] while the clubs like Shobhabazar, Kumortuli, Mohun Bagan, Aryan, Mohammedan Sporting, East Bengal etc. had the pure Indian identity. Therefore through the club identities struggles of national clashes started in the football field and there the successes of the local team against the superior European sides generally considered by the common masses and the Indian victory against the colonial dominators. Thus the Footballing successes of the local clubs often treated as the national successes and in this way certain football events boosted the nationalist zeal. In 1892 Shobhabazar Club first time ever as an Indian club defeated the all European side East Surrey with 2-1 scoreline. [5] But the biggest glory in this regard was achieved by Mohun Bagan in 1911. In 1911 in a very crucial year of Indian history Mohun Bagan won the IFA Shield as the first Indian club by defeating all the Euopean sides. This particular even created many nationalist myths among the local masses. This particular victory was celebrated as an Indian success against the colonial masters and thus this event very much boosted the nationalist movements of contemporary India. [6] During 1930s Mohammedan Sporting showed exceptional brilliance in the field of football and virtually ended the European supremacy from Indian football. Mohammedan Sporting not just won the prestigious Calcutta Football League (First Division) in 1934 as the first Indian football club but also won it consecutive five times from 1934 to 1938. In addition to that the club also won the IFA Shield in 1936. [7] All these successes very much boosted the national pride and gradually football became the soul of sporting nationalism in Bengal.

It is also true that in colonial period India also achieved even greater successes in the field of hockey when the national hockey team won three consecutive Olympic Golds in 1928, 1932 and 1936. In 1932 Los Angeles Olympics hockey India even registered a 24-1 win against the host U.S.A. [8] but still it could not left enough influence on Indian nationalism like the Mohun Bagan's IFA Shield victory of 1911. Because the Indian hockey team of that time was generally regarded as a British-Indian team. The team was created both with the Indian, Anglo-Indian and British players so these successes were not considered as pure Indian victories. Besides Dhyan Chand, Rup Chand the English born players like Richard James Allen also played key roles in those victories. [9] Even in domestic level also most of the hockey teams were created with British-Indian collaboration. In 1933 Beighton Cup was won by Jhansi Heroes. Indian hockey legend Dhyan Chand played for this team. This team was also a mixed team built both with Indian and European players. [10] So unlike football hockey could not provide the direct clashes between the national identities. Therefore the Bengali masses became more attracted towards the game of football to get more nationalist inspirations.

Bare foot Football in Colonial Era: The Indian Style

At the beginning football was restricted within the British army regiments and Anglo-Indian communities. Nagendra Prasad Sarbadhikari introduced the Indian touch in the game of football. But in the early stage generally the boys of aristocratic Bengali families became familier with the game. The early exponents of Indian football such as Dukhiram Majumdar and Manmatha Ganguly also opined to follow the English style to play the game. But the simplicity of the game soon attracted the common masses towards the game. Gradually the local people developed their own style in playing this colonial game. The economic condition of the local teams could not bring all the necessary equipments. Most of the local players started to play without boots in their feet. In the beginning it created massive disadvantages against the European teams. But gradually the Indian players attained new kind of mastery with this unique Indian style of the game and in the first half of the 20th century during the Swadeshi era it became a perfect swadeshi style of laying the colonial game. [11] On 29th July, 1911 Mohun Bagan made history as the first Indian club by winning the prestigious IFA Shield. In this team 10 out of 11 players played without the boots. (Only Reverend Sudhir Chatterjee played with boots) This particular success also came in the particular year when the colonial government dropped the matter of proposed partition of Bengal due to the efforts of swadeshi and boycott movement but transferred the capital from Calcutta to Delhi. Therefore the historic victory of Mohun bagan left deep impact among the common masses and thus played a key role in flourishing the nationalist sentiment. [12]

On the other hand sports like hockey and cricket needed the necessary equipments more strictly. Cricket is particularly the game of aristocrats. Even in England the concept of high birth and gentlemanship was associated with the game of cricket. During the mid 19th century in Western India at first the Parsi community adopted the game as a medium to develop their business relationship with the British government and English entrepreneurs. Therefore in India also the concept of high birth and blue blood were associated with this particular colonial sport. [13] In 1932 when the first Indian cricket team was sent to its first official tour in England, Colonel C.K. Nayudu was the fittest man to lead the team. But due to the concept of royality or blue blood Maharaja of Patiala became the first choice. When he removed himself from the side due to his physical issue then also Maharaja of Porbandar; a man of 47 years of age was chosen to skip the team. Dewan of Ghanshyamsinghji was his deputy in the team. When both these two persons became unfit only then C.K. Nayudu received the official credit to lead the team in the very first test match on foreign soil. [14] Because of the same issue glorious talents like Sarobindu Nath Banerjee alias Shute Banerjee was also dropped from the national team on various occasions. In spite of his brilliant performances in all levels of domestic cricket he only received the honour of playing for the national team just once in an official test match. [15] Due to all tese reasons the common masses of Bengal became much closer to the game of football.

Direct Relation between Football and Nationalism in Colonial Era

Than any other colonial sport football had direct connections with the nationalist ideas. Swami Vivekanada himself argued more than once about the effectiveness of football in building up of discipline and national spirit. During his visit to Dhaka in 1901 the eminent lawyer Satish Chandra Roychowdhury met with him. There Vivekananda expressed his support towards the game of football as it was capable of returning the humiliation to the white colonial masters. During 1880s Swami Vivekananda used to regularly visit Calcutta Maidan to witness the clashes of nagendraprasad's Shobhabazar club with its English opponents. Netaji Subhas Chandra Basu was also an urdent supporter of the game of football. [16] Even Mahatma Mohandas Karamchand Gandhi also encouraged the game of football during his stay in Tolstoy farm in South Africa.

Except that during the colonial era in many occasions bloodsheds happened on the football field and this particular game became closer to the national politics. On August 30, 1931 Haripada Bhattacharya; a follower of Masterda Surya Sen killed the notorious Deputy Superintendent of Police of Chittagong Assanullah during a football match. On September 2, 1933 District Magistrate D.E. Burge was shot dead by Anath Panja and Mrigen Dutta during a football match held between Mohammedan Sporting and Town club. [17] Many other similar events were also happened on the football ground during the colonial period. In this way the game of football became closer to the national sentiment among the Bengali common masses. The Bengali society received severe nationalist inspirations from the different Footballing events of colonial era.

Conclusion

Though the colonial games of hockey, cricket and football introduced in the Indian society during the mid 19th century but in Bengal gradually Footballing nationalism emerged to most prominent aspect. There are some specific reasons behind this. The colonial exploitation brought miserable result to the common Indian masses. In Bengal the common peoples needed something to get back their fighting spirit, they needed the inspiration of speed and power to hit back and football provided all these needs to the common masses during the colonial era. It is football, which first showed that the Europeans are not invincible and the Indians are not by any chance inferior to them. It is football, which taught the people of Bengal to protest against the exploitation. The Bengali common masses found the connection of their heart with the game of football and gradually football becomes much more than a game in Bengali society and turns into an inseparable part of Bengali life and culture. Football turned into an eternal soul mate to the people of Bengal. Therefore the way for the rise of Footballing nationalism became much easier in Bengal. So the game of football played a very significant role behind the rise and spread of nationalist ideas in colonial Bengal.

Notes

1. Roselli, John; '*The Self-Image of Effeteness: Physical education and Nationalism in Nineteenth Century Bengal*'; 'Past & Present, No. 86', February, 1980, pp. 10-25
2. Mitra, Soumen; '*in Search of an Identity: The History of Football in Colonial Calcutta*', Das Gupta & Co. Pvt. Ltd., Kolkata, 2006, p. 55
3. www.webindia123.com/sports/index.htm
4. Kumar, Shibram (ed.); RB (Rakhal Bhattacharya) rochito, '*Kolkata Football*', Prabhabati Prakashani, Kolkata, 2002, p. 67
5. Mitra, Soumen; Op.cit, pp. 36-40
6. Nandi, Moti; '*Calcutta Soccer*', '*Calcutta the Living City: The Present and the Future*', Vol. 2, Sukanta Chowdhury (ed.), Oxford University Press, Kolkata, 1990, p. 318
7. Ibid, p. 318
8. www.webindia123.com/sports/olympics/indiaolympics.htm
9. Richard James Allen was the goalkeeper of Indian field hockey team in the Olympics of 1928 (Amsterdam), 1932 (Los Angeles), 1936 (Berlin). In all these Olympics India achieved gold medal. In 1928 Amsterdam Olympics under the Indian goal R.J. Allen did not received a single goal which was an Olympic record. Both in 1932 Los Angeles Olympics and in 1936 Berlin Olympics he received only a single goal. Thus as a goalkeeper in 3 consecutive Olympics he only received 2 goals and it was also an Olympic record in field hockey.
10. www.bharatiyahockey.org
11. Mitra, Soumen; Op.cit, p. 36
12. Ibid, p. 113

13. History of Indian Cricket-Before 1930, www.zeenews.india.com
14. Mukherjee, Raju; '*Cricket in India: Origin and Heroes*', UBS Publishers' Distributors Pvt. Ltd., New Delhi, 2005, p. 14
15. www.cricketarchieve.com
16. Mukherjee, Sumit; '*Football in Colonial Bengal in Nationalist Perspective*', '*90 MINUTES*', Vol. 2, Issue 1, January-March, 2010, Subhransu Roy (ed.), Valerian Soccer Foundation, Kolkata, 2010, pp. 36-37
17. Ibid, p. 3

Alternative Trends in Bengal Football Fandom : From Nationalism to Sub-nationalism

Amitava Chatterjee & Amitabha Bandopadhyay

Research on the nature of sports audience has been predominantly concerned with those attending live events and outlooks, the process through which sports is consumed by the people everyday life. This pattern of research about the nature of football fandom has also offered ethnographic accounts delineating more complex relationships between supporters and their clubs that indicate associations that go beyond match day scenarios. [1] Research on football in particular supports this notion tending as it has done to focus on 'exceptional' forms of support through the mass literature based around hooliganism in and around football ground and interpretations based upon the perceived responses to increased commodification in football by most 'dedicated' types of supporters that contributes to the 'resistance' movement as fanzine writers or members and organizers of independent support groups. [2]

To avoid the dichotomies constructed around authenticity of football fandom, I argue that fan cultures should be conceptualized as 'imagined communities' [3] that their natures are not subject to consideration of truth validity. Acknowledging the views of Readhead and King, I focus on the point that at no time in history has football fandom remained static in such a way that recourse to a traditional mode of support can be made insisting rather that all fan cultures are "an amalgam of historical episodes, myths traditions" and plain in accuracies. [4] King's works in particular shows how important these "invented traditions" are to the identities of certain types of supporters. [5]

The colonial sporting culture of Calcutta crystallized around numerous clubs that came into vogue throughout the nineteenth century. These clubs were mainly formed by the Indian elite, who taking the cue from the British rules organized themselves into sporting clubs. These clubs were usually built around deep cross currents of social tensions, arising in turn out of contemporary anger against the racist colonial rule or out of increasing commercial upheaval and sub-regional feeling. The natural outcome of this was violence while its most obvious forum of expression could be found in the sporting arena. Football arena primarily became the place of unrest. Football field experienced sharpness of racial drives. Editorials and newspaper articles deplored this humiliation. *Dainik Basumati* in one sub-articles reported about growing popularity in football among Bengali's and subsequent religious animosity to say ;

> There is no harm in black and white play, together but if a spirit of social animosity enters in to sports, that can not be of any good. This spirit has been growing in intensity since the time the Mohun Bagan team won the I.F.A shield in 1911. As a result of this spirit black Indians have sometimes to suffer humiliations and insults at the hands of the whites while witnessing the games and even thrashings are restored to. [6]

The Mohun Bagan victory also provided an occasion for communal amity. When the victory procession of tile team was on their way to Thanthania Kali Temple of Calcutta, the Muslims rushed to Dharmatala with a band party to join the same. In fact, they were allowed to lead the rally with their beating drums and bands. *The Mussalman* wrote: '... although Mohun Bagan was a team composed *of Bengali* Hindus, the jubilation in consequence of its success was in fact a sense of universal joy, which pervaded the feeling of the Hindus, the Mohammedans and the Christians alike. The members of the Muslim Sporting Club were almost mad and rolling on the ground with joyous excitement on the victory of their Hindu brethren.[7] Another Muslim journal, "The Comrade", of which Maulana Mohammed Ali was both the founder and, envisaged: 'We hereby join the chorus of praise and jubilation over the victory of Mohun Bagan. The team did remarkably well throughout the tournament and won the Shield by sheer merit.'[8]

The post-victory reactions to the 1911 victory, which included the enthusiastic patriotism revealed the extent to which the city of Calcutta had responded to the triumph. After the match the winning team was taken out in an impressive victory procession from the Maidan to Shyambazar - the nerve centre and cultural hub of the non-white city. There was tremendous excitement with frequent shouting of slogans like `the *firinghees* have lost' while cries of *Bande Mataram* rent the air. Conch shells were blown all along the way by women to welcome the players. The procession stopped for sometime at the Thanthania Kali Temple on College Street to pay homage to the goddess and thank her for inducting strength to defeat the English team. The victory celebrations continued throughout the night and the *Adi Arya Saraswati Samaj* staged a free show of the play *Vishwa Vijaya* in honour of the club. In sharp contrast, the English localities of the city were quiet and unruffled by all the excitement. An interesting reminiscence that throws light on the victory's nationalistic implication was the question asked by an elderly *sanyasi* to a member of the winning team "We are thrilled that you have overcome the military team, but when will you pull that down?" as he pointed at the Union Jack fluttering on top of the Fort William nearby.[9]

Besides, the commercial importance of Mohun Bagan's I.F.A shield victory is no less fascinating. The black market in tickets for Indian sport may be said to have begun with the historic I.F.A shield of 1911. As one Allahabad based newspaper noted, 'the demand for tickets was such that a two-rupee ticket fetched as much as fifteen.' The commercial world of Calcutta too could not remain unaffected by the feat. Calcutta based businessmen and commercial firms widely used the magic of the clubs name as a brand to promote their business and enterprises. The Standard Cycle Company (59, Harrison Road) distributed halftone photographs of the victorious team along with copies of the 31st July 1911 issue of *Amrita Bazar Patrika*. The fruitful equation of sporting success and marketization again became operative after a break of more than two decades when commercial concerns began to use the individual players of Calcutta league leaders Mohammedan Sporting club and their potential contender East Bengal Club for commercial advertisements. This trend of commercialization of sport in the first half of twentieth century Bengal, set by the 1911 victory, totally disapproves the existing notion that commercialization of sports in India started in India only after 1980s. [10] Moreover; it also challenges the conventional contours of economic history of colonial India, which regard sport as unimportant from the perspective of economic history.

Following its nationalist and communal phases, football in Bengal was to be reincarnated yet again, this time as an expression of ethnicity. Even those slightly acquainted with the game know that modern India football can be reduced, in the ultimate analysis, to the rivalry between two Calcutta clubs-Mohun Bagan and East Bengal. The ferocious binary constitutive of Calcutta football came into being in 1924 with the founding of the East Bengal Club. Mohun Bagan was the preeminent Bengali football club of that time, having won the IFA Shield and countless other tournaments. The club's fan base came from the indigenous population of ghotis (West Bengalis) and its patrons included most of Calcutta's native aristocracy. Formed in conscious opposition to Mohun Bagan, East Bengal was meant to represent newly-arrived *bangals* or migrants from the eastern part of Bengal (now Bangladesh). Anxiety about rising Hindu-Muslim tensions in Muslim-majority East Bengal, Hindus from the region began a westward migration which would last till until the Partition and ultimately involve the transfer of almost 4 million people from east to west. This immigrant population constituted a distinct sociological group which stood culturally at odds-in manners, accent or food-with the previously settled denizens of Calcutta and its environs. This antagonism got articulated by the means of football, the many differences between *bangals* and *ghotis* got ritually "played" out on the green soccer fields of the Maidan. The social strains between these two ethnic communities got exacerbated after the Partition when millions of refugees moved to Calcutta. [11] Living in destitute conditions on the platforms of railway stations, and dependent on a government dole for survival, these new *bangals* would come to constitute a volatile, plebian fan base for East Bengal. Older fans of Calcutta football will no doubt recall that throughout the 1950s, and the 1960s (and even into the 1970s) every fixture involving Mohun Bagan and East Bengal had the city teetering on the edge of violence. This intense rivalry and the concomitant supremacy of Calcutta football would last almost till the end of the millennium. By then, several countervailing forces had tended to diminish the importance of Calcutta football and reduce its significance as a cultural phenomenon. Firstly, intermarriage and cultural diffusion had erased many of the differences between *bangal* and *ghoti* thus removing the objective ground for rivalry between the teams. That both Mohun Bagan and East Bengal are today under the same ownership is an ironic acknowledgment of this convergence. [12]

East Bengal brought anger through regional, cultural and language differences in the backdrop of a hostile social, economic and political environment. [13] Press reports of matches between the two clubs in the 1950s and 60s, either in the Calcutta League and

Shield, or in national-Level tournaments such as the Durand Cup in Delhi and Rovers Cup in Bombay; confirm the presence of massive crowds. The IFA Shield final between East Bengal and Mohun Bagan in 1947 had to be abandoned on the first day due to spectator violence. [14] In the shield final between the two clubs in 1950, a huge police force had to be stationed at the ground to avert violence. [15] These skirmishes gradually extended to engulf the whole of the Calcutta Maidan, to the extent that the IFA decided to conduct the league with regular assistance from the Calcutta police in 1951. [16] East Bengal, however, objected to this decision and a bitter rivalry ensued between the club and the police. The matter assumed such a controversial dimension that the Chief Minister had to intervene to settle matters. [17] The Chief Minister also expressed concern over the question of the organization and control of the game in 1955. Disappointed with the IFA's role in the process, he proposed the formation of a central organization to control the game in Calcutta. The very next year East Bengal, along with a few other clubs, filed a petition to the IFA against biased refereeing in the league. The referee's bias, according to the petition, was intended to favour one particular club. They urged IFA to change the scenario thin a week. [18] Needless to say, the favoured club was Mohun Bagan.

Emotional bonding with a club rapidly acquired violent tempers; aggression became more pronounced and victories or losses produced spontaneous euphoria or retaliation. Spectators would stand in queues for days on end to obtain their cherished tickets to matches. Skirmishes and feuds were common during long waits for tickets. People also got injured or fell ill at such times. In the 1975 shield final, East Bengal defeated Mohun Bagan 5-0. After the fourth goal was scored, one East Bengal supporter had a heart attack from sheer ecstasy and had to be taken to the hospital immediately. [19] Umakanto Palodhi a twenty-five-year-old Mohun Bagan supporter, the ignominious defeat aroused so much dejection that he committed suicide that night. The suicide note he left is revealing: "By becoming a better Mohun Bagan footballer, I wish to take revenge of this defeat in my next birth".[20]

In the late 1970s, as noted by a columnist of a leading Calcutta based sports magazine, the transformation in the character of spectator behaviour during the years 1978-79 was sudden and unprecedented.[21] The matter came to a head in 1980 when, during a rather unimportant league match between the two titans of Calcutta football (East Bengal and Mohun Bagan) at the Eden Gardens in Calcutta, clashes between supporters group lead to widespread violence in the stadium resulting in a stampede that costs sixteen fans their lives.[22] Thirteen fans died while several others were severely injured. Three more latter died at the hospital. The next day, the leading Bengali daily *Ananda Bazar* came out with the match report by using the byline "Football: the new killer in Calcutta." The incident was severely condemned by all. This tragedy was a jolt to the rising fervour of Indian football enthusiasm. It cast a heavy shadow on Indian footballing society and brought about unfortunate changes in Bengali football.

This paper therefore makes an attempt to analyze spectator behaviour and participation in the game of football in colonial and postcolonial Bengal. In the process, it tries to present a picture of continuity in spectator behaviour in the colonial and postcolonial era. In the colonial primarily Mohun Bagan, a football club discussed above showed their nationalist zeal against the colonizers which in turn influenced their supporters as is reflected in their behaviour on the field. Finally, Calcutta football came within sub-nationalist parameters on ethnic lines. Here partition politics played the magic. The East Bengal and Mohun Bagan supporters became staunch rivals in the gallery. Thus the crowd displayed tremendous participatory enthusiasm and added a different dimension in the game.

Notes

1. Chris Stone, *The Role of Football in Everyday Life, Soccer & Society*, Vol 8, No 2/3 April/July 2007.
2. G.Crawford, *Consuming Sport: Fans Sport and Culture*, London: Routledge 2004.
3. For details see Benedict Anderson, *Imagined Communities*, London: Verso, 1983.
4. A. King, 'Football Fandom and Post-National Identity in the New Europe', *British Journal of Sociology* 51.
5. *Ibid*
6. *Dainik Basumati*, 19 June, 1920
7. Quoted in the Mohun Bagan Athletic Club Golden Jubilee Souvenir, Calcutta, 1939, p25.
8. *Comrade*, 12 August, 1911.
9. Mohan Bagan Club Institutional Papers.
10. Kausik Bandopadhyay, *Playing for Freedom*, Standard publishers, New Delhi, 2008.
11. For details see Boria Majumder and Kausik Bandopadhyay, *Goalless: The story of a unique footballing nation*, New Delhi 2006.
12. Ibid
13. Moti Nandy, 'Football and Nationalism' In *The Calcutta Psyche* edited by Geeti Sen, New Delhi,1990.
14. *The Statesman*, 5 October 1947.
15. *Amrita Bazar Patrika*, 17 September 1950
16. *Amrita Bazar Patrika*, 31 May, 1951.
17. *Ibid*, 22 and 23 June 1951.
18. *Ibid*, 22 June, 1956.
19. *Amrita Bazar Patrika*, 30 September 1975.
20. *Amrita Bazar Patrika*, 1October 1975.
21. *Khelar Asar*, 3 July, 1979, p 38.
22. The pre match press suggested that possibilities of chaos and violence on the match of the day. In fact the Federation Cup final between the two teams on 8 May 1980 witnessed extremely unruly behaviour from not only the fans but also the players and club officials. For detailed report see *Ananda Bazar Patrika*, 15 August 1980, and *Khelar Asar*, 16 May 1980.

The Politics of Sports and the Myth of the Nation: Selected Novels of F. Scott Fitzgerald

Shubhankar Roy

> What is it that compels these men to attack? Why are men so disturbed by this spectacle? Why do they get involved so entirely? Why this needless fighting? What is sport? (Roland Barthes, 1997:75)

This comment encapsulates the view that sport is probably the most universal aspect of popular culture and it occupies a central space in the transnational cultural industrialization by crisscrossing cultural spectrum. Sport played a pivotal role in shaping modern nation-states. In *Discipline and Punish: The Birth of the Prison* (1977), Foucault demonstrated how elites attempted to solve the interrelated problems of sustaining a productive and compliant labour force during the turbulent period through bio-power. Foucault was meticulous to pinpoint the fact that bodies were subjected to external modes of regulation and more subtle forms of self-surveillance and self-discipline. He also argued how the popularity of sports and gymnastics in the late 19th century dovetailed with the corporal discipline and surveillance associated with the emergence of modern nation-states. A question can be posited both implicitly and explicitly that where is the cultural nation, the nation we experience through feelings, policies and practices. The idea of sport representing a unified national identity is mythical. Significantly, myths embody fundamental cultural values and character types and appeal to deep-seated emotions. According to Barthes, myths depoliticize social relations by ignoring the vested interests surrounding the stories that become attendant in a given culture. And critically, 'myths disavow or deny their own conditions of existence: they are forms of speech that derive from specific sites and power relations but are passed off as natural and eternal verities' (Barthes, 1973). Myths encourage active participation at the physical as well as the ideological level. Many accounts of sport situate it as a central tenet of national culture, in either a welcoming or a critical way. This reifies the term 'sport' denying the social fissures of gender, class, race, ethnicity, age, sexuality, media coverage, public participation, and region that it engages.

F. Scott Fitzgerald is the first of American authors to see sport as a social institution. The novels under discussion *This Side of Paradise* and *The Great Gatsby* are staples of the fact of how sport fit into the larger concepts of social relationships, both relationships of immediate community as well as those of national identification. This paper will demonstrate how both sport and stories told by and about sport worked together to structure concepts of social stratification. While taking into consideration of the fact of how sport has a noteworthy interaction with Fitzgerald's literary methodologies this paper would also exhume the paradox of burgeoning and cohesive American nationalism. A consistent structure of stratification and hierarchy gradually widens even in the face of the critic's polemical justification to dilate the story that sport erases lines of difference and allows for egalitarian social relationships as a model of success. The physical description of sports never finds any space in the novels. Rather, Fitzgerald uses the settings, stories and language of sports specifically as a way to deal with spectatorship, emulation, and ideology. This method is simply a prelude to expressing both the possibilities and complications of trying to correlate the stratified class system with the act of living in a much larger and rapidly changing America.

Fitzgerald matriculated from the University of Princeton and subsequently dropped out of the University to fight in the World War I. His active participation in the War is often considered to be the most significant period in terms of formulating his interests in status, class, and nationhood which appeared predominant in his fictions. In an essay called *College Humour* published in 1927, Fitzgerald labeled Princeton University as a 'myth, a vision' of America. His thinking of Princeton as a mythic representation of America was an important hypothesis for Fitzgerald, because it allowed him to comment not just on the University but also on the nation which would give us a picture of heterogeneity despite the amalgamative forces inherent on football. In consonance with the variety in the public and at the same time personal life, Fitzgerald notes in the same essay in a fitting manner:

> Football became, back in the nineties, a sort of symbol. Symbol of what? Of the eternal immaturity of race? The failure of a culture within the walls? Who knows? It became... the most intense and dramatic spectacle since the Olympic games (quoted in Jarom Lyle McDonald, 43).

Fitzgerald's first novel, *This Side of Paradise* (1920), is an exploration into the world of Princeton. This novel is an attempt into issues of social distinction and social status. The experiences of young Amory Blaine within the novel can be read as Fitzgerald's exploration into the 'culture within the walls', a culture in which Amory wishes to be prominent (49) at school and strives to model himself after the pervasively worshipped 'Big Man'. The hypothesis of America telescoped in the world of Princeton is revealed in his portrayal of Amory Blaine. In this novel, Fitzgerald considered the lifestyle at Princeton and investigated the degree to which it could be seen as a cultural microcosm for a much larger environment. Amory's experiences in the novel depict the desire that modern American youth had to break into the social world. In this way, the novel explores the intricacies of how the activities of the Princeton social system, including the spectacle of football, correspond with or sit in conflict with the emerging American class stratification.

> Fitzgerald's first novel, *This Side of Paradise* (1920), is an exploration into the world of Princeton. This novel is an attempt into issues of social distinction and social status. The experiences of young Amory Blaine within the novel can be read as Fitzgerald's exploration into the 'culture within the walls', a culture in which Amory wishes to be prominent (49) at school and strives to model himself after the pervasively worshipped 'Big Man'. The hypothesis of America telescoped in the world of Princeton is revealed in his portrayal of Amory Blaine. In this novel, Fitzgerald considered the lifestyle at Princeton and investigated the degree to which it could be seen as a cultural microcosm for a much larger environment. Amory's experiences in the novel depict the desire that modern American youth had to break into the social world. In this way, the novel explores the intricacies of how the activities of the Princeton social system, including the spectacle of football, correspond with or sit in conflict with the emerging American class stratification.

But there is a pointer being given in the twist of the story. If Princeton symbolically represents the American culture, and football as a sort of cultural failure, then the implications are clear. That is, football, as it was played at Princeton, provided Fitzgerald a language for identifying failure within the Princetonian way of life. Football is the key for making out the disjunctions Fitzgerald identified even as he attempted to connect the class system at Princeton with the act of living in a much larger America. Though Fitzgerald is not free of culpability from his own insistence that he deeply desired the social life he imagined at Princeton, *This Side of Paradise* reveals that he was simultaneously critical of his own dreams. Fitzgerald's way of looking at football helps the reader refine the way we evaluate his way of looking at America. The novel's meticulous use of football ultimately emphasizes the notion that Princeton's social systems are not representative of the American social landscape. In this way, Fitzgerald reveals some of the dangerous problems inherent in the homogenous demographic make-up of the football-playing student body which Fitzgerald observed and which he has often tried to identify himself with.

Amory's reactions to his first few days of school depict the desire that entering freshmen had to break into the social world. These reactions set the stage for exploring the intricacies of the social stratifications at Princeton. Amory's statement of his goals, by making a detour to the zone of historic realism, is represented fictionally. Upon entering school, all Princeton freshmen were given a copy of the 'Freshman Handbook'. This pocket-sized, leather-sized, leather-bound book, nicknamed the freshman Bible, contained the following admonition:

> Read this little book from cover to cover. Its pages will make you cognizant of things as they are at Princeton. Have a large circle of acquaintances, but go slow in forming intimate friendships (69).

This handbook, this code of socially acceptable behaviour which included a list of the most advantageous freshmen activities as well as a list of things freshmen were prohibited from doing, reinforced the social power of such concepts. This guidebook is demonstrative of the social atmosphere surrounding freshmen students, and it is exemplified through such rhetorical statements as

> the following customs are, of course, unwritten laws, but they have grown up with the history of 'Old Nassau' ... Anyone who enters into the life of Princeton for the first time will of course desire to observe them (63).

By selling out social behaviour, this handbook helped create a discourse of power. It reinforced the role of emulation, and cemented the figure of the Big Man in the minds of incoming freshmen as if it were a natural role for all to strive to assume. Cultural objects such as the Freshman Handbook relied upon indoctrination to perpetuate the social system. Evidently, such a phenomenon was very tangible evidence for the feudal-like society of Princeton life. Most students would subsequently recapitulate this social conduct by accepting and adhering to these customs as freshmen and by imposing them on succeeding freshmen classes as well they would perpetuate the myth.

Observation and emulation are at the core of the idea of the Big Man on Campus. Traditionally, the figure of the Big Man comes back to Walter Camp's rhetoric concerning football's role in a society. The Big Man was always the football player Camp's football player of self-discipline, refinement, courage, and by extension power, prestige, and privilege. Fitzgerald writes:

> All our schools have learned that the best government is that in which the higher-form boys take the major part, and into that government enters as a large factor the very hero-worship of the small-boy for the big-boy the would-be athlete for the school standard-bearer in sport (140).

Thus, in *This Side of Paradise,* Amory, knowing his decision to be prominent at school requires a carefully constructed plan, chooses an activity that best represents his social desires yet which also methodically follows the code established by previous generations of the social system. While other students join the college newspaper staff or become involved with various clubs, Amory asserts that he is 'going to take a whack at freshman football' (44). Amory's choice of activities demonstrates the degree of his aspirations. He does not want to be seen as merely 'going out for anything' (44), but instead 'decides to be one of the gods of the class' (47). As a narrative of Princeton life, *This Side of Paradise* takes a seemingly minor, almost tangential institution college football and makes it central, in that Amory's attempts to succeed at football are a synecdoche within this tale of the possibilities of social mobility.

While Amory Blaine's decision to play football is certainly significant in considering what *This Side of Paradise* says about the entry into the indoctrinated world of social standing at Princeton, more intriguing is his reaction to the already established hierarchy of football players at Princeton. On his first day on the campus, Amory has an experience that provides a glimpse into the way that football controlled the world of privilege and status at Princeton. As his first day winds to a close, Amory sits in solitude on the steps of his off-campus house and he hears a song which echoes through the towering spires of the nearby campus buildings. Chanting about the glory of the school, a group of singers appears and Amory distinguishes 'Allenby, the football captain, slim and defiant' (46). Amory has never met Allenby, yet he recognizes him nonetheless. Allenby, the Romantic figure, is already firmly established in the upper echelons of the social circle. The act of memory recognizing him is a product of Allenby's privileged status, bound up in the collective stories and attitudes about him which entering freshmen would automatically assimilate as part of their initiation into the university's social world. Of course, it is due to Princeton's very overt emphasis on football. Glancing from shop to shop, Amory visualizes Allenby's likeness in a store window montage, where the collection of 'athletic photographs' (42) prominently displays Allenby's picture lager than the rest. Allenby becomes not a person or even a character in Amory's mind, but he becomes an object something to be advertised, something to be acquired. Allenby is marketed, and his com-modification is an integral part of the social indoctrination surrounding football at the university.

Moreover, the intangible status the store advertises through Allenby is not connected to his athletic accomplishments but to his relationship with the culture of Princeton. The language of the text reveals that the photograph is one of 'Allenby, the football captain' (47). The two titles appear as one phrase as if it were all part of his name. 'Football captain' is an appellation describing part of his identity rather than his activities. Bound up in the label 'captain' are notions of prestige, notions of popularity, notions of social status among his teammates, coaches, and especially the fans. It is less a signifier of his athletic achievements and more a signifier of his social ones. Thus, the act of calling him 'Allenby, the football captain', with the two phrases inseparable from each other, equates the character of Allenby with these social connotations. The text is, in effect, calling him 'Allenby the esteemed', 'Allenby the elite', 'Allenby the Big Man'.

In *This Side of Paradise*, Fitzgerald brings about a relationship between football star and football spectator by giving preponderance to social status rather than economic accumulation. John Davies pointed out that Allenby was modeled on the historical figure of Hobey Baker (quoted in Davis, 135). The historical Hobey Baker, in fact, came from a family with limited financial wealth but renowned social standing. Traditionally, in America, football leads to a particular incarnation of the American Dream, one that bestows communal adulation and devotion. The marching, singing phalanxes are a form of social capital. Amory looks to Allenby as his exemplar and guide to reaping social rewards, reacting to the athletic celebrity by sighing in fascination at the sight of the ideals Allenby supposedly represents. Allenby is the type of 'god' that Amory wants to become, literally believing that physical emulation will lead to social emulation. Thus, through representations of football at Princeton, Fitzgerald is raising the questions about the structures of such a dream and the figures that make it possible. Yet, despite the transcendental mythos of Amory's encounter here with Allenby, Fitzgerald also questions the efficacy of such an aspiration. The supposed American Dream that Princeton football promises, 'the culture within the walls' that supposedly offers a social mobility through success on the gridiron. But, in reality, it defines the boundaries of its upper class as limited, prohibited to individuals lying outside of the elite. After all, the pane of glass allowing Amory to view Allenby's athletic photograph from Nassau Street may be transparent, but it is also impermeable. Metaphorically, it signifies that the iconic montage is completely exclusive; it is observable but not touchable.

The phalanx of singers following behind Allenby represents a coalescence of status seekers, and simultaneously giving Allenby his privileged status. The singers hope to amass similar status themselves, but at the same time, reinforce the barriers. Amory 'resents social barriers as artificial distinctions' (46), but quickly learns that despite their synthetic nature, the social distinctions of a world such as Princeton are nonetheless impenetrable. Football is the key in the social distinctions which, in the same feudal metaphor, found throughout the portrayal of football by various cultural forces. They created barriers and simply 'made by the strong to bolster up their weak retainers and keep out the almost strong' (47). Fitzgerald makes out a comparison between football and an age of chivalry. This comparison is paradoxical on two levels. The first irony lies in the fact that the genteel, refined images of a chivalric age should not merge with a game so violent and physically brutal as football. Perhaps this is exactly the reason why Camp sought to downplay the violence of the game in the way that he did. Yet, at the same time, by requiring such levels of physical strength, football is able to utilize that physicality to hoard social strength. In conjunction with this, the second visible paradox in the feudal analogy lies in the logic of a story of meritocracy itself as it relates to football. What Fitzgerald begins to identify as the failure of a culture within the walls is that rather than training boys to be conscientious, socially responsible citizens, football selects those who are at the top and who uses concepts of observation and emulation to keep others in line with the system. There is no social mobility, only stories of mobility. Amory, days after his romanticized dream-encounter with Allenby, wrenches his knee in practice and is thus forced to retire. Amory is kept in check by physical limitations, and unable to become a football star himself.

The words of the handbook, as well as the sequence of choices that young Amory makes, demonstrate a hierarchy in terms of the prominence of a given activity. Before this, Fitzgerald stated,

> Every entering man feels ambitious to enter some undergraduate activity. The publications hold a place of high importance, respect, and influence in social life and offer opportunities for the energies of men who do not possess athletic ability (58).

However, there is a stratum of social life in Princeton's feudal system, signified by one's extracurricular activities. Significantly, the novel's character of Kerry Holiday serves as a divergent voice to all of Amory's social aspirations beginning first and foremost with Amory's desire to play football. Kerry functions as an anomaly at Princeton, a critic of rigid social system and the class tension it creates. As such he gives voice to Fitzgerald's critical eye and thereby complicating the seemingly simple picture which the 'Freshman Handbook' paints about Princeton's social life. A self-proclaimed outsider by choice, Kerry

> chides Amory gently for being curious ... about the intricacies of the social system (48).

After hearing Amory confess that he does not 'mind the glittering caste system' as long as he gets to be on top, Kerry engages Amory in a series of conversations in which he attempts to identify a structural fallacy in Amory's aspirations for social mobility. When Amory claims that he still wishes to be prominent, Kerry deridingly calls Amory a 'sweaty bourgeois' (50). In other worlds, Kerry recognizes that Amory buys into the concept that social status is something that can be achievable through proactive effort. Fitzgerald points out that,

> Amory wants to bring a girl to the prom and be damn debonair about it introduce her to all the prize parlour-snakes and the football captain (51).

This is the way to garner status. Amory's goals of social mobility hinge upon the results accomplished by exercising his social agency. By calling such mindset bourgeois, Kerry Holiday is, in effect, telling Amory that working for being prominent will never place someone in the aristocracy.

Though not explicitly textual, such a goal is especially connected to Amory's desires to physically emulate Allenby. Football is a game all about the result; the final score, the winning team and the hero of the game. Amory finds himself in a position where he is unable to achieve the athletic results of a football player. It is almost as if he feels that parroting the other outward signs of elitism, he will garner some sort of acceptance. Kerry criticizes this paradigm as misguided and he warns Amory that he is 'just going around in a circle' (51). Kerry's choice of words here is vital. By describing Amory's aspirations as circular, Kerry acknowledges that class lines are drawn in such a way as to prohibit utterly the kind of mobility from one level to another. In attempting to climb the social ladder, Amory, instead, endeavours to follow a flat plane which leads him back to where he began. In effect, Kerry provides an ideological voice speaking out against the class systems in general. Fitzgerald manifestly shows that struggling for social mobility just reinforces Amory's own position as an outsider. Such an ideological position maintains that actions will not cultivate status, but that status is somehow innate. All of Amory's aspirations for social mobility are wrapped up in a sense of defeated movement. Thereby, the dreams of Amory lead to what keeps him firmly locked in the middle class.

In *The Great Gatsby* (1923), Fitzgerald makes an experiment in depicting the contentions and ambivalences between the upper class and the middle class over what best represents America. Through this dichotomy and the binary opposition between the two classes Fitzgerald endeavours to explore tensions between different groups of people who would like to be characterized by the rubric of Americanness. In chapter four of *The Great Gatsby*, Jay Gatsby, while privately conversing with Nick, makes an effort to clear up some of the stories circulating around the history of his rise to fortune. Nick has already excavated the magical elixir behind the success of Gatsby and pointed out that, 'I don't want you to get a wrong idea of me from all these stories you hear' (51). Gatsby was aware of the bizarre accusations that flavoured conversations in the halls. In an effort to provide tangible evidence of his history Gatsby proceeds to empty his pockets with 'souvenirs' that he conveniently has on hand. Gatsby states,

> It was a photograph of half a dozen young men in blazers loafing in an archway through which were visible a host of spires (53).

While studying the photograph Nick discerns that among the gentlemen is 'Gatsby, looking a little, not much, younger with a cricket bat in his hand' (53). This Oxford photograph, which Gatsby 'always carries' around him, opens Nick's eyes and it is charged with the larger conflicts between the Buchanans' elitism and Gatsby's opulent attempt to rise from the middle class.

Though it was not an oversimplified fact that in the 1920s only two classes existed in America. The decade also exhibited enormous anxiety amongst blue-collar factory workers, farm workers, recent immigrants etc. since this paper would explore the complex relationship between sport, social status and nation building, it is pertinent to deal with the notion of culture in relation with sport and the polarity between the glamorous upper-crust society of leisure to which Fitzgerald continually aspired in his personal life, and the ever-growing middle-class society that characterized his upbringing. As Bill Brown notes,

> by the turn of the century, play, not, work, appeared to be the mode through which a culture expressed itself' (qtd. in McDonald, 112).

However, it is intriguing that in *The Great Gatsby*, football plays a minor role. The single reference to that sport is the mention of Tom Buchanan as a former Yale football star. The reference is not insignificant, in that it draws on the inherent violence in the game which is meant to deepen the portrayal of Tom as a 'hulking brute of a man' (10). Nick's assessment of Tom Buchanan is noteworthy:

> Her husband, among various physical accomplishments, has been one of the most powerful ends that ever played football at New Haven a national figure in a way, one of those men who reach such an acute limited excellence at twenty-one that everything afterwards savours of anti-climax... Tom would drift on forever seeking, a little wistfully, for the dramatic turbulence of some irrecoverable football game (5).

These characterizations certainly pave the way for the exposition of the novel. And beyond this moment, football is conspicuously absent. Instead, baseball figures prominently in Fitzgerald's examination of emerging American self-characterization in a unique way. Fitzgerald does not give the reader any physical description of the game of baseball. *The Great Gatsby* contains only a few scattered allusions to baseball and these allusions are pivotal in understanding the role played by baseball in early 20th century ideologies of class and nationalism. By interrogating moments in the text where allusions or references to baseball intersect with the cultural history and significance of the sport, this paper would excavate how the novel recognizes the complexities of the connection to baseball to class tension and anxiety.

It would be pertinent to delve into the fact of how baseball came into prominence in America. Gatsby's photograph of his Oxford cricket-playing days is as much a product of an American cultural history as it is a British one. In the 1840s and early 1850s the most popular team sport in the United States was not baseball, but was instead cricket, a game most often played by British immigrants and used as a method for the English Community to preserve its own ethnic identity. The popularity of cricket stemmed primarily from the fact that the game's players were, for the most part, upper-class, wealthy businessmen who could afford leisure time and who was hailing from Britain. However, in the 1860s, the popularity of cricket began to wane due in large part to cultural forces that ultimately lay outside of sport, most notably the complex intersection between social hierarchy and a growing sense of nationalism. John Higham analyzed how American cultural nationalism in the mid-nineteenth century was partially fostered by images of 'Brother Jonathan' challenging 'John Bull' in various athletic competitions. Higham writes,

> When it came to cricket, the demographic and economic composition of those involved as cricket players created a particularly large obstacle for the game's spread outside of major metropolitan areas such as Philadelphia or Boston. The ethnic component of cricket playing was hostile to the developing sentiment of political and cultural nationalism in 19th century America (*Strangers in the Land,* 12).

Baseball claimed the space on the other end of the spectrum, adopting the characterization of being an American sport that eschewed attitudes of elitism. Baseball created inclusive community though sports. Consequently, baseball encouraged middle-class values by prohibiting the sale of alcohol at the game as a form of improving and educating the masses. Jarom Lyle McDonald writes,

> As the century moved closer to 1900, the serious class tensions present in American life, as clashes over issues of class and status underscored baseball's social significance ... the sporting world was a world of class tension, as upper-class citizens struggled with the growing, coalescing middle class for the right to say what could be defined as 'American' (118-19).

In chapter Nine of *The Great Gatsby* it can be noticed that baseball frames Gatsby's past. When Gatsby's father produces the written record of the schedule of the ball-playing world of 1906 inside a copy of Hopalong Cassidy during a conversation with Nick following Gatsby's death, he provides his own analysis of the schedule. His father's statement shed light on the significance of the middle-class definitions of the American character. His father comments,

> He had a big future before him, you know. He was only a young man, but he had a lot of brain power... 'If he'd of lived, he'd of been a great man ... He'd of helped build up the country' (134).

The schedule and general resolves which follow are worthy of careful study:

Rise from bed...	6.00 A.M.
Dumbbell exercise and wall-scaling...	6.15-6.30 A.M.
Study electricity, etc. ...	7.15-8.15 A.M.
Work...	8.30-4.30 P.M.
Baseball and sports...	4.30-5.00 P.M.
Practice elocution, pose and how to attain it...	5.00-6.00 P.M.
Study needed inventions ...	7.00-9.00 P.M.
Rise from bed...	6.00 A.M.
Dumbbell exercise and wall-scaling...	6.15-6.30 A.M.
Study electricity, etc. ...	7.15-8.15 A.M.
Work...	8.30-4.30 P.M.
Baseball and sports...	4.30-5.00 P.M.
Practice elocution, pose and how to attain it...	5.00-6.00 P.M.
Study needed inventions ...	7.00-9.00 P.M.

GENERAL RESOLVES

> No wasting time at Shafter's or [a name, indecipherable].
> No more smoking or chewing.
> Bath every other day.
> Read one improving book or magazine per week.
> Save $ 5.00 [crossed out] $ 3.00 per week.
> Be better to parents (139).

The implication in the phrase 'baseball and sports' makes us aware that a greater weight is imported to this activity than other sports. Jimmy Gatz's phrase, as a part of the daily regimen, speaks to the cultural narratives concerning the spread of baseball throughout the middle classes in the early part of the 20th century.

Young boys who would have followed such a schedule would have grown up to be the critical mass of American baseball fans migrating to the cities and filling the ballparks, seeking out other fans with similar historical background and working together to help 'build up the country' according to their own set of values and democratic ideals. It must be pointed out that the impression of young Jimmy which Mr. Gatz wants to leave behind, belongs to the middle-class family.

Jarom Lyle McDonald corroborates the view when he elaborates the pontifical notion that,

> By portraying young Jimmy as a baseball player rather than a spectator, Fitzgerald assigns him a sense of agency, in that Jimmy desires to place himself at the centre of the spectator's attentions (2007:120).

Jimmy Gatz's schedule is certainly a construction of a social persona. It was Gatsby's first effort of self-definition. Significantly, there is no portrayal of young Jimmy actually playing baseball, it is just a narrative record of his thoughts. Fitzgerald does not make it explicit whether Jimmy actually followed the schedule or whether he even liked baseball. So far as the problematic of this paper is concerned, it is immaterial. What can be inferred from this part of the schedule as supposedly maintained by Jimmy is that it is a representation of his desire at a young age to posit himself as a member of a particular class. He ultimately strove to represent himself not as a product of main-stream America, but as part of the 'orgastic future' which he contemplated which could be found in 'gleaming, dazzling parties' (1944). Gatsby made it a point that it was practically unachievable to the realm of fantasy by means of monetary accumulation alone. That was exactly the reason why he sought after representational signs of being upper class by becoming an icon of baseball. The image which Gatsby presents to Nick for review uses a visual representation of cricket, along with the associations of British privilege and elitism that had been associated with the game, to rebuild himself as a member of a new class.

These two vignettes encapsulate a tension that goes beyond the two sports. Jimmy Gatz's schedule is no less a cultural sign than the Oxford photograph. As Jimmy, he constructs a persona of the average middle-western, middle-class boy; as Gatsby, he constructs himself to be the elite American cricket player. In both cases, however, Gatsby has constructed a self that is based on metonymic representation, using sport to build himself up just as that sport could 'build up the country'. It must be kept in mind that towards the end of the 19th century and into the 20th century, owners of professional teams continued to use ideologies of morality, social class, and community status as a way to sell tickets. At the same time, analyses of baseball as a social sport often focused on abstract descriptions of how baseball ideologically fit some concept of a sensibility belonging to a middle-class American type. The French sociologist Bourdieu has recognized a historical connection between cultural class tension and sport. Tracing the emergence of sports in the strictest sense, Bourdieu notes that class 'defines the meaning conferred on sporting activity, the profits expected from it' (qtd. in Jarom Lyle McDonald, 126). In other words, participation in sport is not exclusively a matter of preference or taste. Instead, participation is largely governed by economic means and, more importantly, social expectation. Bourdieu argues that tennis, golf, and sailing, as individualized sports that bestow gains in distinction and honour a notion of leisurely amateurism, make up an ethos which is that of the dominant fractions of a dominant class. Bourdieu notes that,

> Baseball, on the other hand, a sport of middle-class participation and fanship, developed in the form of spectacles produced for the people.... more clearly as a mass commodity (1960:318).

Given Bourdieu's statement, sport becomes an ideological tool, linking class standing to social character. Fitzgerald understood the solid relationship between the sport and the middle-class. Rather than making the leap from that relationship to idealistic rhetoric of baseball as a sign of American middle-class sensibility, however, Fitzgerald instead uses the sport to scrutinize the larger notion of Americanness as a tool for middle-class social structuring. By examining the baseball allusions in *The Great Gatsby* it can be perceived that Fitzgerald posits baseball not as representative of the American middle class, but as representative of his larger assessment of the 'American Dream'.

By referring to the 1919 World Series, one of the most well-known historical baseball events, Fitzgerald exposes the complexities and ironies in both the upper-class privileged life and in the middle-class privileged life and in the middle-class dream for an equal opportunity. Consequently, the myth of a unified nation based on homogeneity and egalitarian opportunity gets tremendous overhauling through Fitzgerald's critiquing of the deep conflict between the middle class and the upper class. This conflict is culturally informed by the clash over the issue of athletics and Americanism. When Gatsby struggles to overcome his baseball playing middle-class heritage, the man who recognizes him as a 'fine appearing gentlemanly young man' and 'made him' in business (137), Meyer Wolfshiem is profiting from baseball the easy way. Once Gatsby met with Meyer Wolfshiem and the latter confided to the former the fact of how he hijacked the World Series. Nick comments that 'he's the man who fixed the World Series back in 1919' (58). Nick's internal monologue narrates the significance of the historical event to his own perception of the masses involved as fans of the game:

> The idea staggered me. I remembered, of course, that the World Series had been fixed in 1919, but if I had thought of it at all I would have thought of it as a thing that merely happened, the end of some inevitable chain. It never occurred to me that one man could start to play with the faith of fifty million people with the single-mindedness of a burglar blowing a safe (58).

The national class tensions in baseball are evident in Nick's phrase 'fifty million people' which Wolfshiem's actions signify. The World Series represents not just the best of baseball but serves as the locus of spectatorship for early 20th century America. In his book, *The Content of the Form: Narrative Discourse and Historical Representation*, Hayden White writes that,

> The baseball that these fifty million were watching was the culmination of the enterprise in which owners-builders were interested in establishing their sport as the personification of middle-class values, which, at the time, were synonymous with morality, respectability, and civic-mindedness (1986:86).

The way Meyer Wolfshiem plays with the vulnerability of the middle-class American, it becomes synonymous with the tenuous democracy being established in America. Perhaps the promise of equality that democracy offered was at risk. Most importantly, perhaps the middle class was indeed powerless in the face of greater wealth than they could accumulate. Hence, Nick's expressed astonishment is not just at the fact that a baseball game could be tampered with. Rather, Nick perceives middle-class American life in peril by taking into his ambit their identification with the game. Their desires for identification, their desires to have shared experience and their desires to further an egalitarian ideology are all melted away by the complicity of the bigwigs like Meyer Wolfshiem. Nick blurts out,

> We drew in deep breaths of it as we walked back from dinner through the cold vestibules, unutterably aware of our identity with this country for one strange hour, before we melted indistinguishably into it again (141).

Fitzgerald narrates another episode involving Jordan Baker's alleged cheating in a local golf tournament to bring home the fragility of the framework of the nation. This episode, along with the actions of Wolfshiem, exposes the apprehension of middle-class America. The amateur golf players themselves are responsible for their own scoring and submission of scorecards. Despite being endowed with wealth, talent and status, Jordan still feels compelled to attain an advantage over other competitors. This is solely meant for reaping for social profit, honour and status which are accorded to a champion in a golf tournament. Jordan Baker's action in altering the lie of her ball is perhaps more profound than Wolfshiem's involvement in throwing the World Series. Yet these two instances exhibit radically different conceptions of how citizens in competing classes function with their associates. Jordan's deception ostensibly hurt 'the spirit of the sport' and her fellow competitors, who would have been on the same class level as she had been from her youth. Yet Meyer Wolfshiem's connection to the World Series scandal can be construed not just as taking advantage of a sport or personal honour, but as economic exploitation of a lower class through the destruction of America's game. It is an attempt to take baseball, and thus by extension, take America away from the middle class. In fact, Nick's very first visual perception of Wolfshiem characterizes him as a figure perhaps not quite human, but closer to an animal:

> A small flat-nosed Jew raised his large head and regarded me with two fine growths of hair which luxuriated in either nostril. After a moment I discovered his tiny-eyes in the half-darkness (55).

By labeling the fix of the 1919 World Series 'inevitable chain' in his earlier statement, Nick makes a point about the connection between baseball, class, and the nation. Wolfshiem's attempts to take America away from the middle class expose the reality that middle-class life itself is responsible for the downfall of the sport they are trying to champion. In other words, by accepting the stories about baseball's exceptionalism and its embodiment of their version of American values the middle class is powerless to effect a change in the inevitable chain.

In *The Great Gatsby* Fitzgerald critiques the complex interrelationship between class relations and emerging nationalism during the tumultuous decade of the 1920s. The novel also unearths a number of allusions by means of which we are to understand the power of an institution such as baseball in defining the roles and boundaries of those who claim to make up the American society. Nick's estimate of what the future of the country might be for the middle class in the penultimate pages of the novel, it would be evident that Gatsby's escape from the image of the green island, representative of the cultural past, is as inevitable as the fixing of the World Series. It can be pointed out that if baseball represents middle class America, then Nick, in looking at the World Series, foreshadows the ways in which the 'green breast of the new world' would be replaced by the 'dark fields of the republic'.

> Its vanished trees, the trees that had made way for Gatsby's house, had once pandered in whispers to the last and greatest of all human dreams... He did not know that it was already behind him, somewhere back in that vast obscurity beyond the city, where the dark fields of the republic rolled on under the night (144-145).

The middle class may cultivate 'the last and greatest of all human dreams', dreams of success, wealth and status. Their attachment to a land is profound which promised the prospects and opportunity for social mobility. But their hopes for 'the new world' are elusive, receding, and ultimately unreachable thereby the cohesive unity of the nation is at risk.

References

Bryer, R. Jackson, Ruth Prigozy and Milton R. Stern. Eds. *F. Scott Fitzgerald in the Twenty-First Century*. The University of Alabama Press: Tuscaloosa & London, 2003.

Fitzgerald, Scott F. *The Great Gatsby*. Intro. M. Sivaramkrishna. New Delhi: OUP, 1999.

—, *This Side of Paradise*. New York: Noble & Barnes, 2007.

Foucault, Michel. *Discipline and Punish: The Birth of the Prison*. Trans. A Sheridan. Harmondsworth: Penguin, 1987.

McDonald, Jarom Lyle. *Sports, Narrative, and Nation in the Fiction of F. Scott Fitzgerald*. New York & London: Routledge. 2007.

Messenger, Christian K. *Sport and the Spirit of Play in American Fiction: Hawthorne to Faulkner*. New York: Columbia University Press, 1981.

Miller, Toby, Geoffrey Lawrence, Jim Mckay, and David Rowe. *Globalization and Sport: Playing the World*. London & New Delhi: Sage Publications, 2001.

Riordan, James. *Sport, Politics and Communism*. Manchester and New York: Manchester University Press, 1991.

Umphlett, Wiley Lee. Ed. & Intro. *American Sport Culture: The Humanistic Dimensions*. London & Toronto: Bucknell University Press, 1985.

Vinokur, Martin Barry. *More than a Game: Sport and Politics*. New York and London: Greenwood Press, 1988.

Sports in Colonial India: Vignettes from the Past

Souvik Naha and Amitava Chatterjee

An understanding of sport, which is inextricably tied to corporeality and movement, would be nigh impossible without the testimony of images that appear in numerous media such as paintings, lithographs, posters, coins and medals, ceramic arts, stone and metal sculptures, photographs and films. (Douglas Booth, *The Field: Truth and Fiction in Sports History*, London: Routledge, 2006, p. 98.)

Jagadindranath, Maharaja of Natore (middle row centre) at the head of the Natore team in 1907

Modern sports such as cricket and football in colonial India were funded primarily by the princes and landed magnates, the aspiration being escalation of political influence or subversion of imperial hegemony. Nevertheless, the uneasy accord of class and caste towards forming representative teams was the seminal outcome of this patronage.

Balai Chatterjee heading the ball to Hemanga Biswas in an exhibition match in Java.

Unlike cricket, football and hockey overgrew the identifier of an English game in quick time. Victories over European teams and audiences at home and abroad not only elevated the sports in public imagination and commercial value, but also fomented a field in which the domains of colonial power and hegemony was continuously negotiated on social terms.

Dhyan Chand accepting a silver cigarette case from Mrs. Fletcher, wife of the president of Bengal Hockey Association, after what turned out to be his last exhibition match.

The basketball team of Victoria Institution, Calcutta, winners of the inter-college 'Hindustan Standard' Challenge Cup.

The aesthetic form and moral content of a 'lady' were arguably informed by nationalist discourses of creating the ideal female in response to colonial critiques. The domestic position of women changed as encounters with colonial policies continually modified women's relations with men, giving rise to new agencies, innovations and restrictions.

Leila Chatterjee (centre) beaming with winner's elation after the All-India 100 Metres Freestyle Swimming for women, flanked by R. Sen Gupta (left) and S. Pal.

Students of the Calcutta Blind School in drill practice.

Cultivation of strong physique did not necessarily carry a nationalist overtone, but a well-built body and a strong-willed mind evoked appreciation. Arguably projections of muscular bodies were premised on a potential convergence of middle class rectitude and working class defiance.

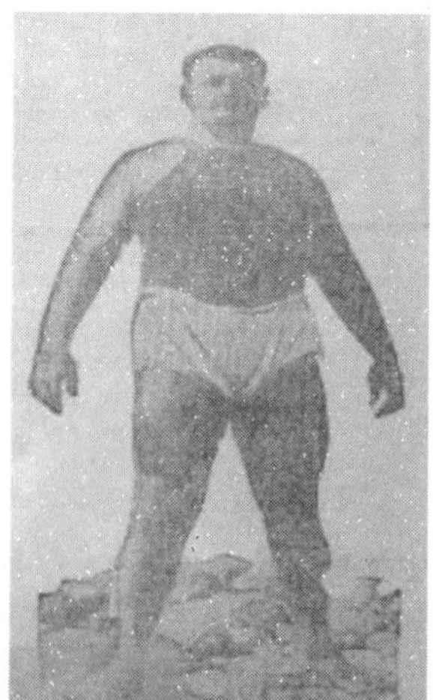

Gobor Guha, the only wrestler from Bengal to have been acknowledged the world heavyweight champion.

Mushtaq Ali, the famous cricketer, advocating the qualities of a multinational brand.

Adoption of English games symbolically reinforced the theory that following English rituals was the assured way of elevating the mental and physical faculty of Indians. At the same time, brown bodies subverted the sanctity of Western attires, and decolonised their values as well as the game these bodies represented.

In addition to promoting India's cricketing prowess, C.K. Nayudu endorsed the National Tea Board.

Gurdas of Hoshiarpur and Lal of Amritsar in the All-India wrestling tournament at Simla.

The confluence of pure body and the sharp mind through regimented exercises promoted a charismatic psychosomatic self which became a metonymy for resisting colonialism, articulating 'Indian' aspirations as opposed to the disciplinary mechanics of imperial power, at least in some quarters of Bengal and North India.

A wrestling competition at Cossipore, Bengal. Winners of the tournament would be eligible to participate in the international championship in Bombay.

List of Contributors

Amitava Chatterjee is an Assistant Professor of History at Ramsaday College. He is working on the evolution of sporting culture in colonial Bengal. He has published extensively in reputed journals of India and abroad viz. *Calcutta Historical Journal; Journal of History*, Jadavpur University; *Soccer & Society, Sport in Society* etc. He is a Charles Wallace Fellow (UK), 2012. He is assigned as a Guest Editor of *Sport in Society* and referee of *Soccer & Society* (International Journal, Routledge).

Boria Majumdar, a Rhodes Scholar, is a Senior Research Fellow at the University of Central Lancashire, UK. He has taught at the Universities of Chicago, Toronto, Western Australia and Monash and has written extensively on the history and politics of sport in India and across the world. Developmental Editor of the *International Journal of History of Sport* and Executive Academic Editor of *Sport in Society* and *Soccer & Society*, he is General Editor of the Routledge Series, 'Sport in the Global Society'. Some of his books include *Twenty-Two Yards to Freedom: A Social History of Indian Cricket* (2004), *Goalless: The Story of a Unique Footballing Nation* (2006), *Olympics: The India Story* (2008) and *Sellotape Legacy: Delhi and the Commonwealth Games* (2010).

Sean Brown teaches at the University of New Mexico and is due to finish his PhD at the Northeastern University. His thesis explores questions of sport popularity in the United States. He edits *Soccer & Society* and is an Associate Editor of *Sport in Society*. He has edited two books and has published extensively on sociology of sport. His research interest includes globalization, political economy, sport and nationalism, sport studies (sociology, anthropology, history), religious studies (particularly pertaining to sport and Muscular Christianity) and Qualitative Methods.

Souvik Naha is a doctoral research fellow at the Centre for Historical Studies, Jawaharlal Nehru University. He has been a part of the research team in two international projects, undertaken by the University of Ulster, which seek to devise optimal coaching methods for Special athletes. He is an academic referee in two international journals. His research and review articles have been published in the *International Journal of the History of Sport, Soccer & Society* and a umber of edited collections of essays.

Jishnu Dasgupta is an Assistant Professor of History at Serampore College, Hooghly. His research interests cover sports and (social history of) politics, and the fascinating state of Bihar. He has written regularly for *Global South: the Sephis e-Magazine* and used to write a fortnightly column for the *Bengal Post*. His articles have appeared in the *International Journal of the History of Sport*.

Avipsu Halder is a UGC Junior Research Fellow at the Center for International Politics, Organization and Disarmament Studies at Jawaharlal Nehru University. His ongoing doctoral research explores the theoretical aspects of globalization in the realm of sport with reference to International Political Economy, changing role of states, state-market interaction and sports diplomacy.

Suparna Ghosh is the Head, Department of History and Assistant Professor in History at Loreto College, Kolkata since 2000. Her thesis, on women of Bengal in sports, was awarded a PhD in 2008 by Jadavpur University. She has published in national and international journals and books. Two of her articles were published in *The International Journal of the History of Sport*. Her key interest areas include sports studies, women's studies and popular cultureparticularly rural culture, customs and traditions.

Binayak Dutta is an Asistant Professor of History at Assam University, Diphu Campus and Visiting Fellow, OKD Institute of Social Change and Development, Guwahati, Assam. Formerly he was at St. Edmund's College, Shillong and the North Eastern Hill University.

Debashis Majumder completed M.Phil in sports history from Jadavpur University in 2011. His main area of research is different aspects of history of Indian sports, especially Kolkata football. In addition to article in noted journals, he has published a monograph, *The History of the Football Clubs in Calcutta: Bengali Identities since the Partition: 1947-1985* from Readers Service Publishing House, Kolkata in 2012. He is an Assistant Teacher of History in Kantalia High School, Bhangore.

Amitabha Bandopadhyay teaches Bengali at Ramsaday College. He specializes in Bengali folk literature and has profound interest in sports history.

Shubhankar Roy obtained his Ph.D in English in 2012 from Ranchi University, preceded by an M.Phil. from the University of Calcutta. Earlier he topped in his PG examination in 2003 from RBU. He has contributed articles on different journals and books of repute. His areas of interest include post-colonial literature, 20th Century American Fiction and Border Literature. Presently, he is a faculty member in the Dept. of English, Vidyanagar College (CU), teaching both UG and PG courses in English.